CAPITALISM, VALUE AND EXPLOITATION

A Radical Theory

GEOFF HODGSON

Martin Robertson · Oxford

First published in 1982 by Martin Robertson & Company Ltd.,
108 Cowley Road, Oxford OX4 1JF.

British Library Cataloguing in Publication Data

Hodgson, Geoff
    Capitalism, value and exploitation.
    1. Value
    I. Title
    335.4'12   HB201
    ISBN 0−85520−414−1

Typeset by Freeman Graphic, Tonbridge
Printed and bound in Great Britain

To my teachers

CONTENTS

PART IV   CAPITALIST PRODUCTION

PREFACE

The purpose of this book is to provide an analysis of the capitalist economic system. It is, however, at an abstract level of discourse. There is little discussion of different capitalist systems, or their historical development. More accurately, this book is about the tools of analysis that are required to analyse real capitalist systems. It is not suggested, however, that such an abstract analysis is *sufficient* for an understanding of the capitalist epoch, or for providing prescriptions for political or economic policy. These can come only by the infusion of the study of real history, and real political structures.

The analysis in this book is descended from a certain tradition of economic thought and it assumes some familiarity with it. This tradition is Marxian Political Economy. The works with which it is assumed that the reader is acquainted are: Marx's *Capital,* especially the first volume; the important debate between Böhm-Bawerk and Hilferding in *Karl Marx and the Close of His System* (edited by Sweezy); Dobb's *Political Economy and Capitalism*; and Sweezy's *The Theory of Capitalist Development.*

In addition, this work is influenced by writings in the tradition of Keynes. This, incidentally, contrasts with the so-called 'Keynesian' tradition which has been persuasive in the last 30 years. The classic work is, of course, Keynes' *The General Theory of Employment, Interest and Money.* The modern re-evaluation of Keynes is constructed in Leijonhufvud's *On Keynesian Economics and the Economics of Keynes.* Two extremely important economists stand, at different points, between the writings of Keynes and Marx. They are Joan Robinson and Kalecki. Robinson's *Collected Economic Papers* and Kalecki's works (see Feiwel, 1975) include discussion of both Marx and Keynes and are worthy of mention. Radical political economy would be by far the weaker without the original efforts of these two theorists.

Sraffa's *The Production of Commodities by Means of Commodities* has revolutionized economic theory in the past two decades. It has been an important influence on the present work. However,

Sraffa's slim volume is difficult to negotiate, and the reader would be best advised to read Steedman's *Marx After Sraffa* first. In the latter work there is not only a discussion of the impact of Sraffa's theory of relative prices on Marx but also a clear account of the essentials of the Sraffa system.

In the last decade there has been an explosion of publications which are interpretations or accounts of Marx's thought. This present book is not such a work of interpretation. However, it is useful to note a number of important and influential works of both a critical and interpretative nature which can be found amongst the debris of the explosion. They are Colletti's *From Rousseau to Lenin,* Lippi's *Value and Naturalism in Marx,* and Howard and King's *The Political Economy of Marx.* All three are most stimulating and relevant reading.

Along with the explosion of Marxology in the last few years has been the reprinting of a few relatively unknown classics in Marxian thought. In economic theory the most notable is Rubin's *Essays on Marx's Theory of Value*; a major and highly informed study, with an interpretation of Marx which remains persuasive even today.

This present work, however, is some distance from the orthodox Marxian tradition, especially in its rejection of the labour theory of value. This rejection raises questions which have not been discussed adequately elsewhere, except, as far as the author is aware, in the work of Cohen (1979); Ellerman (1978, 1980); Levine (1977) and Lippi (1979).

It may be of some interest to note the genesis of some of the ideas in this book. In 1973 and 1974, under the supervision of Ian Steedman of the University of Manchester, the author was engaged in research on the problem of joint production. This led both student and supervisor to unearth the possibility, under a certain definition of value, of 'negative surplus value' in a capitalist economy. From this point it seemed that efforts to rescue the labour theory of value, in the traditional formulation at least, were forlorn.

The efforts to cope with the abandonment of the labour theory, in December 1973 and afterwards, are still vivid in the author's mind. The theory had to be abandoned, on logical and scientific grounds, yet such an abandonment called into question the notion that the working class suffered some sort of exploitation under capitalism, and, indeed, the whole class view of modern society. Furthermore, standard Marxian approaches to the theory of capital accumulation had to be modified or even discarded. The author was impelled to investigate the real meaning of such notions as exploitation, which had been explained, in an unsatisfactory and tautological fashion, by the labour theory. It was a striking revelation to find that very little had been written on the subject. The orthodox, neoclassical analysis had started from the presumption that capitalism, under free market conditions, was the best of possible worlds, and thus exploitation would not exist if the competitive market held sway. Orthodox Marxism, still retaining the labour theory of value, did not feel the need for an independent investigation into exploitative social relations. Even sophisticated works, such as an essay by Eatwell (1975) and, later, a book by Morishima and Catephores (1978), both of which have the word 'exploitation' in their titles, simply *assume* that exploitation involves the *existence* of some sort of surplus product. Such abrupt, and somewhat cavalier, definitions of exploitation had little persuasive power. The same trick was performed as had been with the labour theory; those writers had *assumed* what had to be *proved,* they had simply stated the *effect* of a phenomenon which had to be *explained.* Only concrete studies of the labour process, such as those which are found in the first volume of *Capital,* and Braverman's *Labor and Monopoly Capital,* provided any real illumination of the relations and processes involved.

An initial attempt to reformulate the notion of capitalist exploitation was made in a paper presented at Birkbeck College, University of London, in February 1975. Two later versions of this paper were published in the *Bulletin of the Conference of Socialist Economists* and, in Danish, in *The Nordic Review of Political Economy.* A still later version appeared in *Science and Society* in 1980. The account of exploitation in this volume is a further development and modification of those ideas.

Parallel with the development of a theory of exploitation was the elaboration of a relationship between monetary and value theory. Some ideas on this were presented in a paper given at the Universities of Copenhagen and Aarhus in October 1976. A modified version of this essay is to appear in *Australian Economic Papers,* and Chapter 15 of the present work draws upon material in this paper. In addition, Chapter 8 draws, in part, on some material included in an essay scheduled to appear elsewhere. Permission from the editors concerned, to utilize some of this previously published material, is gratefully acknowledged.

Many of the ideas in this book have been discussed, and often constructively criticized, in conversation with others; also a number of people have made useful comments on sections of the manuscript. In at least one of these ways I have benefited from the time and attention of Samuel Bowles, Christian Groth, Geoff Harcourt, Barry

Hindess, Jan Kregel, David Levine, Edward Nell, Theo Nichols, David Purdy, Robert Simmons, Thanos Skouras and Ian Steedman. There are others, too numerous to mention; and the intensive work of anonymous referees. The help of all these people is acknowledged with warm gratitude. Needless to say, however, many of them will wish to differ with the approach taken in this work, and none of them can be held responsible for its errors. The author alone has this burden.

Finally, I must acknowledge a debt to Bennington College for luring me away from the temptations of political activity in Britain, and for providing me with both time and congenial environment in which to complete this book. Most of all my thanks are due to Vinny, for her patience and help, in ways that she may not know, in dealing with a turbulent author.

GEOFF HODGSON
Bennington College
Vermont, USA
January 1981

PART I
FOUNDATIONS

CHAPTER 1

INTRODUCTION

*The crisis consists precisely in the fact that the old is dying and the new
cannot be born; in this interregnum a great variety of morbid symptoms
appears.*

ANTONIO GRAMSCI, *The Prison Notebooks*

There is more of a relationship between the development of economic
theory and the state of the modern economic system than is often
recognized. The majestic edifice of classical economic theory was
constructed not simply out of a desire for truth and understanding
but also with a concern to provide the theoretical justification for
competitive capitalism and unrestricted free trade. In those days the
discipline was not called 'economics' but 'political economy'. The
literal etymology of the latter term is: 'the rules governing the
management of society', from the greek *polis* (= social unit), *oikos*
(= household), and *nomos* (= rules, or law). A modern translation of
the term could be: 'the theoretical basis of economic policy'. The
classical economists were not solely concerned with abstract theoriz-
ing, nor could they be. Their work was prompted by the growth of
industrial capitalism and the expansion of trade, it was directed
towards a furtherance of such economic progress, and it caught the
minds of their generation precisely because, with serious analysis and
clear prescriptions, it addressed the central policy issues of the time.

Subsequent to this, it is no accident that Marx often described his
work as 'a critique of political economy'. Marx's analysis in *Capital*
and other works found faults *within* the works of the classical
economists, and also showed opposition to the *direction* of their
theoretical endeavours. His critique of classical economics was not
conceived as simply a technical one. He rejected also an analysis
which was based on the assumption that the capitalist arrangement
of production was the natural order of things. With this he rejected
policy prescriptions which were simply adjustments within the
capitalist mode of production and did not recognize the historical
and economic limits of that system. By showing that capitalism had

3

such inbuilt limits, Marx aimed to provide a critique of the orthodox economic policy of his time. Within his economic theory a unity is intended: from the theory of value at the foundation, through to the theory of production, accumulation and crises, reaching a point where a strong policy stance is implied, albeit unelaborated. In Marx, economic theory and policy are linked.

The neoclassical school

It is with the neoclassical school that the break is made. In the 1870s, with Jevons, Menger, Walras and others, the labour theory of value is rejected along with the radical political conclusions with which it had become associated. In the hands of Marx, and Ricardian socialists such as Thomas Hodgskin, the labour theory had been used to indicate the exploitation of the working class under capitalism. Attempts after 1870 are made to turn political economy into a science, akin to the natural sciences of physics and chemistry. With the rise of positivist philosophy towards the end of the nineteenth century, the neoclassical counter-revolution in economic thought finds its explicit methodology. The science is to be purged of value-judgements. Normative bias, at least at the theoretical foundations of the subject, has no place. Even a new name for the discipline is successfully advocated by the great neoclassical theorist Marshall: 'political economy' is to be renamed 'economics'. No doubt the unsatisfactory etymology of the latter word was recognized; but to its advocates it served the purpose of emphasizing the break from the sordid world of politics.

In fact, as we shall show in the next chapter, the neoclassical school did not free the subject of an attachment with ideology. Whilst their value-judgements were silenced they had a more pernicious influence behind the scenes. Like classical economic theory itself, the capitalist market was seen as natural and even immutable. A coarse doctrine of *laissez faire* was implied. In severing the link from political practice, neoclassical economics advocated, in effect, an absence of political or government intervention in the economic sphere. Whilst Smith and Ricardo had used powerful tools of theory to demonstrate the alleged superiority of the market mechanism, in the neoclassical economics its superiority is accepted by default. In the political silence stalked an elaborate justification of the *status quo*.

Keynes

Only the sounds of the period of greatest economic crisis in the history of the capitalist system broke that silence. Keynes, a former pupil of Marshall, became impatient with the political and practical impotence of orthodox economic theory. During the 1920s and 1930s, in every capitalist country, unemployment took an increasing toll of human misery and starvation. In the early 1930s world trade collapsed. In these two decades the neoclassical economists continued to preach their doctrine, and gave support to the notion that the best policy was to leave things alone. With their theory of a self-regulating market they believed that the market itself would bring the economy back to full employment. Keynes was sceptical. He successfully undermined the neoclassical theory of the market and advocated enhanced government intervention and regulation of aggregate economic demand. Such policies were accepted by many governments after the Second World War and for some time, perhaps as a result, the world was free of the peril of a slump.

But neoclassical theory was not replaced. On the contrary it enjoyed a new lease of life. This was due to both the success and the failure of Keynes. Keynesian policies had contributed to a period of near-full employment and economic growth within the framework of the capitalist economy. Government intervention was increased but private ownership survived and the market still remained the dominant mechanism. So the very prosperity of the system brought new confidence in the power and efficiency of the market, and of capitalist enterprise. Keynes' failure was that, whilst he had shown in his writings that the market was in fact a deficient mechanism, he had not related this to a theory of value or production which was substantially different to that held by the neoclassicals. In Keynes there is a theory of money, but no original theory of value and no original theory of production. He had left a void.

Even before his death in 1946, this void was being filled by the preceding conservative theory. Keynes' success in creating policy prescriptions for advanced capitalism ensured that his macroeconomic analysis would form an uneasy synthesis with neoclassical orthodoxy. But his failure to develop an extensive theoretical alternative, particularly to orthodox microeconomics, meant that the so-called Keynesian Revolution was a half-hearted affair. So developed the absurd situation where, in the pages on microeconomics in the post-war economics textbooks, an analysis was put forward which implicitly or explicitly predicted an automatic tendency to *full employment* in the capitalist economy; whereas, in contrast, in the pages on macro-economics, a theory was put forward, due in the main to Keynes or his followers, which predicted *unemployment* in the absence of adequate government expenditure.

In the last few years economists have become increasingly aware of this discrepancy. However, the contradiction has not been re-solved by a radical development of Keynes' work. On the contrary, the tendency has been to attempt to put macroeconomics on the foundations of orthodox neoclassicism, rather than to supersede the latter. A resurgence of neoclassical thinking has taken place. This reversion to pre-Keynesian orthodoxy has been aptly described as a counter-revolution in economic theory.

The New Right

Recently, there has been the emergence of monetarism. Behind the plausible statement that there is some relationship between the supply of money and the rate of inflation a whole host of other judgements stand. This monetarist view of the inflationary process is usually combined with the pronouncement that it is the government (not the private banks or other creators of money) which has to be restricted in its powers, and in particular, its propensity to 'print' money. This hostility to government intervention in the economy is generalized to the extreme, most particularly in the pronouncements of the high priest of monetarism, Milton Friedman. A plausible academic theory on the causes of inflation becomes the mask for a wholesale opposition to public expenditure, public ownership, and the welfare state. Another step is taken backwards into the pre-Keynesian world, where it is believed that the capitalist market is a magic cure for all economic ills. With the cracks in the Keynesian consensus now visible, a New Right in Western politics is born.

The relationship between this reinvigorated support for the capitalist market and the neoclassical theory of that market is not a simple one. It is doubtful if value-judgements as to the superiority of the market mechanism can be derived directly from the neoclassical analysis of supply and demand. What is more likely is that the neo-classical analysis concentrates on some aspects of the capitalist system and ignores others; it makes oversimplified assumptions which admit rather than promote such bias. Furthermore, the notion of the market as a self-regulating entity is firmly based on a highly mechanistic and deterministic neoclassical view of the economic process. In his outlook the economy works much as a machine: its behaviour is predetermined, and although individuals make choices those choices themselves are fixed by rigid mathematical functions of preference or utility. This mechanistic outlook sustains not only the view that the market is a self-righting mechanism but also the view that governments can do little to alter the real, long-run, development of the economy other than to divert it from an optimal path.

The crisis in economic theory

The first crisis of neoclassical theory, in the interwar period, was largely brought about by the failure of neoclassical economic policy to restore full employment and promote economic growth. A second crisis is now upon us. Developing economic problems in the capitalist world in the 1970s have undermined the efficacy of Keynesian prescriptions. The Keynesian era is drawing sharply to a close. In Britain, the sickest economy in the developed world, the end of that era is most apparent. In the meantime, it never must be forgotten, Keynesian 'demand management' has *never* been a solution to the more extreme economic problems of the underdeveloped world. Keynes, it has been widely remarked, is dead.

In the meantime it is becoming increasingly clear that the New Right is providing no suitable alternative. Already, by the end of the 1970s, the new fad for the purist, and most anti-Keynesian, version of neoclassical theory had reached its limit in many of the most prestigious ivory towers. In the meantime, most acutely in Britain under the Conservative Government of Margaret Thatcher, and also in the United States, it is becoming increasingly clear that monetarist policies, combined with blind faith for the curative powers of capitalist competition and the market, quite simply do not work. Like the 1920s and 1930s, neoclassical theory has failed on the test of its policy.

Inflation rages, and throughout the world over 100 million people are unemployed. Nor, it must be said, will an easy economic solution to these problems be found; but, however daunting the problems may be, economists can never be absolved of a duty. Whilst economic theory can never be a panacea for economic or social ills, it too must play its part. One is reminded of the famous passage from Keynes:

Practical men, who believe themselves to be quite exempt from any
intellectual influences, are usually the slaves of some defunct economist.
Madmen in authority, who hear voices in the air, are distilling their frenzy
from some academic scribbler of a few years back (Keynes, 1936, p. 383).

This passage can always be invoked by economists, even those of the most abstract and theoretical kind, to try to show that they are doing something useful; yet it still has a ring of truth about it. Keynes explicitly and grossly underestimated the power of vested interests. For example, his own policy prescriptions were not adopted on the basis of a conversion by those in power to the arguments and conclusions of Keynes' *General Theory*. They were adopted because the vested interests within the system saw his policies as the most likely way to make capitalism survive, and thus preserve the vested interests of the property-owning elite. Yet the recent abandonment of Keynesian ideas by business interests in the West, and their courtship of the New Right with its monetarist austerity, does not seem to be in their best long-run, or short-run, interests. There are many in authority who hear voices in the air, and the scribbler wins prizes and has prime time on television.

The power of economic theory, especially that which poses as a surrogate for effective action, can be exaggerated; but nearly all of the great movements in such theory have had their effect on humankind. As well as curbing his exaggeration, however, Keynes should have added that the *lack* of innovation in economic theory can be a force for good or ill, usually for ill. It is the lack of an adequate alternative to neoclassical theory which has helped to perpetrate the mythology of the magical capitalist market. It was the lack of what we could call a microeconomic basis, or a theory of value and production, in Keynes' own work which limited the gains of the Keynesian Revolution and made the counter-attack so much easier. That is the crisis of modern economic theory: whilst economic reality is afflicted by acute problems, the old theory is way beyond its time and the new cannot be born.

In search of an alternative

New theories and approaches are not born out of thin air. In fact, what often passes for the new is little else but a mixture of the old. In this sense, novelty and originality can be overrated. A search for the beginnings of a new approach must start with a reassessment of past theories. It is no accident that in the 1970s the History of Economic Thought once again became a popular subject, and great attention has been paid to economists of the nineteenth, as well as the twentieth, century. Whilst, most emphatically, this present book is not a contribution to the history of economic thought, it is, in part, a search through the old in an attempt to begin to build the

new. No apology is made for an extensive discussion of past economists, in particular Karl Marx, and no attempt will be made to rebut
the obvious charge of eclecticism.

It is the view of the author that we must turn mainly to Marx, and
partially to others such as Keynes, Kalecki and Sraffa, to begin to
build the basis of an alternative to neoclassicism. The reasons for the
emphasis on Marx are quite simple. Within his work there is the only
developed alternative theory of value to neoclassical economics.
Admittedly this has serious flaws and has to be reassessed in the light
of the work of Sraffa and others; but as a defined and developed
starting point it cannot be rivalled. Second, it is *only* in Marx that
there is a developed theory of production which has any semblance
to what is really going on within the capitalist system. Furthermore,
it is a theory of production which has crucial links with both the
theory of value and the theory of crises. The vast analytical lacuna in
modern economic theory, which has played such a significant role in
its recent crisis, will be filled at first after reference to *Capital,* and
above all its first volume.

The danger in this lengthy excursion back to Marx is that some
Marxist observers will totally misunderstand the whole point of the
journey. With the resurgence of Marxism in the 1960s the disease of
Marxian Fundamentalism has hit the Left. One of its symptoms is
the exposition of the view that Marx cannot be wrong. A corollary,
or subtle variant of this, is that any attempt to develop or enlarge the
Marxian analysis is seen as an *interpretation,* valid or otherwise, of
what Marx wrote himself. It is thus easy to dismiss an attempt to
build something new as an invalid interpretation of Marx. It should
go without saying, but, with the exception of one or two clearly
noted passages, this work is not such an attempt of interpretation.
Where the man himself speaks, he does so within quotation marks.

The aims of this work

Within this work, the object of analysis is the capitalist mode of
production. However, it is an analysis of fundamentals and not a
complete analysis of the system. Particular capitalist systems, and
their historical development, are excluded. We concentrate on these
fundamental areas of analysis: the theory of value, money, the production process, exploitation, and profit. In addition some attention
is paid to the process of capital accumulation and the possibility,
within the system, of crises. Less justice, however, is done to the
latter issues. Excluded from the analysis is an extended discussion of

the theory of economic growth, the credit system, and the phenomenon of rent. It could be said, therefore, that the concerns of this work are broadly similar to much of the first volume of *Capital*.

One of the most striking differences between the analysis in this work and that in *Capital* is that in the former the labour theory of value is rejected. However, it is the view of the present author that the extent to which many of the propositions in *Capital* depend upon the labour theory of value has been overestimated by both supporters and opponents of Marxian analysis. The debt that is owed to Marx, in his pioneering analysis of the capitalist system, is still great without the labour theory of value.

Some ideas of other important theorists are discussed and incorporated. These include Keynes and some modern neo-Keynesians. As would be expected, the impact of Sraffa's seminal work is discussed. The aim is to begin to weld together an alternative theoretical structure: a labour of both incorporation and reconstruction.

This rather eclectic approach may be rejected by some Marxists, at least those of fundamentalist habits. However, it is clear from Marx's own scholarship that he, himself, drew a great deal from the more important economists of his time and before. In particular, he recognized the strengths of the classical theorists, and the ideas not only of Smith and Ricardo but also John Stuart Mill and many others. These had their influence on his work. For example, Marx's theory of value is founded on the analyses of Smith and Ricardo, and many of Marx's ideas on the future development of capitalism are taken from Mill.

In terms of analytical results an aim of this work is to aid the development of a fruitful approach to the theory of value, drawing on much work which has been done elsewhere. The goal will be to break with all mechanistic and naturalistic notions of value, and with a conception of value rooted exclusively in technology. Instead is asserted a notion of value which embraces social relations; involves, to some extent, technical data; recognizes uncertainty; and thereby includes money and some monetary phenomena. Such a goal may be ambitious but it is to be re-emphasized that the analysis here is tentative and preliminary.

It has been recognized since the work of Machlup (1967) and others that the neoclassical theory of the firm is not a theory of production at all but merely a theory of the market. The gap is filled by the neoclassical production function which simply posits a certain relation between outputs and inputs, in a mechanistic fashion, without reference to real processes or relations of production. A similar accusation can be made against, for example, neoclassical labour economics; it is merely a theory of the labour market, not of the characteristics of labour itself. In this work a small attempt is made to remedy these deficiencies. In a general sense, relations of production under capitalism will be discussed, and the measures affecting, for example, the level of output. In addition, and this is at least as significant, the peculiar characteristics of labour will be examined.

The latter will lead to a reformulation of the notion of exploitation: one which is not dependent on the labour theory of value. This is one sense in which what is here proposed is a *radical* theory: one which does not endorse a symmetry of substance and interests between labour and capital. The ethical consequences are obvious. Capitalism is an exploitative system and this exploitation will be diminished or removed only by a fundamental change in social relations, bringing about a quite different economic system.

However, this work is not simply an ethical critique of capitalism (although ethical concerns are often too downgraded in radical literature). Even at a level of analysis as abstract as this it is possible to show that there are limits or barriers to capitalist development. It is futile to suggest that the collapse of capitalism is inevitable and predetermined. It is more realistic to show that there are limits and problems in the process of capital accumulation. A full analysis of the course of capitalist evolution is impossible without a study of real history, and specific capitalist systems. Clearly, that is beyond the scope of this work; but, again, tentative notes and suggestions can be made, based on an established body of analysis.

The scope and standpoint of this work

On the whole, the content of this work is not formally complex. Efforts have been made to avoid a complex mathematical treatment, and in any case many of the ideas here proposed are extremely simple. The novelty of this work lies, first and foremost, in its attempt to synthesize certain previous theories and results. In a few places a more original analysis is put forward. Such an attempt of synthesis has to remain, quite often, at the level of pure exposition, so that previously unrelated elements of theory can be effectively combined without confusion or misunderstanding. Logical consistency and clarity become at least as great concerns as theoretical originality.

It is easy to anticipate the criticism that this work is unoriginal. Whilst this is not entirely true, it would be of less concern to the author than the accusation that the analysis here is wrong. Unfortunately, it is also easy to anticipate the latter verdict on this work. Perhaps this criticism will come most often from Marxian Fundamentalists, so-called 'Keynesians' who still deny that money plays an active role in the formation of relative prices and the overall level of output, die-hard advocates of the labour theory of value, and advocates of neoclassical orthodoxy. Perhaps, also, criticism might come from others, not included among the above, who find genuine fault with this work. In the case of the latter alone is repentance on behalf of the author to be anticipated.

There are many, unfortunately, whose habits of thought require not a careful and critical assessment of the analysis proposed, but a rapid attempt to label the work as belonging to one or other well-established category or deviation, and thereby dismissing it with ease. It is tempting, therefore, to make a weak attempt to forestall such a dismissal by adopting a label for the present work, at the start. In fact, labels can help the process of understanding by alerting the reader to the features of a certain approach. Regrettably that is too rarely the case. Furthermore, the difficulty of providing a useful label for this work is partly a result of the general crisis of economics referred to above. The new will only be born when it is recognized as new, and has an emblem of its novelty. No such appropriate label can be found. However, it should be clear that an older label is still of some considerable use: this work is largely within the Marxian tradition. However uneasily it fits within that category it owes most to the work of Marx and a number of later Marxists. A discussion of the value and importance of Marxian economic analysis is the substance of the next chapter; but it can be stated here that the author is less and less convinced that the Marxian label is, elsewhere, being applied to a consistent, coherent, and original body of work, and less and less to one which leads to an identifiable body of practical economic prescriptions. As an alternative the term 'neo-Marxism' comes to mind. That is, perhaps, the best label that can be chosen. It is becoming increasingly clear that a resolution of the crisis of economic theory will have to supersede Keynes, the neoclassicals and perhaps even Marx himself.

The structure of this work

This work is divided into four parts. It would be useful to comment on the logic behind this. The first part deals with the fundamental concepts associated with the theory of value, including a critical discussion of the neoclassical approach. A 'Neo-Marxian', 'cost of production plus profit' approach is established. Part II is concerned with a necessary critique of the labour theory of value. The first two parts, therefore, serve to distance this work from both the neo-classical and orthodox Marxian traditions. The third part deals with money. Finally, the fourth part establishes a general analysis of capitalist production, in brief outline. However, some of the elements of this final part are more 'fundamental' than others, and could find a place in the first part of the book. Indeed, there is a small measure of repetition between the first and final parts. However, a more logical structure would be misunderstood by some readers, because the conceptual basis would be established before the labour theory of value was rooted out of the theory. Fundamental elements would be 'read' in labour theory of value terms, and other readers would assume that in some sense the content would be dependent on that theory. It is regrettable, but in this case it is necessary to destroy before one can build. The legacy of confusion provided by the labour theory makes an escape from the old modes of thought exceedingly difficult. One is tempted to agree with Steedman when he writes:

It can be scarcely overemphasised that the project of providing a materialist account of capitalist societies is dependent on Marx's value magnitude analysis only *in the negative sense that continued adherence to the latter is a major fetter on the development of the former* (Steedman, 1977, p. 207).

CHAPTER 2

THE VALUE OF MARXIAN ECONOMIC ANALYSIS

Why could not Marx's system have been freed, by constructive criticism, from irrelevance and contradictions and clearly shown to be the original and penetrating system of analysis that, with all its blemishes, it certainly was?

JOAN ROBINSON

Since the late 1960s the advanced capitalist nations have been afflicted with growing economic problems. Old policy prescriptions are evidently inadequate, as inflation, unemployment, and stagnation remain, or are intensified through time. Old theories are being challenged from all sides: by monetarists, Cambridge radicals, and Marxists. The orthodox economists' world is in disarray: both theory and reality are blighted.

In this environment Marxian economics has grown in influence. The number of publications in this field has increased dramatically. Marxian economists are found teaching in institutions of higher education all over the world. Their ideas have once again become an influence on the mass social-democratic and socialist parties of Western Europe. They have influenced key debates on the causes of our economic malaise. This is largely a new situation, with precedent only in the years immediately preceding and following the First World War.

Whilst neoclassical orthodoxy has remained dominant in the economics profession, it has lacked the flavour of immediacy, relevance and realism which is found in Marxism. Mainstream economics has tended to degenerate into an empty algebraic formalism on the 'theoretical' side, and into a limp and naive empiricism on the 'applied' side. The construction of such theory has almost become a mere logical game. In its explicit methodology it finds its test in the validity of its 'predictions' only. Little or no attention is paid to the realism of its *assumptions*. Reading the orthodox texts, we are almost led to believe that perfect competition prevails in the real world,

14

that individual tastes and preferences are immune to manipulation and mass advertising, and that vast oligopolistic firms do not exist. For a long time such unrealistic theory was justified on the basis of its utility as an instrument of prediction or policy, but now these claims seem less and less justified. Orthodox economics has failed. In the meantime, however, whilst the storms of crisis wreak havoc in the world outside, its proponents play elaborate (even interesting) but useless games with their 'models' of a non-existent world.

The resilience of Marxian economics

In contrast to modern neoclassicism, the economics of such influential figures as Adam Smith, Ricardo and Keynes paid attention to the realism both of its assumptions and its theory as a whole. The same can be said for Marx, and those others like Kalecki, who lie broadly in the Marxian tradition. Furthermore, despite the frequent accusation that Marxian economics has failed in the test of its own predictions, its success in that respect is probably *greater* than that of neoclassicism. Let us consider a few examples. First, Marx predicted the concentration of capital into the hands of fewer and fewer oligopolistic firms. In fact, today, only a few hundred vast firms dominate the entire capitalist world. Second, Marx predicted the gradual separation of the functions of ownership and control of capitalist firms, leading to the rise of the new social strata of company managers distinct from the main body of shareholding owners. Today this is a recognized fact. Third, Marx predicted the erosion of peasant agriculture and other antiquated forms of production, leading both to the domination of capitalist relations in the agricultural sector and a human migration from the countryside to the town. This process is virtually complete in the developed capitalist countries. Fourth, Marx predicted the creation of an integrated world capitalist system and a world-wide working class. Today capital penetrates the entire world, with the exception of China and the Soviet Bloc, creating an economically unified world system of production in which the most significant proportion of the population live by selling their labour-power. Fifth, Marx saw the continuance and exacerbation of capitalist conflict and chaos in the world economy. To an important degree, these elements are still with us.

The theoretical resilience of Marxian economics has been recognized by a number of important non-Marxian economists. Nobel prizewinner L. R. Klein, for example, saw Marxian economics as 'probably the origin of macro-economics'. In a similar vein, E.

Domar, one of the fathers of the modern theory of economic growth, wrote: 'Of all the several schools of economics the Marxists have, I think, come closest to developing a substantial theory of economic growth.' Joan Robinson, a major theorist who has done a great deal to rehabilitate Marxian economics, has remarked that Marx gives 'more insight than any other economist into how a capitalist system actually operates . . . no-one has ever produced any alternative view of the system which is anything like as powerful or enlightening as the view which Marx gives us'.

Despite its relative success in the field of prediction, the main strength of Marxian economics lies elsewhere. It lies in a powerful system of concepts which illuminate the real processes and relations of the capitalist mode of production. In contrast, neoclassical economics is based on ahistorical concepts such as 'society in general', or the isolated individual, thus losing connection with the particular economic system which is under investigation. In *Capital*, Marx attempts to develop categories which correspond to the reality of the capitalist system, rather than ideal abstractions which have no base in social reality. Also he takes a historical view, analysing the genesis of the capitalist system, as well as suggesting the internal developments which will help to lead to its downfall. Despite some weaknesses, Marx's theoretical structure and methodological approach has enormous strength and vitality.

Marxian fundamentalism

It is highly unfortunate, however, that Marxian economics has not been able to rectify its more blatant and serious theoretical weaknesses. In many Marxian circles it is still highly unpopular to criticize Marx, or to have the apparent audacity to suggest certain modifications to Marxian theory. There is a kind of symmetry between the lack of balanced consideration of Marxian economics by non-Marxian orthodoxy, on the one hand, and the denouncement by Marxists, as heresy, of all attempts to criticize sympathetically and improve Marxian economics, on the other.

A mildly amusing list of statements can be found in certain Marxian publications which attempt to show that *Capital* is flawless. One technique is to quote statements of Marx where he asserts that mainstream economic theory has degenerated since Ricardo, and use these to 'prove' that Marxian economics cannot be updated by the inclusion of any element of modern economics. Another is to state that Marx's theoretical system is a paradigm which stands and falls as a whole, and which cannot withstand any theoretical tinkering; all those who revise Marx, are, therefore, dismissed as non-Marxist. Another is to state that the logic of *Capital* is 'dialectical', and thus it cannot be refuted by formal, consistent, logical argument. It may be surprising, but all the above arguments are to be found in worthy theoretical journals. Unless Marxism can break from these quasi-religious methods of defending Marx's work, it will remain the exclusive property of a blinkered priesthood, and never penetrate into mass political culture.

As yet, the Marxian theoretical movement is not saturated by a scientific, enquiring, and self-critical outlook. Marxian economic theory has shown a large degree of incapacity to develop in an original direction, to come to terms with, and perhaps even accommodate, some of the developments in economic theory and reality which have occurred since Marx died. One major exception is the economic works of Lenin. He utilized the analysis of imperialism developed by the non-Marxist Hobson in his famous work *Imperialism*. Lenin also added to Marxian economic theory with his work on *The Development of Capitalism in Russia*. Other Marxists have been much less willing to accommodate non-Marxian analysis. Yet Marx himself incorporated large elements of the analyses of Quesnay, Smith, Ricardo, Mill and others, albeit after some criticism and modification. Latter-day Marxists have shown little propensity to reproduce the methods of constructive scholarship of Marx and Lenin in matters of economic theory.

As a result, the legacy of non-Marxian modern economics, and the realities of a structurally modified postwar capitalist system, have hardly been faced by contemporary Marxism. Yet, on the theoretical side, most of the more significant and relevant developments in non-Marxian economics have occurred since 1930. Keynes, Sraffa and others have brought revolutionary developments into economics; but, with one or two notable exceptions, there has been no attempt to integrate the bulk of these important developments into the corpus of Marxism, nor to criticize seriously, nor face the consequences of, such developments. A deep-rooted fear of contamination has overtaken Marxism. Placing itself in voluntary isolation, it has denied itself the healthy air of outside influence.

The isolation of Marxism

There are historical causes for the isolation, and consequent dogmatism, of Marxian economics. The first was the victory of the newly formulated neoclassical economic theory in the 1870s and its implantation in academic institutions as the orthodox creed. Largely for political reasons, Marxism was excluded. The second, more important cause, was the repression of Marxian theory that followed from fascism and Stalinism, in the very countries where Marxism was most strong. The geographical consequence was that Marxism was exiled to Britain and the United States, where it had always failed to gain roots in mass culture. The temporal consequence was that Marxism was much less able to appraise the post-1930 developments in non-Marxian economic theory and devise a critical synthesis where possible. The third cause was the real success of capitalism in its long and unprecedented boom after the Second World War. In this situation the Marxian assertion of the limitations and contradictions of capitalism seemed to be pure fantasy. Above all, however, the isolation of Marxism is a heritage of the *defeats* of the socialist movement in the period subsequent to the First World War.

The result of this isolation was that the Marxian movement was bound together in defence of the creed, in defiance of the reality which appeared to contradict it. Antibodies quickly identified, isolated, and expunged any taint of dilution or revision. Facts were not faced, and 'empiricism' became a cardinal sin. Claims to identify theoretical inadequacies and logical inconsistencies in the texts were simply rebutted as 'non-Marxist'. Marxism survived, virtually by repetition and incantation of the classic works of Marx or Lenin.

The changing theoretical situation

With a background of economic crisis and relative stagnation in the world capitalist system, Marxian economic theory is showing strong signs of revitalization. Of course the underlying stimulus of this change is the extent and severity of the ructions within the capitalist economic system. At the purely theoretical level, however, there have been two important seminal movements. The first is the more recent trajectory of Marxian philosophical work, especially in France and Italy. Althusser, for example, has argued that Marx's work is not entirely consistent as a whole, and that there is an 'epistemological break' in Marx's theoretical development. Whatever the veracity of this thesis, it has certainly stimulated an unprecedented degree of scrutiny of Marxian theory, and generated an important debate within Marxism. In addition, Althusser and his followers have developed an important philosophical analysis of *Capital* and Marxian economics (Althusser and Balibar, 1970). From a different point of view, Colletti has emphasized the links between Marx's theory of value and his theory of fetishism. Again this has stimulated examination and development of Marxian economics (Colletti, 1972, 1973).

The second movement resulted from the publication of Sraffa's classic work in the theory of value (Sraffa, 1960). Although the first effect of this work was to wreak havoc in neoclassical economic theory, it also gave rise to a critical examination of Marx's theory of value. We shall argue in this work that Sraffa's analysis highlights severe inadequacies in Marx's *Capital,* but at the same time it provides some necessary material for the reconstruction of Marxian economics. We repeat some of the Sraffian criticism of Marx which have been laid down elsewhere (Steedman, 1977) but also we pay attention to the urgent task of conceptual reconstruction—a task that cannot be accomplished by formalism alone.

'Neo-Ricardianism'

The more dogmatic Marxian economists have forcefully rejected Sraffa's work, dismissing him as a heretic. Too often his work is not even seriously examined. The prosecution adopts a simple alternative technique. Evidence is brought up of Sraffa's associations with the work of Ricardo. Thus exhibit A is Sraffa's editorship of the definitive ten-volume edition of Ricardo's works. Exhibit B is a textual reference in Marx's works where he fiercely criticizes Ricardo's economics. Sraffa is found guilty by association, and 'refuted' by repetition of Marx's text. He is scornfully labelled as a 'Neo-Ricardian'.

We do not assert that Sraffa and his followers are beyond theoretical criticism: we shall come to this below. It is true that Sraffa's work has unwillingly and by default helped the development of imperfect theoretical tendencies close to, or within, Marxism. But sins of imperfection and false emphasis are of a different nature to the disease of fundamentalism.

At this stage it is important to note that it is not appropriate to label Sraffa's work as 'Neo-Ricardian'. There are resemblances between Sraffa and Ricardo, but they are akin to the degree of resemblance between Stravinsky and Bach. Stravinsky makes witty imitative references to Bach and other Classical composers, but his works remain distinctively modern. What Stravinsky and Bach have in common is their equal distance from the intervening Romantic movement in music. Like Stravinsky, Sraffa uses classical constructions as the motifs of his work; but in this case they are the motifs of classical economics and in particular the central preoccupations of

Ricardo's *Principles,* namely the concern to construct a standard of absolute value and to investigate the distributive relations between wages and profits.

Sraffa, however, whilst sharing a similar compass of enquiry, has not, on the whole, vindicated Ricardo's formal analysis. Sraffa has demonstrated that the standard of 'absolute value' cannot be labour, as Ricardo was prone to suggest, but it must be the Sraffian 'standard commodity'. The standard commodity is a particular mixture of the basic commodities in the economic system. Second, Sraffa *demolishes* the concept of embodied labour by showing its *redundancy* in the formal determination of prices and profits, thus embarrassing the attempts of both Ricardo and Marx to erect a formal theory of prices and profits on the basis of this concept. The 'labour theory of value', so central to Ricardo's *Principles,* is no longer tenable as a result of the Sraffian revolution in economic theory.

It is true that there is a focus in Sraffa on questions of economic distribution, and this does reflect a similar emphasis in Ricardo; but Ricardo's exposition rests on several key propositions, which, incidentally, are mostly repeated in Marx's *Capital,* but which are refuted by Sraffa. For example, Ricardo asserted that prices will be proportional to amounts of embodied labour within 'six or seven' per cent, and Marx seemed to agree that deviations of price from embodied labour value would be small (Marx, 1962, pp. 147, 184). These assertions are shown to have no theoretical basis, as a result of Sraffa's analysis. Second, Ricardo believed that a reduction in the amount of labour embodied in a commodity, through a technical change, would always lead to a reduction in its price, other things presumably being equal. This proposition was later dubbed by Marx as the 'law of value' (ibid., pp. 174, 176). Sraffa's analytical system can also be used to refute this 'law'.

On one important point, however, Sraffa and Ricardo both correctly endorse a common proposition that was unconvincingly rebutted by Marx. We refer to the statement that in stationary economic equilibrium the general rate of profit is determined by the conditions of production in those industries which directly or indirectly produce the real wage, and not by the conditions in other industries. It is relatively easy to produce arguments and examples to support this Sraffian proposition (Hodgson, 1974b, pp. 366–8, 389–90).

At the formal level, therefore, it is clearly the case that the 'Neo-Ricardian' label should not be applied to Sraffa. In many respects his own work is the antithesis of Ricardo's.

Symptomatic silences

However, Ricardo and Sraffa share a number of what might be called 'symptomatic silences'. The production process, for example, is ignored in Sraffa and hurriedly evacuated in Ricardo. The driving forces of profit and competition are apparently assumed, without discussion, at the outset of both works. The analysis of money is vulgarized in Ricardo and sidestepped in Sraffa. These are all serious omissions.

In the case of Sraffa, unlike Ricardo, there is a strong case for clemency. Sraffa's work is clearly subtitled *Prelude to a Critique of Economic Theory*: a modest inscription which virtually justifies all sins of omission. Ricardo, on the other hand, attempted to write a complete text on the *Principles of Political Economy and Taxation.*

Furthermore, the recognition of such silences in Sraffa's work does not, in any sense, undermine the *formal* correctness of his theoretical edifice. It remains a valid logico-theoretical work; the necessary syntax of any adequate theory of value, distribution, accumulation and exploitation. The cost of abandoning Sraffa's work is nothing less than the cost of abandoning *logical consistency.*

The inadequate emphasis which is given to the latter point in a recent important essay by Rowthorn has generated much confusion (Rowthorn, 1974). Rowthorn accepts the basic achievements of the Sraffa school (ibid., p. 73) but misleadingly adopts the 'Neo-Ricardian' label for this school. There is no formal inconsistency in Rowthorn's position; it simply suffers from a lack of committed emphasis and clarity on one important point. It must be stated, clearly and un-equivocally, that Sraffa is formally correct, and that the logical con-sequences must be faced. The substance of Rowthorn's article is not an attack on Sraffa, therefore, but it does include a viable critique of formalistic *interpretations* of Sraffa.

In a later work, Rowthorn has made his position more clear. Referring to his earlier article, he remarks that it was not his inten-tion to show that Sraffa and his followers 'were completely wrong, but rather that they were very limited in their approach, and that their exclusive emphasis on the distribution of income had led them to ignore the social aspects of production' (Rowthorn, 1980, p. 8). It would have been better if the word 'completely' had been omitted, but here the appraisal of Sraffa is more to the point. The approach *is* limited, and in many of the writings of the Sraffa school the social aspects of production *are* ignored. The point, however, is that Sraffa himself would probably admit that this was true. At the same time, the devastating impact of the Sraffa system should not be ignored.

Nevertheless, Rowthorn's work has highlighted some important omissions. In particular, two important issues are emphasized. First, the need for a dynamic study of the sphere of production and the labour process within it; and second, the essential role of the concept of a 'mode of production' bequeathed to us by Marx. We shall assess the former at a later stage of this work. The second issue can conveniently be discussed here. The idea of an economic system, or 'mode of production', corresponding to a set of structures in the real world, is one of Marx's most fundamental and illuminating contributions to economic theory. When analysing the modern world this idea plays an important role in arranging and structuring the analysis. Other writers, particularly Colletti (1972, 1973) have explored this in more depth, but we can give a brief summary here.

The capitalist mode of production

Marxian economic theory is constructed in relation to a real object: the capitalist mode of production. Its aim is not to examine 'society in general', nor universal laws of societal life, but the specific laws and character of the capitalist system.

The relevance of such an analysis is based on the fact that the capitalist mode of production is dominant in the modern world, and that the laws of capitalist development are the major determinants of economic, social and political change on a world scale; but, of course, the capitalist mode of production has never existed, and will never exist, in a pure and unadulterated form. It is usually combined with other subservient modes of production, and forced into a matrix of nations and cultures, all with different institutional and ideological inheritances. A different social formation exists in every major country of the capitalist world, but in each social formation the capitalist mode of production is dominant.

At the most abstract level, therefore, the task of Marxian economics is to analyse the structure and dynamics of the pure capitalist mode of production. As such a pure mode does not exist, references to empirical reality can only be made in circumstances where the empirical material is generated by economic forces of a predominantly capitalist genus. For this reason, Marx chose empirical material from mid-nineteenth-century Britain for use in *Capital,* because at that time the capitalist mode was most developed in this country; in no other country was capitalism so strong.

After completing an analysis of the capitalist mode of production it is then possible to analyse specific capitalist social formations. This secondary stage of analysis includes the mediating social and historical connections which explain the origin and development of a particular capitalist society. The developing socioeconomic structures of such a concrete society can then be illuminated both by the abstract concepts of the capitalist mode of production and the related specific features of concrete reality.

In this particular work we confine ourselves to the primary and most abstract level of analysis; it is concerned with the dissection of the pure capitalist mode of production. However, as such an analysis must adopt some responsibility for the later task of constructing analyses at the secondary level, it will be a major concern to develop feasible analytical connections between the two levels. This will be reflected in the attempt to develop a conceptual framework which permits measurement and empirical testing. Furthermore, a sustained attempt will be made to make the theory operational at a secondary level: to provide suitable building blocks for derivative theory.

In our basic analysis of a notional pure capitalist system, one important dimension of the capitalist mode must be excluded. We refer to the international dimension, and the associated phenomena of international trade and imperialism, both of which have been so crucial right through the whole history of capitalism. It would clearly be beyond the scope of this work to include a theory of international trade and capital accumulation. Unfortunately, Marx did not write his intended volume on international capitalism. Neither have subsequent Marxists produced an adequate analysis of this issue.

Capitalism: a definition

Having established the centrality of the concept of the capitalist mode of production in the analysis of the modern world it is necessary to conclude with a Marxian definition of capitalism. Marx, himself, was not prone to putting such a definition on paper, but perhaps the best one that has been established in the Marxian literature, by Mandel and others, is 'generalized commodity production'. However, this definition of capitalism needs explanation and a degree of qualification.

First, a commodity is a good or a service which is brought to the market for sale. When sold, it can be either bartered for another commodity or exchanged for money. The latter, of course, is most often the case. The word 'generalized' in the definition applies to the fact

that, under capitalism, labour-power, i.e. the capacity to work, is also
a commodity. People work, after a 'freely' negotiated contract with
their employer, for a wage or salary. This is not the case under
feudalism or slavery. Neither serfs, nor slaves, strictly speaking,
receive wages, and their labour-power is not a commodity.

For labour-power to be hired on the market its owners must be
deprived of an alternative source of livelihood. In other words they
cannot have ownership or direct access to the means of production.
It follows, therefore—from the statement that labour-power is hired as
a commodity—that workers are separated from ownership or control
of the means of production. The means of production are privately
owned by the capitalist class. 'Generalized commodity production'
can be taken to imply a class-divided society, in which the workers
are separated from the means of production.

However, both labour-power and money are peculiar commodities.
In the case of labour-power this has several unique qualities which
are discussed in Chapter 16 below. One of the most important is
that, unlike most other commodities, it is not itself produced under
capitalist conditions. The significance of this is elaborated later.

If money exists as gold coin then its special features are limited to
the general nature of money itself. These are discussed in Part III of
this work. If, however, money exists in its modern form, not as a
precious metal, then it is almost universally produced by the state.
This production too is not strictly under capitalist conditions. It is
not motivated for profit, whereas, unlike the commodity labour-
power, it is possessed by the institution in which it is produced,
before it is transferred to the market.

Whilst accepting the definition of capitalism as generalized commodity production it is important to stress that both money and
labour-power are unique commodities, and they have a unique and
central role in the system. This, precisely, is done by Marx.

Another strength of the Marxian analysis of modern society is that
it unifies, rather than compartmentalizes, social science. The definition of capitalism, elaborated above, has included references to
aspects of the system which cannot, in the orthodox sense of the
word, be considered pure 'economics'. For example, we have made
reference to the 'sociological' category of *class,* and a class-divided
society. Second, for a commodity to exist it must be owned. Hence a
system of *property rights,* and a legal and state apparatus to support
them, is implied. This trespasses into the realm of politics and law.
As we shall also see below, there are points where the frontiers of
what may be called psychology are crossed. Marxian analysis is not

confined to the realm of 'economics' alone. This is clear, even from the very definition of capitalism itself.

With the concept of 'mode of production' in general, and 'generalized commodity production' in particular, emphasis is placed on *production* within the system. This is true in two separate, but related, senses. First, we are led to examine the mechanisms through which the *system* sustains and reproduces itself. In other words, a focus is created on the reproduction of social relations. Second, the question arises as to how the system produces the goods and services required for human survival, comfort and enjoyment. Attention shifts, therefore, to the sphere of production within the system, and its connection with distribution and consumption. The emphasis on production within Marxian analysis is in complete contrast to neoclassical orthodoxy, where the emphasis is on the sphere of exchange.

Conclusions

On the one hand Marxism is burdened by dogma, and a good measure of irrelevance. Furthermore, until recently, its polemics were exhaustingly strident and many of its leading advocates were of narrow Fundamentalist persuasion. Marxism has not readily learnt from or incorporated new advances in political economy. After visible daubing, with labels such as 'Neo-Ricardian', these have been consigned by the more narrow and dogmatic Marxists to the dustbin.

However, on the other hand, a careful evaluation of Marxian thought reveals that it has a penetrating and powerful system of concepts, which, at the present time, provide the most useful way of analysing the advanced economies of the Western world. Whilst the label 'Marxist' is open to a wide and conflicting number of interpretations, in the thought of Marx himself we find a method and approach which should be valued. It is here that we must start, even if, at the end, we have something that would best be given another name.

CHAPTER 3

IDEOLOGY AND ORTHODOX ECONOMICS

Relationships of ownership
they whisper in the wings,
to those condemned to act accordingly
and wait for succeeding kings . . .
        BOB DYLAN, *Gates of Eden*

In this chapter our main concern is with orthodox economics. In particular, the back-door intrusion of ideology into the mainstream school is discussed. Despite claims to be scientific, and free of such ideology, modern orthodox economics is based on false and inappropriate canons of scientificity. These, in turn, invite a conservative, pro-capitalist ideology to enter through the back door.

The dominant tendency within orthodox economics is, of course, the neoclassical school. This swept the bourgeois intellectual world after 1870, loudly claiming that it was 'scientific', 'objective' and, furthermore, separate from any political persuasion. In particular, most neoclassical economists were keen to disassociate their 'science' from the socialist and radical ideology which had tainted the preceding classical school, and, especially, Marxism. The neoclassical economists argued that the same standards of scientific validation which were found in the physical sciences must be applied to economics. Above all, they thought, this meant that economics must free itself from historical particularities and develop principles and categories of a universal character. An attempt was made to develop a systematic analysis which would be applicable to all economic systems, all forms of human society, and all history. They abstracted, therefore, from history itself. The binding links with politics and the study of particular social systems were severed. Economics, in order to become a science, had to be ahistorical, asocial and apolitical.

Even today, when we open any orthodox economics textbook, such as Samuelson (1975) and Lipsey (1975), it is immediately clear that orthodox economics is meant to apply to all forms of economic system. It bases itself on features which it claims are common to all of them, whilst ignoring or underemphasizing the specific features of particular forms of economic system. Particular phenomena which are peculiar to specific systems, such as the labour market, slavery, or feudal relations, are pushed into the background. Instead, abstract and allegedly universal concepts such as 'choice', 'scarcity', 'ends and means', 'production possibilities', 'factors of production', 'utility' and so on, pervade and dominate the whole analytical system. It is these abstract and universal concepts, rather than concepts which apply to particular economic systems, that become the raw material to build most of the arguments and theorems of neoclassical analysis.

The same universal and ahistorical concepts are applied to the ridiculous illustrative example of Robinson Crusoe, all alone on his desert island. He too has 'unlimited wants', 'scarce means', a 'production possibility frontier', and a 'utility function'. Neoclassical analysis feels equally at home with this shipwrecked entrepreneur. And then, with no difficulty, it can provide a theoretical and formal analysis, with the same categories and the same theorems, that applies to Ancient Egypt and stone-age tribes, as well as to modern capitalist society.

Neoclassical formalism

Especially since the Second World War, neoclassical economics has become highly formalized, and sanctified in complex mathematical splendour. The claim to scientific objectivity thus appears to be reinforced by the utilization of the virtues of mathematics. In general, of course, at the purely mathematical level, this formal apparatus is mathematically valid and not without content and significance.

On the other hand, we invoke different criteria of validity if we make the claim that such a formal mathematical model corresponds to real processes in the real world. For example, it is certainly possible to construct a consistent mathematical model where 'individuals' maximize some quantity which is called 'utility'. Such a model, however, subjects itself to more than purely mathematical and logical standards of validity if we argue that real-world individuals actually attempt to maximize their individual utility. Here we invoke the additional assumptions that the individual is a self-contained entity, and that satisfaction is something to do with homogeneous units called 'utility'. These are highly questionable assumptions. If we go further, into the realm of 'welfare economics', and assert that when all individuals in society achieve a certain equilibrium and satisfy a certain arbitrary criterion of 'optimality', and that equilibrium situation is *actually* optimal, then the whole exercise becomes open to doubt. Neoclassical economists have become mesmerized by their own mathematical constructions, turning their eyes away from the real world and the latent ideological assumptions of their own economics.

The infiltration of bourgeois ideology

Consider the common neoclassical model of individuals as independent atoms of desire, all seeking to maximize their individual satisfaction, their aggregation being the substantial nature of society as a whole. It is sometimes forgotten that this view of human society is a highly particular and relatively recent development. It became prominent in utilitarian philosophy and in the ideology of the nineteenth-century bourgeoisie. Neoclassical economics, for all its claims to scientific objectivity, embraces this assumption and endows it with almost universal validity, with no explicit justification other than to remark that alternative assumptions would make the mathematics much more complicated. Science is sacrificed at the altar of mathematics, whilst the high priests of bourgeois ideology stalk in the shadows.

Another example of the infiltration of bourgeois ideology is the very frequent adoption of the criterion of 'Pareto optimality' in welfare economics. A few decades after the birth of neoclassical economics in the 1870s it became apparent that the sum total of individual utility might well be maximized in a more egalitarian society, as the sum total of utility would probably increase if a slice of income were transferred from the rich to the poor. The rich would lose, but not as much as the poor would gain. In fear of making a dangerous concession to the socialist creed it was asserted that the maximization of total utility was not, after all, the concern of the welfare economist, and another alternative criterion of optimality was adopted. This criterion, originally engineered by Pareto, the Italian scholar of pronounced conservative views, had the redeeming feature that it did not erode the existing income of the rich. Income redistribution was sanctioned only if the rich (or poor) did not lose in the process. Welfare economics became a highly conservative theory, giving the stamp of 'optimality' to the inegalitarian *status quo.*

It is true, of course, that one reason why Pareto optimality was adopted was that interpersonal comparisons of utility are difficult, if not impossible, to make. This, in turn, should lead us to scrutinize the ideological content of the individualistic concept of utility itself. In the next chapter we shall posit an alternative concept which does not relate to the individual alone but to the fundamentally social character of human satisfaction and desire.

Ideology can also be traced in the terminology of orthodox economics. Consider the concept of 'capital'. This is defined by orthodox economists as a stock of potentially productive wealth. However, there are two distinct aspects to 'capital' which are liable to be confused. First, there is the physical, asocial and ahistorical aspect: 'capital' as *means of production,* as things. Physical means of production have existed in all forms of human society, including the most primitive. Second, there is the social form and function of 'capital' within capitalist society in particular; here it is *privately owned,* and its ownership is concentrated into the hands of a small social class. Capital is not just a set of *things,* it is also a part of a set of *social relations* within capitalist society; involving the separation of the mass of the labouring classes from ownership and control of the means of production, and involving specific social relations between the workers and capitalist owners.

Orthodox economics sidesteps this point with neoclassical general equilibrium analysis. Here it is assumed that individuals have an 'initial endowment' of goods or capital: the concentration of ownership of capital in the hands of the few is thus ignored because it is a 'special case'. Marxists have continuously pointed out that this starting point is ahistorical, and the *actual* distribution of property, in capitalist society, is not explained in orthodox theory. The neoclassical response is typified by Hahn:

[It is not] easy to see why so much fuss has been made about exogenously given endowments. No sensible theory would, as I have already noted, start with Neanderthal man. At whatever date we start, we had better take the available resources at that date, and their distribution, as given by history (Hahn, 1980, p. 127).

In other words, the historical point at which the model 'starts' is data in the model: it is not embedded in the model itself. This cavalier attempt to construct a 'general', universal and ahistorical theory is strange if we consider the analysis itself. For example, the analysis is based on a very special type of perfectly competitive market, in which, according to Hahn, money has 'no role' (1980, p. 130) and economic agents are effectively 'without economic power' (p. 132). So the accusation can be turned back upon the neo-classicals themselves: to what point in history can your general equilibrium analysis apply? A casual look at the many thousand years since Neanderthal man finds no such period to which it could be applicable. For thousands of years developed markets were lacking; for much of the time tribal despots or national rulers were more important in the distribution of economic wealth than the market; and in the last few hundred years the role of money has been crucial. In abandoning history, general equilibrium analysis abandons reality as well.

Surely it would be more fruitful to concentrate, explicitly, on *capitalist* society, recognizing the specific social relations involved. It would then be perceived that the 'supply of labour' has a magnitude which derives from the fact that people are deprived of ownership of the means of production, and must work in order to live. But to do this is simultaneously to recognize the concentration of ownership of the means of production in the hands of the few. Unable to face these real facts, orthodox analysis falls short in its own terms. It fails to perceive the economic power behind the distribution of property, and fails to appreciate the functional effect of this distribution on prices, wages and profits themselves. As Preiser shows in his analysis:

What matters is indeed the relative scarcity of the factors of production
. . . such scarcity is not a natural, but a social phenomenon. It depends on
the distribution of property, and the degree of stability of this social
datum determines the degree of stability of the distribution of income
based upon it (Preiser, 1952).

Whilst neglecting the distribution of wealth under capitalism, and its functional effects on the distribution of income, the productivity of capital is seen as a technical or physical quality: having nothing to do with the social relations of production. Inputs, such as 'capital' and 'labour' are, in the neoclassical view of production, mysteriously transformed into an output. Production is conceived as a natural or asocial process (see Rowthorn, 1980, p. 15). Social relations within production fade out of sight.

At the same time, torn from its social environment, 'capital' becomes ahistorical and timeless; it appears to have existed for all history. Its concentration in a few hands seems natural and immortal, a fact of human life. It is then but a short step to a conservative political outlook and a justification for the *status quo*. Although such an ideology does not follow logically or automatically from careful and 'positive' statements of neoclassical theory, it is no accident that most neoclassical economists are conservative in their outlook. It would have been better if the pretensions to universality had been abandoned, and the ideological assumptions stated clearly from the outset.

Without paying heed to such warnings, neoclassicism leads to the approach of seeing all history through the lenses of capitalist ideology. This, in turn, endows the existing capitalist system with the attributes of a natural, immortal, and optimal social system. A 'this is the best of all possible worlds' approach develops. The spurious 'value-free' claims of neoclassical economics turn into a system of partly concealed apologetics for the existing social order.

Having jettisoned real history and real social relations of production, neoclassical economics has no firm object upon which to anchor its own analysis and axioms. The result, in most cases, is a thinly disguised ideological defence for the capitalist *status quo*.

Economic science must have a concrete object

We have noted how neoclassical economics imports bourgeois ideology under the cover of an attempt to render economics a universal and a historical science. Analysis is based on abstract concepts such as 'society in general' or 'human nature'. However, although it may *appear* to all inhabitants of Western consumer society that, for example, there has always been a conflict between 'unlimited wants' and 'scarce means', as the neoclassical economists tell us, a different picture emerges when other concrete economic systems are analysed. In fact, as Sahlins (1972) has pointed out, in primitive tribal economies there is no social process by which wants are continually generated and extended without limit. Wants remain stable and relatively *limited*. Furthermore, the means to satisfy such wants are easily available: they are *not scarce*. In contrast, a tension between *unlimited* wants and *scarce* means is very much a feature of capitalist society, in which wants are generated and increased through the whole process of production and distribution. The assumptions of neoclassical economics are *not* universal: to assume that they were would be to impose an alien and inappropriate ideology upon a quite different mode of production.

This example should show that not only are the key axioms of neoclassical economics ideological in character, but that it is also necessary to abandon spurious claims to universality. The basic assumptions in economic science must be related to a concrete mode of production. A major defect of any analysis which bases itself on ahistorical and allegedly universal abstractions is that it cannot, itself, explain the social basis and origin of such categories. Economics, instead of being rooted in real-world conditions, becomes attached to unverifiable and unreal abstractions. These, in turn, become part of a theory which claims to say something important about the real world. In fact it is not a *realistic* theory at all: it is a process of logical deduction from basic assumptions *within thought* (see Hollis and Nell, 1975, ch. 1) even if, *at a later stage,* an appeal is made for empirical verification.

Such a method of developing theory is unable to descend to the level of concrete objects, and remains imprisoned within the realm of ideas and ideology. As Colletti puts it:

The relation between the theory and its object contracts, due to the ideal character of the latter, into a mere relation of idea to idea, an internal monologue within thought itself. The object of analysis thus slips through our fingers; it is . . . impossible for us to undertake any study of the facts, *of social processes, precisely because we are no longer confronting a society, a real object, but only the* idea *of society, society in general* (Colletti, 1972, p. 3).

In contrast, it is clearly evident from the opening pages in *Capital* that Marx is attempting to analyse a particular society only: capitalist society. In other words, *Capital* is not a study of the abstract 'economy', detached from social relations and a location in history, but the study of the capitalist economy and its inherent social relations.

On the materialist method

Orthodox economics explains social reality from predefined ideas; it does not explain ideas, including its own concepts, from real social relations and forces. Marxian economics, on the other hand, proceeds from the real processes and relations of the capitalist mode of production. A premise of this, of course, is that there is such a thing as capitalism in the real world outside our heads. But capitalism itself was built by man, and is recognizable as such in the institutions of commerce and law. There must always be some social system by which the material conditions of life are reproduced in human society, and this must be expressed in particular social relations.

Such a premise, therefore, is not arbitrary. Marxian economics claims to be scientific on the basis that its central categories are abstract expressions of real social relations found within the capitalist mode of production. Such categories remain operational only as long as such relations exist.

The point is not to ignore the sphere of ideas, and attempt to confine ourselves to a fictitious 'purely material' social reality, but to avoid the isolation of the ideal from the material. It is necessary to recognize, within the terms of the materialist method itself, that the economic system does not just produce *things*, but also it produces and reproduces all sorts of *ideas*, some which have a foundation in science and some which do not. Furthermore, the Marxian approach sees production as a combination of natural forces, human consciousness, and social relations. These cannot be separated out. Orthodox economics, on the other hand, concentrates exclusively on the natural–physical aspect of production, consigning the elements of consciousness and social relations in a sealed package to the Department of Sociology.

The effect of this damaging division of labour within social science is, as Blackburn (1972) points out: 'to prevent the underlying determinants of the social formation coming into view' (p. 10). Economics becomes a formalistic game, and sociology soars skywards in irrelevant abstraction. The analysis of a concrete socioeconomic system requires a unified system of social science. The production of things is inseparable from the social relations in which men and women interact in order to accomplish this production, and the distribution, of the product. Hence the analysis of the production of things is inseparable from the analysis of social relations. Marx was the first to recognize this, and he then laid down the basis of a historical, materialist, and unified, social science.

CHAPTER 4

COMMODITIES AND THEIR UTILIZATION

For so it is, oh Lord my God, I measure it; but what it is that I measure I do not know.

SAINT AUGUSTINE, *Confessions*

Capitalism, as we have discussed above, can be defined as generalized commodity production. The analytical starting point, the capitalist mode of production, thus provides us with a real object as the foundation stone. In the opening words of Marx's *Capital*:

The wealth of societies in which the capitalist mode of production prevails appears as an immense collection of commodities; the individual commodity appears as its elementary form. Our investigation therefore begins with the analysis of the commodity.

The importance of this starting point lies in its ability to generate a number of key categories. In particular, Marx adopted the classical distinction between use-value and exchange-value, seen as two facets of the commodity.

Neoclassical economics has a different starting point. Instead of the commodity, a specific social form, there are goods and services, conceived ahistorically. From the consumption of such goods and services individuals derive *utility*. This, alone, is the primary aspect of the commodity. Then, of course, the concept of marginal utility is established, and related to price. In rejecting this neoclassical approach our aim is to help to re-establish some earlier, classical and Marxian analytical categories, despite the passage of over a century of neo-classical thought. Our discussion of the exchange-value of commodities is left to the next two chapters: here the discussion centres on use-value.

The social and natural aspects of the commodity

We could first examine a commodity-producing society from a technological and naturalistic point of view. We would note that in the

34

production process particular substances and objects are combined with others, with the help of human labour in many instances, to produce a final product. This would be an examination of the physical and technical methods by which man interacts with, and modifies, his natural—physical environment. It would be a study of the ecology of the human species.

Such a view would portray the movement and metamorphosis of substances, the creation and fission of objects, the flow of energy in the production process, the mechanical linkages, the chemical reactions, and the work-methods of people engaged in productive activity. But this ecological, technological, and naturalistic view would not be sufficient to grasp the nature of the commodities which moved in and out of production. The commodity itself would remain a mystery; for it is not a purely naturalistic phenomenon.

We could even extend our naturalistic view from the production process, and widen it to include the hustle and bustle of the market. We could observe that people seem to be impelled to produce goods in order to exchange them for strange tokens called money; but the commodity would still remain an enigma. The simple physical exchange of object for object is not a sufficient characterization of commodity exchange. After all, the bee and the flower carry out an exchange; when the bee enters the flower to collect the nectar it deposits a 'payment' of pollen. Such an act of exchange, however, is clearly not an exchange of commodities.

What are the obvious features of a commodity? First, a commodity takes the physical form of an object, or an activity which changes the form or disposition of objects. In the former case the commodity is a good; in the latter case it is a service. In every case it has an objective physical—sensuous form which can be recognized by two or more human persons. Without such a sensuous form the exchange could not be mutually recognized and accepted.

If we probe more deeply other features are detected. It becomes evident that the commodity is not a purely physical entity. In short, the definition of a commodity is something that is produced for sale on the market. So here we have introduced a particular type of exchange, and the institution of the market, within the definition of the commodity itself. We shall now elaborate on these two concepts.

The specificity of commodity exchange

The word 'exchange' cannot be here interpreted in the wide and rather vacuous sense of 'exchange theory' in orthodox sociology (see, for example, Homans, 1961; Blau, 1974). According to this body of theory an enormous number of social activities, in all forms of society, are acts of exchange. The tribal tribute from the member of the tribe to the chief is 'exchanged' for the benefits of the security and cohesion of the tribal system. The work of a modern housewife is 'exchanged' for a share of the wealth, earnings and accommodation of the wage-earner. The work of a slave is 'exchanged' for the benefit of not being whipped by the slave-driver. The smile of the stranger is 'exchanged' for the endearing conversation of a suitor.

These acts are not acts of commodity exchange. Exchange, in the sense that it is used in this book, involves not only the exchange of goods and services, but also the exchange of *legal property rights,* within a social system of *private property relations.* The tribal tribute is not *privately* owned by either the chief or the members of the tribe: it is an object of collective property. The husband does not come to own the services of the housewife, neither are most domestic services subject to private ownership within the family. The slave has no ownership whatsoever of his body or his labour-power; hence these cannot be exchanged in the strict sense of the word. If smiles, endearing conversation, and other pleasantries became objects of property then the suitor would not be a suitor at all: he would be the client of a prostitute.

The exchange of commodities requires a legal system which has the following features:

(1) the legal right of personal or corporate ownership of private property, and, within broad limits, the right of the owner to sell or dispose of the property as he or she wishes;
(2) a body of law relating to contract between persons or corporations;
(3) a general system of law under which the human parties to a contract are equally accountable, i.e. 'equality under the law';
(4) legal criteria to assess whether or not the contract has the necessary voluntary agreement of both parties, voluntary agreement being a necessary feature of a legally valid contract.

Such a system of law is found, of course, in many countries today; but it is a relatively new creation. In England it did not become securely established until the seventeenth century, although aspects of this law can be traced back to Roman times. Even in modern capitalist societies there are important parts of the social formation which do not come under such law. The tax system is a notable example; the exacting of taxes is not an exchange as there is an asymmetrical legal relationship, i.e. taxes must be paid even without the consent of the citizen.

The Soviet Union is also worthy of examination in this light. Without attempting to categorize this particular social formation, it is sufficient to note that commodity exchange is not dominant but peripheral in the USSR. Objects are continually transferred from one sector to another, e.g. steel from the steel industry to the tractor industry, according to the national plan. But these goods are not privately owned. Neither are the objects transferred by mutual agreement; their movements are directed by the central planning agency. The bulk of production in the Soviet Union, therefore, is not commodity production.

Many argue, however, that labour-power is a commodity in the USSR. Let us examine this question briefly. Labour is compulsory for those that are eligible and able, so there is no completely voluntary agreement between the state-employer and the worker. Furthermore, there is a pronounced lack of symmetry between the legal status and position of the employing agency, i.e. the state, and the worker. For example, the employers' rights to hire and fire labour are more effective than the workers' right to go on strike for higher wages. It appears that labour-power is a quasi-commodity in the Soviet Union: a weird amalgam of private and statified forms, and not a commodity proper.

The commodity and human society

Inherent in the system of legal relations which provides the institutional basis for commodity exchange is an implicit demarcation between human possessors and non-human objects of possession. The legally recognized members of the human species, insofar as they own commodities, are, as we have seen, 'equal' under this system of law. Hence the analysis of the commodity cannot be a purely naturalistic one; the commodity must be viewed from the standpoint of human society. We cannot study the commodity in the manner of the physical sciences alone, nor from the spurious viewpoint of a supra-human objectivity. The social science of modern society must base itself on this humanistic premise.

However, this premise is neither arbitrary nor subjective. It is based on two important objective facts. First, the existence of a legal system of the type we have described with 'equal' possessing agents. And second, the existence of an identifiable human species, i.e. a species which, despite clear physical differences from individual to individual, has a set of commonly held natural characteristics. These include the various common biological needs, for food, warmth and shelter, and the various commonly held potential or actual capabilities. The latter conditions have, of course, existed for an extremely long period of time; but it is only in the recent epoch that the common biological identity of the human species has been reflected in a common social identity in terms of law. As we shall see, a common *economic* identity has yet to be created in reality; but we should never underestimate the consequent change of man's view of himself when the seemingly egalitarian political and legal institutions of the bourgeois revolutions were thrust upon the world. Man, instead of being an object of nature, became the subject of social life.

Forces and relations of production

We have noted that a commodity is a good or service that is produced for exchange, and this exchange involves a specific system of social relations. So, even at this early stage of our analysis we have encountered the combination of two distinct elements of economic reality within the guise of the commodity. The first is the set of production techniques which are available to produce the commodity. These are not independent, of course, of the laws of the natural—physical world which man can investigate but not change. Neither is technology independent of the human social world: it is conditioned by the development of human capabilities and the system of organization of the production process itself. This conception of a socially conditioned technology, expressing the interaction of man's creative activity with nature, is summed up in the phrase 'the forces of production'. Second, as we have seen, the commodity corresponds to a definite system of social relations, expressed particularly in the legal system, but also involving the method of social organization upon which production is based. These are summed up in the phrase 'the relations of production'.

The division of labour

The division of labour between separate tasks of production is a necessary social basis for commodity production. Without a division of labour no form of exchange would be necessary. However, as Adam Smith pointed out a long time ago, the division of labour under capitalism has allowed important developments in the productive forces, i.e. increased social productivity. So the division of labour is an example of a strong interaction between the forces and relations of production.

It must be emphasized that the division of labour is a necessary, but not sufficient, condition for commodity production. Quite frequently orthodox economists give commodity production the semblance of immortality by suggesting that the division of labour is limited by the extent of the commodity market. It cannot, therefore, exist outside commodity production. This error is found in the writings of Adam Smith, and it is still repeated today. It was clearly refuted by Marx:

This division of labour is a necessary condition for commodity production, although the converse does not hold; commodity production is not a necessary condition for the division of labour. Labour is socially divided in the primitive Indian community, although the products do not thereby become commodities. Or, to take an example nearer home, labour is systematically divided in every factory, but the workers do not bring about this division by exchanging their individual products (Marx, 1976, p. 132).

Another way in which orthodox economists unintentionally or intentionally obscure the historically specific social relations associated with the commodity form, is to identify economic *goods* with *commodities* in all circumstances. Economic goods are present in all forms of human society; in contrast, the production of commodities involves a specific type of social system.

Use-value

The commodity has two facets. The first is its use-value and the second is its exchange-value. The use-value of a commodity relates to the natural properties of the commodity and their capacity to satisfy human social and biological needs. Hence goods which are not commodities also have a use-value. Marx explains this aspect of commodities in the following passage from *Capital*:

The commodity is, first of all, an external object, a thing which through its qualities satisfies human needs of whatever kind. The nature of these

*needs, whether they arise, for example, from the stomach, or the
imagination, makes no difference* (ibid., p. 125).

Note that the use-value of an object does not reside purely in the
mind of the human consumer or owner: it has an external manifesta-
tion in the object itself. This passage makes it clear that, for Marx,
use-value was not a purely subjective concept:

*The usefulness of a thing makes it a use-value. But this usefulness does not
dangle in mid-air. It is conditioned by the physical properties of the
commodity and has no existence apart from the latter* (ibid., p. 126).

Use-value is not, however, an asocial category. It is not derived
simply from individual biological needs. A use-value is an object
which can satisfy particular human wants, and hence is socially
conditioned insofar as these wants result from society: from social
pressures and circumstances. In modern capitalist society the vast
majority of wants are created socially rather than springing from an
isolated human individual.

However, despite the fact that a use-value is conditioned by social
circumstances, it does not usually bear the clear hallmark of a particular social system. Many objects have had a broadly similar use-
value in different forms of society. Bread, water, wine, air, leather,
knives and horses are all examples. Also, as we have mentioned, all
objects that are useful to human beings have a use-value, but it is not
the case that all objects that are useful are commodities. Air has a
use-value, but it is not, as yet, a commodity.

To assess a particular use-value it is necessary to examine the
physical properties of the object, as well as the physiology and psychology of the human owner or consumer. This assessment may vary
from individual to individual, or it may be the same for all members
of the human species. It is quite possible for an object to have an
important use for one person but to be of little use for another, due
to eccentricities of taste. This still does not mean, however, that use-
value is a subjective category; such eccentricities result from heredi-
tary, environmental, or class differences, on the whole, and these
explain most of the deviations from the mean.

In the writings of Smith, Ricardo and Marx, the concept of use-
value is social and objective rather than individual and subjective. Use-
value, to them, was the objective social worth of an object, not the
subjective satisfaction that was derived from its consumption. Use-
value, to them, was not totally extrinsic to the goods themselves; it

was largely an intrinsic property of objects. This conception of use-value is illustrated by the fact that they sometimes used the term 'value-in-use', with equivalent meaning; and a phrase such as 'satisfaction value' is absent from their works. They refer to the use-value *of an object*, rather than satisfaction obtained.

If we too adopt this social and objective conception of use-value then we have to deal with the question of individual variations in the nature of the use-value of particular goods. A cigarette, for example, has a different use-value for a smoker than a non-smoker. This problem can be dealt with quite easily. As in the definition of use-value employed by Smith, Ricardo and Marx, use-value relates, fundamentally, to the whole society and only secondarily to the isolated individuals within it. The use-value of a cigarette, therefore, is the use or worth of a cigarette for society as a whole. This would be expressed by a description of *both* the repulsive and unhealthy features of a cigarette, *and* of its functions in calming nerves and perpetrating certain social conventions.

This does not imply that the examiner of a particular use-value must make a moral judgement about the usefulness of an object when he subjects it to analysis. The analysis of a use-value requires a purely scientific examination of the physical nature of the object and the biological and socially determined needs which the object can satisfy.

The existence of an indentifiable human species of interdependent individuals with common characteristics means that, despite variations from individual to individual, there is an objective substratum of wants and needs. Furthermore, in modern capitalist society wants owe a great deal to social conditioning and the social culture. This social determination of wants has been explored by a number of writers (Galbraith, 1962; Marcuse, 1968) and Marx, himself (1973, pp. 408–10). These elements provide the objective and concrete foundation for the scientific study of use-value in relation to society as a whole.

Use-value and utility

Ever since the rise of the neoclassical school of economics, with its emphasis on the concept of subjective marginal utility, the mistake has been made of identifying that concept with the concept of use-value found in the writings of Smith, Ricardo and Marx. As a result many contemporary Marxists obscure the distinction between the two concepts, thus granting an unwarranted concession to the subjective individualism of neoclassical economics. In the history of economic thought, however, a clear break was made when, in 1871, Jevons dropped the idea of relating the worth of an object to an 'intrinsic quality', as the classical economists had done before him, and founded his concept of utility solely on the subjective satisfaction of the consumer. On this question at least, there is a sharp discontinuity between the economics of the classical and neoclassical schools.

Subjective utility is the degree of satisfaction obtained, by an individual or household, from the consumption of a good or service. It is supposedly quantifiable, either in the ordinal or cardinal sense. (Under conditions of uncertainty it *must* be quantified in the cardinal sense.) According to the axioms of neoclassical economics, each consumer will behave as if he or she had a set of ordered preferences for different combinations of consumer goods (see, for example, Ferguson, 1972, pp. 17–33). From this preference function it is possible to assign a number to each feasible combination of goods consumed, and this number would be the utility, or degree of satisfaction, obtained from the consumption of that bundle of goods.

On the whole, this seems to be a dubious exercise. It may seem plausible in the textbooks of economic theory which consider a world of two, or at the most three, goods. However, in the real world, with many, many more commodities to consider, the argument seems to wear a bit thin. Such real-world decisions, furthermore, would involve comparisons not between goods themselves, but choices between diverse *bundles* of goods. A 'preference' would have to be established for a well-done fillet steak *plus* glass of wine *plus* ride by bus *plus* hot shower with shampoo *over* lamb casserole *plus* small liqueur *plus* half-mile walk *plus* ten-minute soak in a warm bath. Individuals will surely choose one rather than the other of such combinations, and they may even do this with consistency, transitivity, and the other neoclassical qualities. It would be a different matter, however, to suggest that a clear *preference* is involved. Such choices would come about more by whim and suggestion. Individual consumption is a complex, socially determined process which cannot be readily embraced by an explicit and calculated set of preferences.

In attempting to reduce all consumer behaviour to the process of maximizing a single index of satisfaction, neoclassical economists ignore the fundamentally heterogeneous nature of the qualities of goods. In addition, the notion of cardinal or ordinal utility does not express the qualitative category of use-value. The notion of utility is inconsistent with the idea of use-value, as found in the works of

Smith, Ricardo and Marx. Neither can use-value be summed up in a 'preference function'. These points can be easily demonstrated. For example, even if a preference ordering exists, so that we can impute a quantity of utility to different objects, then if two different objects have the same utility for a particular individual they still do not have the same use-value. A loaf of bread could be seen as having the same utility as a packet of cigarettes; but the use-value of the former is the edible bulk and nutritional content which can satisfy human hunger and biological need, whereas the use-value of the latter is its capacity to satisfy the craving for the drug nicotine, or its use in the social ritual associated with smoking in company, and so on.

In short, therefore, utility does not embrace the intrinsic features and qualitative aspects of goods; it is simply a subjective index of satisfaction. Use-value is *nothing else* but the useful qualities of goods in a given social environment. Marx emphasized the qualitative rather than the quantitative nature of use-value when he wrote: 'As use-values, commodities differ above all in quality' (Marx, 1976, p. 128). Any step from use-value to homogeneous utility involves the adoption of questionable assumptions about 'rationality' and the detachment from the objective, physical and qualitative features of the object.

It is implicit in our argument above that the concept of use-value cannot be reduced to a single quantity. However, it must be admitted that Smith, Ricardo and Marx did, on occasions, refer to use-value in a purely quantitative rather than a qualitative sense. We regard this as an aberration: a proto-scientific monism not dissimilar to the early physicists' notional reduction of all matter to a single fluid. An inspection of the works of Smith, Ricardo and Marx shows that the qualitative and objectively based notion of use-value prevails over any purely quantitative conception. Even when they use the word 'utility' it is mostly in the qualitative and objective sense.

To make the distinction clear, we shall use the word utility to mean the quantitative and neoclassical conception and the words use-value to refer to the objectively based qualitative conception, which we have discussed above. Use-value is objectively based because it rests upon a scientific analysis of the physical properties of goods and their capacities to satisfy human physiological, psychological and socially conditioned needs. Utility, on the other hand, is largely intangible. It can only be assessed by observing consumer behaviour on the market. We cannot detect an atom of utility by analysing commodities or even by observing the act of consumption itself. 'Utility' appears to be an idea imposed upon reality, rather than a concept which is paralleled in reality itself. As Joan Robinson (1974) puts it:

Utility *is a metaphysical concept of impregnable circularity;* utility *is the quality in commodities which makes individuals want to buy them, and the fact that individuals want to buy commodities shows that they have* utility (p. 48).

For the above reasons we reject the concept of utility as unscientific. It is unwarranted to found a theory of price or consumer behaviour on such an inadequate category. Whilst the concept of use-value is more complex and difficult to analyse in many situations, it rests on a more solid scientific foundation. Utility is abstract, intangible and asocial. The use-value of a commodity is the set of its useful qualities, in a given social environment. Such qualities can be investigated with the methods of the sciences, in an objective manner, not divorced, of course, from the social integument in which the commodity is bound. In contrast to utility analysis we are no longer confronting ideal objects, mere products of thought; we are engaged in a theoretical and empirical process of investigation which has as its object social and material reality. Lenin's remarks against the alternative, 'metaphysical', approach are apposite:

The metaphysician—chemist, still unable to make a factual investigation of chemical processes, concocts a theory about chemical affinity as a force. The metaphysician—biologist talks about the nature of life and the vital force. The metaphysician—psychologist argues about the nature of the soul. Here it is the method itself that is absurd. You cannot argue about the soul without having explained psychical processes in particular: here progress must consist precisely in abandoning general theories and philosophical discourses about the nature of the soul, and in being able to put the study of the facts about particular psychical processes on a scientific footing (cited in Colletti, 1972, pp. 4—5).

A theory based on such an intangible concept as utility cannot really explain social reality at all. In fact, as Hollis and Nell (1975) have pointed out, it cannot, in the true sense of the word, make *predictions* either. Utility theory is not predictive; it is merely a formal set of propositions derived from arbitrary axioms. It is in the form: 'If we assume A, B, and C, then X, Y, and Z will follow.' That is not a prediction, and it cannot be, it is merely a formal logical deduction. All utility theory can really say, as many critics have pointed out, is: 'a person does what a person does'.

CHAPTER 5

EXCHANGE AND PRODUCTION

*All progress is based upon a universal innate desire on the part of every
organism to live beyond its income.*

SAMUEL BUTLER, *Notebooks*

In chapters 5–11 we shall make the simplifying assumption of excluding money from our analysis. The necessary modifications to this
analysis when money is incorporated will be raised in chapter 12 and
beyond. Here we consider a simple barter economy, where commodities are traded one for another.

Exchange-value

We have discussed the use-value of a commodity. Use-value, as we
have seen, is both qualitative and elusive. It is neither measurable by
a single quantity, nor is it immediately apparent on the surface of
things. In contrast, the obvious public face of the commodity has a
single and misleadingly simple quantitative dimension. The Latin
origin of the word reflects this: *com* = with; *modus* = measure. The
public aspect of the commodity, expressed in a single quantity, is its
exchange-value. As Marx (1976) puts it: 'Exchange-value appears
first of all as the quantitative relation, the proportion, in which
values in use of one sort are exchanged for those of another sort'
(p. 126). In other words, exchange-value appears as the set of ratios
in which various use-values exchange for each other in commodity
markets. Hence, for example, ten loaves of bread may exchange for
one shirt, which, in turn, may be exchangeable for two knives. The
exchange-value of a shirt, therefore, can be expressed as being either
ten loaves or two knives in this case. It is possible, of course, to express the exchange-value of a particular commodity in terms of all
the other commodities in the economy.

As we have already noted, a necessary condition for commodity
exchange is a division of labour in production. Second, there must be
a set of private property relations including individual or corporate

45

property rights. In such circumstances ownership of commodities is absolute in the sense that the owner has a legal right to dispose of his own property as he wishes. He is free to sell and free to buy from others.

The neoclassical explanation of exchange

Why does one individual, legally free within the system of commodity exchange, part with one commodity in order to obtain another? The neoclassical answer is that the two property-owners involved in the exchange each do so in order to increase their own individual utility. It has been argued already that this is a spurious explanation. We can only impute utility to objects on the basis of observed acts of exchange.

A further criticism of this approach can be made by conjoining the two aspects of exchange and production. Traditionally, neoclassical theory divided the world into two hostile regions. On the one hand there were 'factors of production', i.e. labour, capital and land; on the other there were goods for consumption. Goods were produced in one camp, then exchanged, and then consumed in the other. This is the 'one-way avenue that leads from "factors of production" to "consumption goods"' (Sraffa, 1960, p. 93). The final goal, the maximizing of utility within the sphere of consumption, was seen to be the animating spirit of the whole process. Hence, whilst goods and services moved, *via* exchange, from production to consumption, i.e. from 'firm' to 'household', the consumer was 'sovereign', and ultimate causality flowed in the opposite direction.

This division of the capitalist economy was more important in the earlier stages of neoclassical thought, before the extensive mathematical formalization of their analysis gave the 'production function' and the 'utility function', in the firm and household respectively, identical, or very similar, mathematical properties. Consumption was the dominant realm: the realm of the individual. Production, the realm of the firm, was the servant of consumption. This division obscured an essential unifying element of the capitalist mode of production: the fact that it is generalized commodity production. Units of capital, land and labour-power are all *commodities.* Furthermore, the *production* of a commodity is simultaneously the *consumption* of other goods, e.g. raw materials, and the consumption, of course, of labour-power. Conversely, the *consumption* of goods in the household is simultaneously the *production* and *reproduction* of labour-power.

Production and consumption

The latter view involves an element of circularity in the economic system. There is no one-way avenue: instead, the 'production of commodities by means of commodities'. This circular view of the economic process was prominent in the works of Quesnay, Smith, Ricardo and Marx. Furthermore, the classical idea of circularity finds an echo in the Keynesian idea of the 'circular flow of income'. (Although the latter presentation was not made clear by Keynes, himself, in the *General Theory*.) More explicitly, of course, the conception of production as a circular process can be found in the input—output tables of Leontiev and the work of Sraffa.

However, whilst there is some circularity in the unified process of production and consumption, it would be an error to equate the two. Marx dismissed the identification of production with consumption as a Hegelian error. Within this misconception, there is a God-like view of society, from the outside, and without adequate regard to internal relations. Marx wrote:

Thereupon, nothing simpler for a Hegelian than to posit production and consumption as identical. . . . To regard society as one single subject is, in addition, to look at it wrongly; speculatively. With a single subject, production and consumption appear as moments of a single act. The important thing to emphasise here is only that, whether production and consumption are viewed as the activity of one or many individuals, they appear as moments of one process, in which production *is the real point of departure and hence also the* predominant moment. *Consumption as urgency, as need, is itself an intrinsic moment of productive activity. But the latter is the point of departure for realization and hence also its predominant moment:* it is the act through which the whole process again runs its course. *The individual produces an object and, by consuming it, returns to himself, but returns as a* productive *and* self-reproducing individual. Consumption thus appears as a moment of production* (Marx, 1973, pp. 93—4; emphasis added).

Consumption and production are, therefore, a unity, and each contains an aspect of the other; but production is 'predominant' within this unity.

In recent years, by abandoning their previous one-way avenue, neoclassical economists have become increasingly 'Hegelian' in their approach. In the works of Cairncross (1958), Becker (1965), Hirshleifer (1970) and others, the household is regarded as a kind of firm which, amongst other things, can produce the 'services' of labour. In addition, both firms and households alike seek to maximize utility. In short, therefore, the firm and the household are made identical. It should be noted, first of all, that this approach is not compatible with the traditional dogma of consumer sovereignty. In such an analysis the firm is just as 'sovereign' as the household. In addition, unlike the work of Marx and Sraffa, the maximization of utility is still the goal, or end-point, of the process; only this time, however, the concept of utility is spread so widely that it loses its previous meaning. The approach of Cairncross *et al.* does violence to the nature of the firm by treating it as an individual, and does violence to the concept of utility by applying it to the firm.

The above discussion is important, and we shall return to this theme later in this work. At this stage it is relevant to note that the economic process must be conceived as neither purely 'circular' nor simply as a 'one-way avenue'. In addition, as was pointed out by Marx, production should be regarded as the predominant moment. This is in clear contrast to the traditional and modern neoclassical approaches which regard *consumption* (in the household and perhaps also the firm) and the consequent maximization of utility as the goal. In both versions of neoclassical thought, the motive for exchange is found in the maximization of utility.

Exchange and production

It is possible to begin to sketch out an alternative approach here, using some traditional and elementary theoretical tools. In figure 5.1 we start with the familiar budget line. Assume that the point I represents the initial endowment of the two commodities A and B.

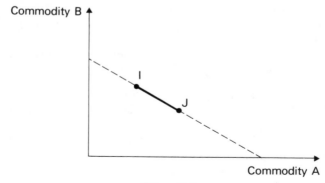

Figure 5.1
The budget line

In principle, one of these commodities could be labour-power, but that particular commodity presents special problems which are discussed at a later stage. This is a world in which only two commodities exist; also, as we stated earlier, money proper does not exist—it is a barter economy. At a later stage we shall show that money proper is incompatible with the traditional budget line analysis.

An exchange takes place and our commodity-owner ends up at point J. He has lost some of commodity B in return for an increased endowment of commodity A. As the elementary textbooks explain, the ratio in which the two commodities A and B exchange (i.e. their relative price, or the exchange-value of one in relation to the other) is represented by the slope of the budget line itself. The exchange-ratio is taken as given.

According to neoclassical theory the commodity-owner ends up at J because the utility he obtains from the consumption of his endowment at that point is maximized, and greater than the utility obtained at I; but this view treats consumption as the end of the process. It excludes the possibility of the exchange taking place not for the purpose of consumption at all. It completely separates production from exchange. Production, therefore, has to be brought into the picture.

The two commodities A and B could be used to produce a different amount of A and B. For example, horses and corn can be used in various ways including horse-feeding, horse-breeding and corn-growing, to produce more horses, more corn or both. At least one commodity must be produced in a greater amount, otherwise there is no motive for production; but the endowment of one commodity could decrease.

Production, therefore, is partly represented by a movement in commodity-space from one point to another. In our diagram it is shown by a movement from J to K (figure 5.2). Clearly, point K could not be reached from J simply by the process of exchange; the *production* of commodities must be involved. After the movement to K there is another act of exchange, bringing the endowment to L. The movement from L to M represents the *consumption* of both commodities (not an act of exchange or production) by the owner of the firm. Thereafter, MN represents exchange, NO production, and so on. The net effect of the endless cycle is a progressive move away from the origin in a direction between 'north' and 'east'. Production has the effect of moving the consumer to a greater budget line, representing a budget no less than that achieved before. If this did not happen there would be no motive for production and also, therefore, no motive for the previous exchange.

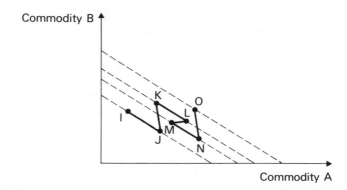

Figure 5.2
After exchange and production

When the combined process of production, consumption and exchange is viewed as a whole, consumption is the subordinate moment. The progressive movement in the direction between north and east comes about only by the effective dominance of the production vector over that associated with consumption. Production is both the end and means of the process.

The notion of production is necessary to understand exchange. The neoclassical approach—by starting from, and concentrating upon, the spheres of consumption and exchange—cannot explain the dominant role of production. In figure 5.2 exchange explains movements along the budget line only, not a shift in the budget line itself. Levine makes a similar, but more elaborate, point in regard to consumption. In the neoclassical system, instead of production, we have consumption

viewed as an individual act which directly connects the undetermined individual with the object of his need where both individual and object are taken as given. Nothing is of greater importance to the critique of the neoclassical analysis of value than to grasp the difference between consumption taken as an individual act and consumption as an aspect, or moment, of a social process. . . . Implicitly, consumption becomes a discernible economic function only when it opposes itself to production within *an ongoing process of reproduction* (Levine, 1977, p. 178).

The above analysis—which combines production, consumption and exchange, viewing them 'within an ongoing process of reproduction'—enables us to make a clear distinction between the three moments in the process. This is in opposition to the modern neo-classical view. At the same time, however, this same analysis rejected the 'one-way avenue' and regarded each commodity, potentially at least, as an item for production *or* consumption.

The reproduction of the possessing agent

What does the consumption moment represent if it is not, as the neo-classicals would have it, the end of the process? The trajectory in figure 5.2 represents the transformation of the wealth of a commodity-owner through a combined process of production and consumption. We shall call the commodity-owner the possessing agent. The act of consumption is not simply for the satisfaction of the consumer; it must also be necessary for the *reproduction of the possessing agent.* Without consumption the commodity-owner would die and the process of *his* wealth creation would come to an end. The process must not only ensure a non-decreasing stock of wealth; it must also ensure the reproduction of the possessing agent. That is the main justification for the temporary regression towards the origin, during the act of consumption, in figure 5.2.

In much of classical and neoclassical analysis the possessing agent is subsumed into the commodity itself. It is a ghostly spirit that haunts the movement and transformation of goods. Exchange is seen as simply the exchange of goods: little attention is paid to the necessary concomitant exchange of property rights. Levine points out this error in the work of Ricardo:

For Ricardo the particularity of the owner plays virtually no role and Ricardo fails altogether to explicitly recognize the specification of the exchange relation by the individual commodity owner. Ricardo's failure to grasp the relation of the commodity to its owner involves an implicit restriction of the social character of the commodity which is typical of classical political economy and to a lesser extent of Marx (Levine, 1977, pp. 176–7).

The significance of the distinction between the commodity and the possessing agent, and the separate but related analysis of these two aspects of a commodity-producing economy, will be seen below, at several points in our analysis. We can, however, come to one major application of the distinction immediately: the analysis of commodity ownership, production, consumption and exchange applied to a member of the working class.

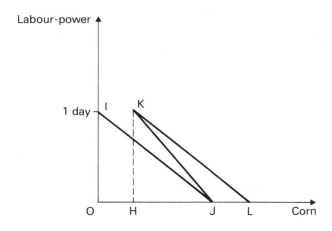

Figure 5.3
The production and exchange of labour-power

The production and exchange of labour-power

We continue to consider a two-commodity world. One commodity is
labour-power and the other we shall call corn. Our possessing agent is
now a worker, a member of the proletariat, who, initially at least,
possesses nothing but his labour-power. Figure 5.3 illustrates the
situation. The initial endowment, represented by the point I, lies on
one axis as the worker possesses labour-power alone. He hires his
labour-power for a period of time (say a day) for an amount of corn.
This brings him to J. He then consumes some or all of the corn to
feed him or her and their family. The act of consumption serves a
dual purpose: it reproduces the possessing agent (and offspring), and
it restores the capacity to work, i.e. it restores his or her endowment
of labour-power. This is one peculiar property of labour-power as a
commodity. It is fused with its possessing agent. Consequently, the
non-production of labour-power means the non-survival of the
possessing agent. Capitalism, it is supposed, just brims with 'free
choice'; but in the case of labour-power the 'choice' is between the
survival and non-survival of the possessing agent. If life is to be preserved this is no choice at all.

In figure 5.3 we have assumed that the worker is able to save a
small amount of corn from his or her wages. After consumption,
therefore, the endowment is a small distance, equal to OH, away
from the vertical axis. From that point, K, labour-power is sold once
more and the worker is brought to L. The process may then continue.

(It may be useful to note that figure 5.3 assumes a linear technology for the production of labour-power. Amount of corn HJ produces 1 day of labour-power. The wage rate is the slope OJ/OI and the 'subsistence' wage is HJ/HK. The difference between the wage rate and the 'subsistence' wage in corn terms is simply OH.)

Clearly, utility analysis cannot be applied to the production and exchange of labour-power. There can be no continuous process of utility maximization in the trade-off between life and death. A dead person has no satisfaction: his or her utility cannot be maximized. (See Blatt (1979) for a formal discussion of this point.) Instead of utility, it is production which dominates the process (at least if all the wage is consumed). For the worker to attain a greater budget line it is necessary to save goods and reproduce labour-power. The act of consumption is not important with regard to a means of satisfying wants and needs in this respect. It is only important, from the point of view of attaining a higher budget, in regard to the production of labour-power itself. Two elements dominate, therefore: primarily and universally the *production* of labour-power, and secondarily the *non-consumption* of some of the goods received as a wage.

In short, utility analysis cannot be applied to the household or individual which depends, for its survival, upon the sale of its labour-power. Likewise, some would argue, it would be wrong to regard the capitalist firm as a utility-maximizing unit. It is difficult to bring the canons of individual preference into the complex social institutions of capitalist business. It could be concluded that neither the firm nor the household can accommodate utility maximization as an adequate theory of their behaviour. The only area in which it would appear to have the remotest chance of meaningful application would be the household of the capitalist, who does not depend upon the sale of his labour-power for the source of his income. Perhaps in that there is an object lesson for neoclassical theory.

Our combined discussion of production and exchange has led us to distinguish two types of commodity-owner. On the one hand there is the worker who produces his labour-power and depends upon its sale in order to live. On the other hand there is the capitalist who does not, necessarily, bring his labour-power to market. Instead, he arranges the combination of factors of production so as to produce a commodity other than labour-power. In most circumstances we shall assume that the capitalist must purchase labour-power in order to produce, and thereby rule out, full automation. Second, we shall generally disregard the capitalist who works in a useful way in his own firm, alongside the labour force.

In distinguishing between worker and capitalist we have, even at this early stage of analysis, introduced, in part, a concept of social class. So far, however, the distinction is not adequately drawn, and we shall return to it at a later stage of this work.

CHAPTER 6

EXCHANGE-VALUE AND COSTS

The market is a place set apart where men may deceive one another.
ANACHARSIS OF SCYTHIA, *c.* 600 BC

In the last chapter we noted that it is the goal of all commodity-owners to avoid a real reduction in their budget. More specifically it is the goal of the capitalist to progressively increase his budget, and the goal of the worker at least to avoid a reduction. From this point on we shall assume that the workers do not save. They do not increase their wealth; they simply reproduce themselves as possessing agents. They do not make profits in any sense. The reproduction of the possessing agent cannot be considered as a profitable activity, whatever the level of the wage. Profit, properly defined, is a part of a revenue from the sale of a commodity on the market. Under pure capitalism possessing agents cannot be sold. If they were they would cease to be possessing agents and become slaves instead. This is an important point, and it is elaborated at a later stage of this work.

In contrast to the worker's household, for the capitalist firm the principle of budget maximization is expressed in a familiar form. It is the principle of production for profit. More specifically, if we disregard other suggestions as to goal of capitalist firms, it is the principle of *profit maximization.* The cost of factors of production must clearly be less, in most circumstances, than the price that the produced commodity will obtain on the market. This is not a psychological law: it is a condition for capitalist survival.

Interlinked production costs

Capitalist X produces commodity A. He requires commodity B as a raw material input. Measured in terms of some common *numéraire,* the exchange-value of A must be greater than the exchange-value of B, if profits are to be obtained. Commodity B is produced by capitalist Y who uses commodity C as an input. In addition, therefore, the exchange-value of B must be greater than the exchange-value of C.

Hence, if we consider a single produced commodity, produced by means of other commodities, a chain of costs is derived. These costs, as in the above example, are related in the following way:

> Exchange-Value of A
> \> Exchange-Value of B
> \> Exchange-Value of C, etc. . . .

A long, sometimes infinite, chain of inequalities is derived. We shall sometimes refer to commodities such as B and C as the *embodied inputs* of commodity A, and sometimes simply as *costs*.

We now face a problem. We have moved from the consideration of the situation facing the individual capitalist, i.e. the microeconomic context, where costs and exchange-values can be taken as given, to a more overall perspective where one capitalist's cost is another capitalist's revenue and exchange-values cannot be taken as given. As a result we have no given basis for the comparison of costs which are represented by dissimilar commodities.

Smith, Ricardo and Marx lead us to an answer to this problem. They chose to find the sum total of labour that was directly or indirectly utilized to produce a given commodity, i.e. the total labour-cost, in terms of past and present labour performed in the production of the commodity and all its necessary inputs. No knowledge of exchange-values is required to calculate this amount of 'embodied labour'. Now the given commodity can be exchanged for labour-power on the market. The precise amount of labour-power that can be purchased will depend on the wage-rate. Smith, Ricardo and Marx saw the wage-rate as being determined by the cost of those items that were necessary, according to the given biological, social and cultural conditions, to reproduce labour-power. We shall not enter into a discussion of what proportion of the wage can be regarded as 'necessary' in this sense, as there has been much controversy here. It is sufficient to note that for labour-power to be reproduced the wage must be *greater than or equal to* the cost of reproduction of that labour-power. Now it should be clear that for every capitalist directly or indirectly involved in the production in the given commodity, to make a profit the labour cost of (labour embodied in) that commodity must be less than the amount of labour-power that the commodity can be exchanged for on the market. The latter is usually referred to as the 'labour commanded' and is equivalent to the exchange-value of the commodity in question divided by the wage-rate, expressed, of course, in the same *numéraire*.

The reduction of costs to dated labour

The previous analysis of costs has led us to a method of analysis which consists of reducing the exchange-value of a commodity to a series of elements of labour, plus a portion of profit. This analysis is alluded to in the works of Ricardo and Marx, but is most explicit in Sraffa's famous work (1960).

Let us take a simple example. A corn-producer harvests 10 tons of corn in a year if 1 ton is sown in the spring. He also requires the labour of five men for the year and 1 ton of fertilizer. The wage-rate is 1 ton of corn per man per year. We shall, for the purpose of this example, assume that labour is homogeneous and that all the wage is 'necessary' for the production of labour-power. Now consider the fertilizer industry, and assume that the fertilizer consists of animal droppings which are collected with unaided labour. One man-year of labour is required to gather 1 ton of fertilizer. The labourers in the fertilizer industry receive the same wages as in the corn industry.

The cost of producing 10 tons of corn is 5 man-years of labour, plus the labour that must be performed in the year before to produce the seed-corn and fertilizer that are necessary, plus the labour that must be performed in the year before that to produce the necessary inputs for that seed-corn and fertilizer, and so on, back into the past. Consider the production of the 1 ton of seed-corn. It takes 5 man-years of labour to produce 10 tons of corn, so 1 ton of seed-corn will take ½ man-year of labour, assuming constant returns to scale. The fertilizer that is used with that 1 ton of seed-corn requires 1 man-year of labour. But also, in the year before that, ¹⁄₁₀ man-year of labour is required to produce the fertilizer that is needed to produce the seed-corn, plus ¹⁄₂₀ man-year of labour to produce the seed-corn itself.

Furthermore, in the year before that, more labour is required to produce the seed-corn and fertilizer needed to produce the seed-corn to produce the seed-corn. The process of reduction of costs to labour consists, therefore, of a progressive fission, going back in time. At each temporal stage an amount of labour-power, with appropriate 'date', is distilled out. This analysis can be illustrated by a diagram (figure 6.1).

As a result, therefore, 5 man-years of labour overall are required in the current year, 1.5 man-years in the previous year, 0.15 man-years in the year previous to that, and so on. The sum of this infinite series can be shown to be $6^2/_3$. Hence the labour-cost of 10 tons of corn is $6^2/_3$ man-years of labour. With the given wage-rate the exchange-value

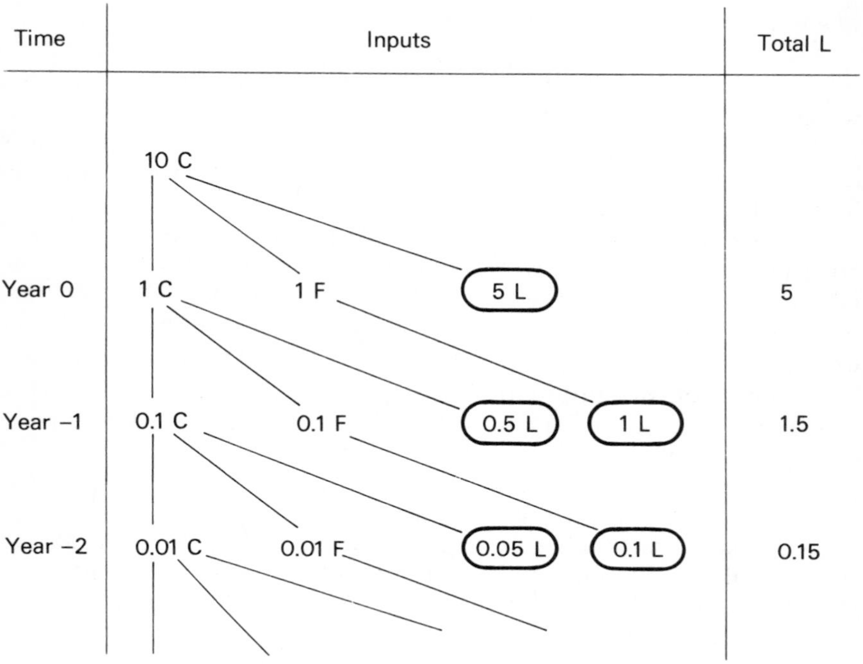

Figure 6.1
Reduction of cost to dated labour (C = corn; F = fertilizer; L = labour)

of 10 tons of corn is 10 man-years of labour-power. Hence the labour-cost in the corn industry is less than the 10 man-years of labour-power 'commanded' by the produced corn. In other words the cost, in terms of labour, is less than the revenue in terms of labour-power. Hence the production of corn is feasible.

We emphasize that this process of reduction does not require reference to a set of exchange-values; but prices must be such that:

(1)   the cost of 1 ton of corn plus 1 ton of fertilizer plus 5 man-years of labour-power is less than the revenue derived from the sale of 10 tons of corn; and

(2)   the cost of 1 man-year of labour-power is less than the revenue derived from the sale of 1 ton of fertilizer.

The former is the condition of profitability in the corn industry, the latter the condition in the fertilizer industry. These two conditions determine a range of feasible exchange-values for the commodities in the system.

The reduction of costs to corn

In general, Smith, Ricardo and Marx had a predilection to reduce costs to labour. Perhaps the major reason for this was that, in the technology of their time, labour was still the most important component of cost at most points in the backward reduction. We shall discuss the background to this in chapter 11 below.

Given the prominence that labour has taken in the writings of these past economists it is necessary to emphasize that costs can be reduced to commodities other than labour-power. In the previous 'reduction' labour was distilled out at every stage and the conditions of production of labour-power did not have to be considered. If we now choose corn, this can be distilled out at every past stage, and correspondingly the conditions of production of that very corn need not be considered. We must now, however, consider the conditions of production of labour-power.

To produce 10 tons of corn 1 ton is required as seed-corn. Hence the corn-cost, in the current year, is 1 ton. Also, in the current year, 5 man-years of labour and 1 ton of fertilizer are required. The 5 man-years of labour-power are produced in the previous year with 5 tons of corn. Hence the corn-cost in the previous year is 5 tons. The 1 ton of fertilizer is produced in this same year with 1 man-year of labour, so, in the year before that 1 ton of corn is required to produce that amount of labour-power. To summarize, therefore, the corn-cost of 10 tons of corn is 1 ton of corn in the current year, 5 tons in the year before, and 1 ton in the year before that. The total corn-cost of 10 tons of corn is 7 tons. In other words, the corn embodied in 10 tons of corn is 7 tons. Note that in this case, unlike the dated labour reduction, the series of dated corn terms is finite. The fact that the corn-cost is less than the corn produced shows that profits can be made in all the constituent industries and that the production of corn is feasible. The process of reduction to dated corn is represented in figure 6.2. Now, to complete the picture, we show that costs can be reduced to the third commodity in our three-commodity economy, i.e. fertilizer.

Reduction of costs to dated fertilizer

In this case the amount of fertilizer is distilled out at every stage, and we must consider the conditions of production of corn and labour-power only. Ten tons of corn are produced in the current year with the use of 1 ton of seed-corn, 1 ton of fertilizer, and 5 man-years of

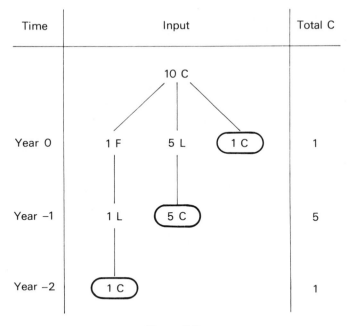

Figure 6.2
Reduction of cost to dated corn (C = corn; F = fertilizer; L = labour)

labour-power. So, in all, 1 ton of fertilizer is required in the current year. In the previous year, ¹⁄₁₀ ton of seed-corn, ¹⁄₁₀ ton of fertilizer, and ½ man-year of labour were required to produce the seed-corn for the current year; also 5 tons of corn were required to produce the labour-power for the current year. So the process goes back in time; whenever a cost is reduced to labour that, in turn, is reduced to corn, and whenever a cost is reduced to corn that, in turn, is reduced to corn, fertilizer and labour. Fertilizer is distilled out at every stage, until all costs are gradually reduced to fertilizer; but, unlike the reduction to dated corn, the process is infinite rather than finite. The process is illustrated in figure 6.3.

In all, therefore, 1 ton of fertilizer is required in the current year, 0.1 ton in the previous year, 0.51 ton in the year before that, and so on, to produce 10 tons of corn. The sum of this infinite series of dated fertilizer terms can be shown to be 2.5. However, unlike the cases of corn and labour, without knowing exchange-values we do not know how much fertilizer will exchange for the produced 10 tons of corn.

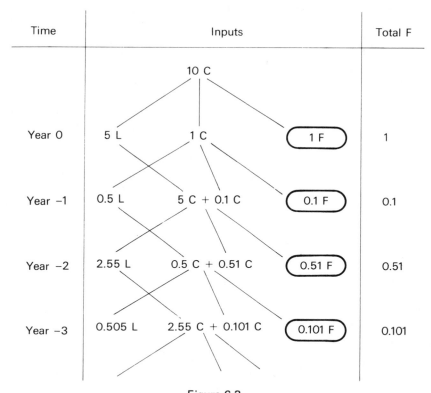

Time	Inputs			Total F

		10 C		
Year 0	5 L	1 C	1 F	1
Year −1	0.5 L	5 C + 0.1 C	0.1 F	0.1
Year −2	2.55 L	0.5 C + 0.51 C	0.51 F	0.51
Year −3	0.505 L	2.55 C + 0.101 C	0.101 F	0.101

Figure 6.3
Reduction of cost to dated fertilizer (C = corn; F = fertilizer; L = labour)

Labour and labour-power

Whilst we have shown that it is equally possible to reduce costs to either labour, or corn, or fertilizer, this does not mean that there is a perfect symmetry between labour-power and other commodities. Some unique features of labour-power have already been mentioned. At this stage it is opportune to make one further observation regarding labour and labour-power. Note that labour-power, i.e. the capacity to work, is produced in the household and hired on the market, not labour itself. However, it is labour, not labour-power, that is used to produce the various commodities. When labour-power is hired the capitalist is never certain that the worker will actually work at the average or 'normal' intensity. Unlike the germinating corn and the activating fertilizer, the labourer can resist. The amount of labour that labour-power will yield is imperfectly specified, and much more uncertain. It is doubly uncertain because the conscious will of a human agent is involved.

Because of this essential difference between labour and labour-power both these categories appear in the reduction process; but we do not have corn and corn-power, for instance. Another result is that despite the fact that the labour-cost of producing a particular commodity is less than the labour-power that can be purchased with it, the capitalist cannot be sure that this purchased labour-power will yield as much actual labour as the labour-cost, especially if the profit margin is small. This inherent uncertainty and variability whilst dealing with labour has been touched upon by other, non-Marxist authors, particularly Leibenstein (1976). This issue will be developed at a later stage.

From costs to exchange-values

Although we shall not make a full general equilibrium analysis in this work we shall show how, with stated assumptions, exchange-values can be determined quantitatively. We shall continue to rely on a Sraffian approach to these problems, but that does not mean that Sraffa can provide all the answers in the analysis of exchange-value.

Consider the reduction to dated quantities of corn. The capitalist in the corn industry buys, amongst other things, 1 ton of seed-corn. The sum of his costs must be less than the sum of his revenue, if he is to make a profit, so it is possible to apportion elements of profit to each element of cost, in proportion to each such element of cost. So if his rate of profit on total capital invested is represented by the fraction r_c the apportioned profit on the 1 ton of seed-corn will be r_c. The cost, plus apportioned profit, of the 1 ton of seed-corn is $1 + r_c$. The cost of the labour-power currently employed, in terms of corn, plus its apportioned profit, is $5(1 + r_c)$. The cost of the fertilizer, however, is not known, and to find this out we must examine the fertilizer industry. Here the rate of profit on total capital invested is r_f; but this capital cost consists of labour-power only, which can be purchased with 1 ton of corn at the given wage-rate. Hence total cost, plus profit, in the fertilizer industry is $1 + r_f$, and obviously this must, by definition, be equal to the exchange-value of the 1 ton of produced fertilizer. This is the cost for fertilizer that the corn capitalist will face. Added to the apportioned profit it will be $(1 + r_f)(1 + r_c)$. By definition, the total cost plus the sum of all the apportioned profits in the corn industry must be equal to the exchange-value of the produced 10 tons of corn. Thus we derive the following equation:

$$10 = (1 + r_c) + 5(1 + r_c) + (1 + r_f)(1 + r_c) \qquad (6.1)$$

Note the derivation of the series of terms 1, 5, 1 from the reduction of costs to dated corn. We can improve the mathematical elegance of the equation at the cost of some economic sense by saying that the 'rate of profit' in the 'industry' that produces labour-power is η. In this case we can derive the more elegant but less legitimate equation:

$$10 = (1 + r_c) + 5(1 + \eta)(1 + r_c) + (1 + \eta)(1 + r_f)(1 + r_c) \quad (6.2)$$

Of course the two equations are equivalent if η is zero, and we have, in fact, assumed that that is the situation. In any case it is not legitimate to regard profit as being made in the labour-power 'industry', for reasons stated above. However, the correspondence between the elegant version and the diagram illustrating the reduction of cost to dated corn should strike the reader.

In a similar way we can consider the reduction to dated quantities of labour and derive the following equation:

$$10 = 5(1 + r_c) + 0.5(1 + r_c)^2 + (1 + r_f)(1 + r_c) \\ + 0.05(1 + r_c)^3 + 0.1(1 + r_f)(1 + r_c)^2 \quad (6.3)$$

(Note the derivation of the coefficients in this equation from the circled terms in figure 6.1.) Whilst being economically legitimate this equation is already in its most elegant form, as during the process of reduction to dated quantities of labour the conditions of production in the labour-power 'industry' are not considered.

The algebraic analysis of the reduction to dated quantities of fertilizer is more complicated. The reader may wish to check that the first terms of the derived series, in 'elegant' form, are as follows:

$$S_f = (1 + r_c) + 0.1(1 + r_c)^2 + 0.01(1 + r_c)^3 \\ + 0.5(1 + r_c)(1 + \eta)(1 + r_c) + 0.051(1 + r_c)^4 \\ + 0.05(1 + r_c)(1 + \eta)(1 + r_c)(1 + r_c) \ldots \quad (6.4)$$

As η is zero this reduces to:

$$S_f = (1 + r_c) + 0.6(1 + r_c)^2 + 0.06(1 + r_c)^3 \ldots \quad (6.5)$$

This series must be equal to the exchange-value, in terms of fertilizer, of 10 tons of corn; but as we do not know this exchange-value the equation cannot be completed. The equations for corn and labour could, however, be completed simply because we knew the wage-rate, i.e. the exchange-value of labour-power in terms of corn and *vice-versa*.

From inspection of equation (6.1) it is clear that there is a strict relationship between r_c and r_f. If both the corn and fertilizer industries are to make a profit then r_c must lie between zero and approximately 0.4285, and r_f must lie between zero and 3. If one of these rates of profit is given then the other is determined; there is 1 degree of freedom.

The quantitative determination of profits and exchange-values

To take this analysis much further we must adopt certain assumptions which are, strictly speaking, premature in terms of a 'deductive' method of analysis. We assume that the economy is in equilibrium and that the rate of profit in every capitalist industry (excluding, of course, the labour-power 'industry') is the same. Hence, in Marx's words, we assume a 'general rate of profit'. Marx left this category aside until the third volume of *Capital* and he criticized Ricardo for introducing it as early as the first chapter of his *Principles* (Marx, 1969, pp. 167–8, 174).

In the previous analysis we did assume that the wage-rate was the same for every unit of labour-power. This assumption is fairly easy to justify in terms of the homogeneity of labour and a degree of competition on the labour-market. However, the assumption of an equalized rate of profit cannot be justified without a discussion of capital mobility, interest rates, perfect competition and monopoly. This, in turn, involves a discussion of money. The introduction of the concept of the general rate of profit involves, therefore, a break from the strict sequence of analysis, incorporating concepts which have not yet been substantiated.

However, with the above reservations, it is still fruitful to press on. We assume that r_c is equal to r_f and, of course, as before, r_l is zero. Let r be the general rate of profit. Equation (6.1) then reduces to:

$$10 = (1 + r) + 5(1 + r) + (1 + r)^2$$

The only feasible solution is $r = 0.3593$ (approximately). Note that this solution is consistent with equations (6.1) and 6.3), pertaining to the dated corn and labour reductions, when substituted for r_c and r_f. Equation (6.5) will give us a rough magnitude for the exchange-value of 10 tons of corn in terms of fertilizer, as long as we trace it back through a sufficient number of terms. However, as we now know the rate of profit it is easier to find this exchange-value by considering the fertilizer industry itself. If p_f is the price of fertilizer in terms of corn then

$$1(1 + r) = p_f.$$

The left-hand side of this equation is the cost of the 1 man-year of labour-power, plus the profit, and the right-hand side is the revenue from the sale of the 1 ton of fertilizer. Obviously $p_f = 1.3593$ approximately. All the exchange-values in the economy, as well as the rate of profit, are now determined.

It has been convenient to approach the Sraffa system via a consideration of costs. Further reasons for this analytical route will become apparent in the next chapter. However, it is useful to present the more usual and direct quantitative determination of exchange-values, using the Sraffa approach. We shall use the numerical example. The economic system can be represented by the following scheme:

	INPUTS			OUTPUTS	
Corn	Fertilizer	Labour		Corn	Fertilizer
1	1	5	→	10	0
0	0	1	→	0	1

The first row represents the corn industry and the second represents the fertilizer industry. Let all the exchange-values be in terms of corn; p_f is the exchange-value of fertilizer, w is the wage rate (exchange-value of labour-power), and r is the general rate of profit.

We have the following accounting identity:

Costs (including wages) + Profits = Revenue.

From this the following equations are derived:

$$(1 + p_f + 5w)(1 + r) = 10$$
$$w(1 + r) = p_f$$

Eliminating p_f we get:

$$w = \frac{9 - r}{(1 + r)(6 + r)}$$

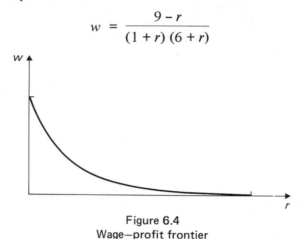

Figure 6.4
Wage—profit frontier

This gives the Sraffian wage—profit frontier, shown in figure 6.4. This frontier can take different shapes, but generally it has negative slope. Alternatively, eliminating w we get:

$$p_f = \frac{9 - r}{6 + r}$$

If the wage is known (it was assumed to be unity in our example) then both r and p_f can be determined. Otherwise, if we treat the wage as variable, both the wage and the exchange-value of fertilizer can be regarded as a function of the general rate of profit. In order to close the system, and render it determinate, either the wage or the general rate of profit must be given by an additional equation. We shall not discuss the question of whether the wage, or the rate of profit, should be taken as the primary and independent variable at this stage. That will enable us to suggest another 'equation' which will determine one outstanding variable and close the system. At this stage, however, we shall not discuss the forces that may determine the magnitude of wages or profits.

   Despite the fact that we have not, as yet, produced a completely determinate general analysis of the quantitative determination of exchange-value, the Sraffa system has taken us a long way. We have developed a conceptual approach which sees exchange-value being determined by a series of costs with an addition of a fraction or profit at every stage, and also a shorter algebraic analysis.

Sraffa's theory of exchange-value is here interpreted as a 'cost of production plus profit' theory; but as Sraffa does not give an explanation of the magnitude of profits this theory is incomplete, despite its elegance and logical validity. The neoclassical economist, therefore, will be keen to graft utility functions and the usual neoclassical apparatus onto the Sraffa system. Consequently, this system will be seen as just one aspect of the more general neoclassical equilibrium analysis. However, the latter, in addition to the illegitimate use of certain categories, such as utility, has the manifest weakness that it can come to not much more of a conclusion than 'everything depends upon everything else'. The primacy of production, and of production-cost in determining exchange-value, is rejected in the neoclassical paradigm.

On supply and demand

At this stage of this work, where money has not yet been introduced, we can give a strong argument against the neoclassical view that exchange-value is determined by the interaction of supply and demand. This conclusion will not be weakened when we eventually come to introduce money; but the argument for it will have to be modified in certain respects.

What is demand? It is the expressed willingness to buy a commodity on the market. In a barter economy this willingness must be expressed by the desire to sell another commodity in exchange for the one that is desired. There is simply no other way of expressing demand. The latter should not be misinterpreted as mere want or need; it is the *expressed* desire to possess something. The only way to express a desire in market terms is by bringing another commodity to the market with the explicit intention of exchanging that commodity for the particular one that is desired. In short, therefore, the only way a demand on the market can be expressed is by the supply of another commodity.

Supply is the expressed willingness to sell a commodity on the market. The expression of this willingness to sell must be the demand for another commodity. The only way a supply on the market can be expressed is by the demand for another commodity.

It follows, therefore, that there is no means of distinguishing supply from demand in a barter economy. Supply *is* demand and demand *is* supply. Apparently (see Dobb, 1940, p. 41) it was James Mill who first expressed this proposition in a clear form; but he, and other classical economists say as Say, applied it illegitimately to a non-barter economy, where money plays its crucial role. This error came about because, unlike Marx, the classical economists did not have a full understanding of the nature of money; but in a barter economy James Mill's argument is nevertheless correct:

A commodity which is supplied, is always, at the same time, a commodity which is the instrument of demand. A commodity which is the instrument of demand, is always, at the same time, a commodity added to the stock of supply. Every commodity is always at one and the same time matter of demand and matter of supply. Of two men who perform an exchange, the one does not come with only a supply, the other with only a demand; each of them comes with both a demand and a supply. The supply which he brings is the instrument of his demand; and his demand and supply are of course exactly equal to one another (Mill, 1821, p. 190).

This creates a problem for neoclassical price theory in a barter economy. If supply is demand and demand is supply it is difficult to talk of the interaction of supply with demand. It is just the same as saying that either demand alone, or supply alone, determine exchange-value. In this case demand and supply as separate and distinct categories lose their meaning.

We shall see later that although the intrusion of money gives a distinct meaning to supply and demand the neoclassical approach is not rescued. In fact the neoclassical equilibrium analysis specifically excludes money proper.

It might seem, given the identity of supply and demand under barter, that it would be legitimate to explain prices either in terms of supply, or in terms of demand, alone. Wicksteed is noted for his attempt to do the latter. It has been shown that if exchange is integrated with production the neoclassical explanation of demand, based on utility analysis, is inadequate and faulty. However, it would be wrong to suggest that we reject demand and concentrate on supply. The 'cost of production plus profit' approach is not one which eschews demand. It explains both supply and the *production* of demand, through the supply of labour-power etc. The unity of supply and demand is embodied in this theory.

Scarcity and reproducibility

We intend our analysis of exchange-value to apply to non-scarce, reproducible goods only; excluding, for example, old masters and rare wines. The definition of scarcity and reproducibility, however, is problematic.

There are two different sorts of scarcity. The first may be due to interruptions in the process of production or commodity circulation, or to a sudden jump in the demand for a commodity which production cannot quickly match by an increased supply. This sort of scarcity can, however, be ameliorated through time and the workings of the market mechanism. Scarcity of this sort will lead to high exchange-values which, in turn, will encourage increased production and an abolition of this scarcity.

The second sort of scarcity cannot be reduced through the market mechanism at the given level of development of the forces of production. The works of rare or unique human genius, such as the paintings of the old masters, fall into this category. Other examples are rare animals and plants which cannot be bred or propagated by man, rare gem stones which are in very short supply, rare wines which are the product of unusual climatic or fermentation conditions, and perhaps the most important example—land.

The two distinct categories of scarcity correspond to a distinction between reproducible and non-reproducible goods. Reproducible goods are those goods which are capable of being reproduced, after a finite period of time, with the currently given forces of production, within the given mode of production and through the operation of its constituent mechanisms. In short, therefore, a good is reproducible if its likeness can be produced by a given economy at a given stage of development.

At present, old masters are non-reproducible for at least one important reason. The attributes of genius cannot be produced within our society partly because the necessary combination of social environment and genetic endowment is not fully understood. Human society may reach the stage where the 'production' of an artist such as Rembrandt, Beethoven or Picasso, is possible. Then the works of such genius would become reproducible; but, as yet, this has not happened. In contrast, however, the works of even a talented painter, graphic artist, or photographer, could be regarded as reproducible within modern capitalist society, as the institutionalized training and creation of such skills does exist.

We have mentioned that wines that result from unusual climatic conditions are non-reproducible. If man could freely control the weather then that would not be the case. Hence, once again, the demarcation between reproducibility and non-reproducibility rests on the extent that man, within a given mode of production, can control the forces of the natural world. The extent to which social man can impose his will on nature is the extent to which goods are reproducible.

It is a mistake, found in some writers, to regard all wines as non-reproducible. The chemical processes through which wines are produced can, these days, be controlled. Hence wines that are produced under average climatic conditions and controllable circumstances of fermentation are reproducible. That does not mean that matured wines are immediately reproducible, of course. The concept of reproducibility includes an allowance for the passage of a finite period of time.

With the limited exception of land that is reclaimed from the sea, land is non-reproducible in a developed capitalist country such as Britain. Little more land is available than that already utilized in some way. However, in earlier times and in some other countries, land could be regarded as reproducible because large tracts of virgin land were available. The fact that only a limited amount of land exists on planet Earth is not relevant (matter cannot be created, so, at the limit, when all resources are used up, *all* goods are non-reproducible). However, the concept of reproducibility does not apply to the limit. It applies to the production feasibilities within, and in relation to, given relations and forces of production.

On reflection it is clear that the bulk of the wealth of modern society consists of reproducible goods. It is justified, therefore, in our abstract analysis of the capitalist mode of production, to confine our attention to reproducible goods. This does not mean that some non-reproducible goods, especially land, do not play a significant role in capitalist society. The correct starting point of the analysis, however, as Marx emphasized, is to abstract from non-reproducibles such as land. This does not, however, deny the importance of a future analysis of non-reproducibles, nor the need to incorporate the fact of limited physical resources, for example, in the concrete analysis of the modern world.

Is labour-power reproducible?

The problem as to whether or not labour-power should be regarded as reproducible is not as simple as it might seem, even if we exclude the labour of geniuses from the discussion. Fresh labour-power, of a particular type, can be produced by the feeding, housing, clothing and training of an individual; but labour-power comes in units of time, and each individual has only a limited amount of time available. The extent to which the capitalist mode of production can reproduce labour-power depends, in part, therefore, upon the availability of time, given that the labourer must rest and relax to the extent that is regarded as necessary under the given social conditions. Under conditions of full employment, when most workers are working overtime for example, more time may not be available given the prevailing social conditions. The only way of producing more labour-power must then lie in the procreation of the human species. Under capitalism, however, human procreation does not take place under capitalist conditions nor for capitalist motives. Labour-power is not and cannot be reproduced through procreation for sale for profit unless there is slavery. In other words the mechanisms of the capitalist mode will not, *on their own,* lead to the procreation of more labour-power if it happens to be in short supply. Shortages of labour-power can only be filled through the mechanisms of this mode of production, such as the market, by using the potential labour-power of existing individuals, attracting them to work more by higher wages, etc. In the history of capitalism, extra labour-power was made available often by the brutal destruction of pre-capitalist and semi-capitalist forms of production, for example the driving of the peasants off the land as a result of the enclosure movement in Britain. When capitalism becomes a dominant and general reality, however, such additional reserves of potential labour-power do not exist. In conclusion, therefore, under conditions of full employment of labour-power, in a social formation where the capitalist mode of production is generalized, labour-power is not reproducible.

However, such conditions are very rare. Even under conditions of full employment in the 1950s British capitalism was able to obtain extra labour-power from other countries where unemployment was greater, or by bringing women from the household into capitalist employment. Furthermore, it is important to note that labour-power is heterogeneous, and it is extremely unlikely that *all* different sorts of labour-power will be fully employed. If just one sort is unemployed, to some degree, then there is the possibility, through retraining if necessary, of reproducing other types of labour-power. Hence, for the purposes of the analysis in this book it would be valid to regard the labour-power of persons other than geniuses as reproducible.

This problem over deciding the status of labour-power stems, once again, from the unique conditions under which labour-power is reproduced under capitalism. Under the slave mode of production the same sort of problem does not exist. Labour-power here is created by the purposeful breeding of slaves, and under the relations of the slave mode of production itself. Clearly, in those circumstances, in relation to that mode of production, labour-power is reproducible.

PART II
THE LABOUR THEORY

CHAPTER 7

LABOUR AND EXCHANGE-VALUE

A science which hesitates to forget its founders is lost.
                                                A. N. WHITEHEAD

Hitherto, the labour theory of value has dominated Marxian economics. In chapters 7—9 we attempt to refute the view that exchange-value, and consequently value as we shall define it, is created or determined by labour alone. Such a detour is clearly necessary given the extent to which the remainder of our analysis rests on the work of Marx. The reader is bound to note the absence of a labour theory of value in this work and this absence must be explained and justified. In addition, in our view, the rejection of a labour theory is a necessary condition for restoring Marxism to a fully scientific status.

Embodied labour and exchange-value

At first we must emphasize the well-known theoretical result that there is no necessary reason for amounts of embodied labour in commodities to be proportional to their exchange-values. This can be illustrated with the example in the previous chapter. The amounts of socially necessary embodied labour time in one unit of corn and fertilizer are ⅔ and 1 respectively. The reader can check these results by verifying that the labour embodied in the inputs, plus the living labour employed, is equal to the labour embodied in the outputs, in each industry. We noted that, according to the calculations in the previous chapter, 1 unit of corn will exchange for about 1.3593 units of fertilizer. This clearly differs from the ratio of their embodied labour values, which is 1 : 1.5. The example is not just a fluke; in general, quantities of embodied labour will not be in proportion to exchange-values.

In addition it must be emphasized that the deviation of exchange-value from embodied labour is not merely due to the fluctuations of exchange-value on the market. The deviation exists *in equilibrium*, when there is no excess demand or supply on the market. The deviation of exchange-values from amounts of embodied labour is, there-fore, structural and permanent, at least in the capitalist mode of production. It does not simply result from accidental fluctuations on the market.

In *Capital,* Marx does not *say* that he is assuming, *as an expository device,* that exchange-values are in proportion to quantities of embodied labour, only to drop this assumption after the first two volumes. However, this is the usual interpretation of the issue made by Marxist scholars. I, myself, am not convinced by this interpreta-tion, because of lack of sufficient clear evidence in *Capital*; but this present work, we must emphasize, is not concerned with the ques-tion of *interpretation* of Marx.

Nevertheless, in this chapter we have been forced to examine the adequacy of the labour theory of value. It is necessary, therefore, to question the legitimacy of any assumption that exchange-values are proportional to quantities of embodied labour. Furthermore, we shall criticize another notion, made explicit in volume one of *Capital,* that labour is the 'substance', source, or sole creator of exchange-value.

Labour as the only substance of exchange-value

In the first chapter of *Capital* Marx sets out on his quest to find a common substance which lies behind the form of appearance of exchange-value. He writes:

firstly, the valid exchange-values of a particular commodity express something equal, and secondly, exchange-value cannot be anything other than the mode of expression, the 'form of appearance', of a content distinguishable from it. . . . This common element cannot be a geometrical, physical, chemical or other natural property of commodities. Such properties come into consideration only to the extent that they make the commodities useful, i.e. turn them into use-values. But clearly, the exchange relation of commodities is characterized precisely by its abstraction from their use-values (Marx, 1976, p. 127).

A few sentences later the crucial conclusion is reached:

If then we disregard the use-value of commodities, only one property remains, that of being products of labour (p. 128).

Objections to this crucial step are widespread in non-Marxian litera-ture. Neoclassical economists, for example, unanimously disagree and argue that labour is not the *only* common substance. All commodities, they argue, possess utility, are scarce to some degree, are products of nature, and so on. This point was made by the neoclassical economist Böhm-Bawerk, many years ago (see Sweezy, 1975, pp. 75–7). In reply, Marxian theorists, such as Hilferding (ibid., pp. 127–37), and Dobb (1940, ch. 1) have attempted to show that these alternative common properties do not measure up to certain scientific criteria. In particular such properties are not objective, social and easily measurable. On the contrary, Dobb and Hilferding argue that utility, for example, is a subjectively determined concept, and it cannot be measured independently as it does not possess an independent phenomenal form. The natural qualities of commodities, for example, are divorced from any social content and, they contend, cannot explain exchange-value which is a particular social form. Dobb and Hilferding thus claim to reject all other candidate 'common substances' as unscientific, and return to the common substance of labour which alone appears to pass the test.

Even if we accept the criteria of Hilferding and Dobb, their argument, as a whole, is not convincing. First, by their own arguments, labour alone cannot explain exchange-value. For labour exists in all modes of production, but exchange-value exists only in a commodity-producing society. The usual retort is to state that it is not labour in general, but abstract labour that is the substance of exchange-value, and abstract labour has something to do with the situation where labour-power is sold on the market, which occurs under capitalism only. But why labour? Many commodities are bought and sold on the market. Why select labour as the *only* common substance? Iron, for example, enters into the production, directly or indirectly, of most, if not all, commodities. Why is iron not a 'common substance'? The production of all commodities requires land, which can be rejected on the basis of its non-reproducibility. Dobb attempts to reject land simply on the basis that it is not homogeneous; but why does the actual heterogeneity of land rule it out as a possible common substance? Dobb gives no reason. After all, we must note, labour is also heterogeneous. There is no reason to suppose that we are searching for a single or homogeneous common substance; simply no reason at all. A multiplicity of substances, heterogeneous or otherwise, could form the common basis of commodities.

There are many types of commodity which enter, directly or indirectly, into all processes of production. For example, in the modern capitalist economy there are few processes which do not directly use steel in some form, and most production processes, if not all, depend upon it indirectly. Perhaps we could go so far as to suggest that some commodities, such as electricity, petroleum, oil, salt, and coal, directly or indirectly enter into the production of all other commodities. Most production processes need electrical power, for instance. It would be quite feasible to consider the 'steel embodied' or the 'electricity embodied' in any commodity, just as it was common during the British drought of 1976 to hear computations of the 'water embodied' in various everyday commodities. Naturally, all these commodities would be measured in their own appropriate units. Our purpose is not to argue that the labour theory of value should be replaced by a 'steel theory of value' or anything like it. That would be absurd. We simply argue that neither Marx, nor anyone else, has demonstrated that that labour is the only social and objective common substance embodied in commodities. Neither do we wish to depart from our previous arguments which show that labour is rather a special type of commodity. We simply state that it has not been demonstrated that the special features of labour have any significance in singling out labour as the sole substance of exchange-value. We are prepared to admit, for the sake of argument, that labour could, in certain circumstances, be regarded as the most important 'substance' behind exchange-value. That does not mean, however, that it is the *only* such substance.

We note, in passing, that there are some processes which do not require direct labour at all. The maturation of wine in a cellar is a famous example. To consider it we must make it clear that we are not considering rare wines, but normal, reproducible wines. Wine undergoes determinate chemical changes, in a more or less 'automatic' manner, in the normal process of maturation. Direct labour is not required. Other 'automatic' production processes that come to mind are the ripening of fruit and the gathering of water in reservoirs. These also do not require direct labour. Yet an average mature wine has a greater exchange-value than an average immature wine; ripe fruit has a greater exchange-value than unripe fruit; and a full reservoir has a greater exchange-value than an empty one.

With the advance of modern automation, more labour-exempt processes are, at least, technically feasible. Even supervisory work can be replaced by computer control systems. The vision of science fiction is not that far beyond our reach: a fully automated society requiring no direct labour at all.

Let us expand on a point made above. Labour, as a productive activity, has been present in all forms of human society; but exchange-value is clearly present in a commodity-producing society only.

Clearly, therefore, some extra elements, other than mere labour, steel, water and so on, must be part of the 'substance' that forms exchange-value. These extra elements are, first, private property relations; second, a division of labour; third, a market. Without these things exchange-value would not exist. This conclusion seems to undermine the very posing of the question: what is the substance of exchange-value? The social basis of exchange-value is not really a 'substance' at all. The use of the latter word involves an implicit analogy with the physical rather than the social world. Such an analogy is both erroneous and misleading. If, in contrast, we ask the question: 'what is the social basis of exchange-value?', then we can answer in terms of the social relations of a commodity-producing society. If we ask a second question: 'what determines exchange-values quantitatively?', then that has already been answered in the previous chapter; it depends on the structural relations of all basic commodities in the inputs and outputs.

It must be emphasized that we do not regard labour as being similar to other commodities. Labour has, indeed, very special features. Our own 'humanist' bias, given that we are all members of the human species, may lead us to favour labour as the sole primary substance of production. However, that would not necessarily be a position based on science. If we consider the 'substance' of exchange-value, what is important is not labour (or labour-power) as such, but that labour-power, like other inputs in the production process, is the object of *property relations*. In pointing to a multiplicity of common 'substances' which could fit the bill regarding the 'substance' of exchange-value which Marx is keen to discover we are not forgetting the *social* character of the category exchange-value. We argue, first, that if one sets out on the quest for the common substance of exchange-value then there is no scientific basis upon which several other non-labour substances can be rejected. Second, the quest for a common substance is, in itself, misconceived because exchange-value is not simply derived from the utilization of 'substances' in production, such as labour. Exchange-value is a qualitative social category which requires the existence of specific social relations.

Labour as the sole creator of value

In a famous argument in *Capital* Marx shows that profit cannot originate as a whole in the sphere of exchange. One person can buy cheap and sell dear, but that is only a redistribution of existing resources, via the market, to that person. The market cannot itself add to existing resources, and thus profit cannot be created in that sphere. Then Marx goes on to make the following remark:

our friend the money-owner must be lucky enough to find within the sphere of circulation, on the market, a commodity whose use-value possesses the peculiar property of being a source of value, whose actual consumption is therefore itself an objectification of labour, hence a creation of value. The possessor of money does find such a special commodity on the market: the capacity for labour, in other words labour-power (Marx, 1976, p. 270).

If, according to some interpreters of Marx, we regard the word 'value' to mean, by definition, 'socially necessary embodied labour time', then the above passage seems banal. If value is labour-time then labour-power is the capacity to create, or 'source', of value. On the other hand it is more convincing to assume that to Marx 'value' meant 'the monetary expression of exchange-value'. In that case the passage would form a key point in Marx's argument in *Capital,* worthy of critical examination. It is certainly in a structurally important section of his discourse: at the point where he makes the transition from the discussion of exchange to the sphere of production. Although we do not wish to bind ourselves to a particular interpretation of Marx's theory of value, it does seem that the proposition 'labour is the source of (the monetary expression of) exchange-value' is worth discussing.

Although the course of Marx's reasoning in *Capital* led him to the appropriate and central destination of production, its route violated the frontiers of theoretical adequacy and scientific substantiation. Marx simply *assumes* that labour is the sole creator of exchange-value. There is no explanation for this assumption other than to credit previous economists (presumably Smith and Ricardo) with its 'discovery' (Marx, 1976, p. 167).

It can be admitted that it is difficult to find processes of production in a capitalist economy which do not require the direct application of labour. However, we cannot conclude from that admission that labour is the source of exchange-value; for it must be noted that it is also difficult to find processes which do not require the use of physical means of production, such as tools or machinery. Both labour and means of production can be necessary for production to take place, but that does not mean that either labour, or means of production, can be regarded as the exclusive source of exchange-value.

To regard the rarity, in contemporary times, of production proces- ses that do not require labour as a vindication of the proposition that labour is the sole creator of exchange-value is to see capitalist social relations through the short-focused spectacles of our present tech- nology. It is quite feasible for a capitalist mode of production to exist with a significant proportion of production under complete automation. Capitalism may be replaced by socialism before such circumstances arise. However, the limited life-span of capitalism is no excuse to deify labour as the whole creator of exchange-value. A single child may die before it is able to walk, but we cannot conclude from that that the exclusive form of locomotion for all humanity is crawling on all fours. The view that labour is the sole creator of exchange-value seems to be influenced by the earliest phase of capitalism, when manual labour was the most prevalent form of productive activity, and mechanized production was more rare.

An analytical approach

Other arguments have been forwarded in an attempt to prove that labour is the prime substance or creator of exchange-value. The so- called 'analytical approach' consists of breaking down the equilib- rium price of every commodity into its various components. At each stage this price divides into the cost of the used-up capital goods, and wages and profits. Wages and profits, called 'value added' in ortho- dox economics, are seen as resulting from living labour alone. We have already questioned that viewpoint, but let us accept it for a while, to examine the 'analytical approach' further. The used-up capital goods were previously produced with labour and capital goods, and their price is divided in the same way. At each stage, therefore, labour costs are identified and extracted. A similar reduc- tion process was discussed in the previous chapter. The process continues until, in the words of Mandel: 'the entire cost tends to be reduced to labour, and to labour alone' (1967, p. 26).

It should be obvious, from the discussion in the previous chapter, that the demonstration of such a reduction to labour does not show that labour is the source or substance of exchange-value. It was shown that it is quite possible to reduce costs to some other com- modity, such as corn or fertilizer. The analytical approach can be easily applied to many other commodities in the real world. The analytical discovery that all costs are reducible to labour costs, can be rivalled by other 'discoveries' that costs can be reduced to other single elements. Once again, the labour theory is based on a circular argument; labour is *selected* as the single prime commodity, and then it is triumphantly demonstrated that all costs are reducible to labour costs. On examination, however, the analytical argument is not convincing.

The post-Sraffa, 'dated labour' theory

Sophisticated supporters of the labour theory of value sometimes use the 'reduction to dated quantities of labour' which is accomplished in Sraffa's famous work (Sraffa, 1960). They argue that Sraffa has both modernized and vindicated the labour theory of value with this 'reduction'. Hunt and Sherman, for example, seem to take this position in their generally excellent textbook (1975, pp. 228—34). The dated labour reduction has given rise to a widespread impression (not justified in Sraffa's work) that Sraffa has bolstered up the labour theory of value. On the contrary the implication of Sraffa's book is at least that the labour theory of value is redundant (see Steedman, 1977). Proponents of the dated labour theory seem not to have read beyond the first part of this book, for in the second part Sraffa shows that, in realistic circumstances, a convergent series of dated labour terms will not always exist, and even if such a series did exist we would have no assurance that all the terms will be positive (Sraffa, 1960, pp. 56—9).

Even in circumstances where the dated labour series does exist it is possible to refute the post-Sraffa version of the labour theory of value. The dated labour series shows relationships between quantities of labour, each with a specific 'date', and prices and profits. It does not relate prices and profits to *aggregated* embodied labour. The *time structure* of past labour inputs is just as significant as the absolute quantities of labour involved. It is not legitimate or theoretically significant to lump all these past amounts of labour together into a homogeneous mass. Furthermore, if this illegitimate aggregation is performed then, according to Sraffa's own analysis, it is quite impossible to derive prices and profits from the aggregated embodied labour. The dated labour series, therefore, does not validate the labour theory, but, on the other hand, illuminates the importance of other elements in the determination of exchange-value: namely the technological and temporal *structure* of production.

We need not dwell on the point, made already above, that other 'dated' reductions are also possible, other than labour. This fact was demonstrated in the last chapter.

Sraffa's system is a purely formal set of logical relationships. That does not, of course, mean that it is either invalid or inconsequential; but it does not embody a description or conceptual analysis of the essential features of the capitalist system. In particular, there is no conceptual analysis of labour and labour-power. Sraffa's work does not claim to be such a conceptual analysis: it is merely a 'prelude' to one.

It would be quite possible to go through the whole of Sraffa's book, deleting the word 'labour' and substituting 'horse-power' (assuming that horses are used to produce at least one basic good). The word 'wages' would become 'the food and maintenance distributed to the horses'. Formally, all this would make sense; there is no logical objection. The result could be a 'dated horse-power series' and a 'horse-power theory of value'! As labour is not analysed conceptually there is no impediment to this procedure. This does, however, emphasize our previous point that the question of the source and substance of exchange-value cannot merely be a formal matter. It must involve a conceptual and interpretative analysis of the essential social relations of the capitalist mode of production.

Mandel's 'reduction to the absurd'

Mandel has related a novel argument in support of the notion that exchange-values are determined by labour-time:

> *Imagine for a moment a society in which human labour has completely disappeared, that is to say, a society in which all production has been 100 per cent automated. . . . A huge mass of products would be produced without this production creating any income, since no human being would be involved in production. But someone would want to 'sell' these products for which there were no longer any buyers. . . . A society in which human labour would be totally eliminated from production . . . would be a society in which exchange-value had also been eliminated. This proves the validity of the theory* (Mandel, 1967, pp. 27–8).

Let us assume that Mandel is referring to a fully automated society in which the means of production are still privately owned by the ruling class. Perhaps this could be the eventual result of progressive automation under a capitalist mode of production, under circumstances where the working class had never managed to place itself in power and institute socialism. The working class would be outcast and economically redundant: surviving on charity or starving to death. However, even if the working class had no income whatsoever we can show that incomes would still be produced in such a society, and commodities would have exchange-values. (We shall assume, furthermore, that there are at least two firms in the economy.)

The private owners of the means of production would buy and sell machines, spare parts, raw materials, and consumption goods, *amongst themselves*. For example, a private owner of an automated electrical power-generating plant would sell his electricity to the owners of other factories, who required this electricity for their own production processes. The electrical power plant owner would thus derive a money income. With this income he would buy luxuries, necessities, and consumption goods, from other factory owners. Money would circulate from owner to owner, and incomes would continually be generated. There would still be commodities, and these commodities would have exchange-values, despite the fact that no labour-time was involved in their production. The elimination of labour is not necessarily followed by the elimination of exchange-value.

Mandel's misconception, in this case, seems to be connected to the underconsumptionist notion that working-class incomes provide the only source of effective demand in the economy. This false notion is very widespread in the labour movement, and has a long pedigree (see Bleaney, 1976). In fact, the underconsumptionist view would seem to be valid if exchange-values were determined by labour alone. This would be the case if there were no investment and capitalists' consumption in the economy. Presumably, profits would be zero, and, as is well known in those circumstances, prices would be proportional to quantities of embodied labour. Underconsumptionism is closely connected, therefore, to a crude labour theory of value and the notion that without labour there would be no exchange-value.

It may be depressing to picture a possible future society in which the proletariat is both powerless and economically redundant. (An approximation to such a society was depicted in the film *Rollerball*.) But it is still necessary to assert this possibility, to warn ourselves of a possible future.

A final word

The unique properties of labour, and labour-power, are important, and should not be neglected. In particular, labour-power is the only commodity which is inseparable from its owner, and under capitalism it is produced under non-capitalist conditions. We shall see the significance of these and other unique features at a later stage; but to say that labour is important and unique is not to say that labour is the source or sole determinant of exchange-value. This does not lead us to embrace marginal utility, or anything else, as a source of value. As Lippi has pointed out, in his excellent *Value and Naturalism in Marx*: 'The possibility that there may be some source of value other than labour is ruled out by extirpating the problem of the "source" of value itself' (1979, p. 91).

Quite often it is suggested that an assumption that labour is the substance of exchange-value is a useful heuristic device. It is supposed to show that the exchange-value of the surplus product, i.e. profit, results from surplus labour. Thus the exploitation of the working class under capitalism is demonstrated. Our discussion above would suggest that such a heuristic device *assumes* what has to be *proved*. It is illegitimate and ineffective to demonstrate the existence of exploitation upon such an assumption. Not only is the assumption false, the existence of exploitation has to be shown by *other* means.

CHAPTER 8

LABOUR, CALCULATION AND CAUSALITY

Here the ways of men part: if you wish to strive for peace of soul and pleasure, then believe; if you wish to be a devotee of the truth, then enquire.

NIETZSCHE

In this chapter we begin a discussion of certain aspects of a recent debate concerning the labour theory of value. Much of this debate resulted from the publication of certain articles by Ian Steedman, David Yaffe and myself in the *Bulletin of the Conference of Socialist Economists,* a journal both inaugurated, and ceasing publication under that title, in the 1970s. Steedman's work was later collected together and published in 1977 in the book *Marx After Sraffa,* the publication of which itself renewed the debate for the remaining years of the decade. By 1980, however, it was clear that the defenders of the labour theory of value were taking increasingly divergent positions, and could be classified into at least three groups.

The first group is aptly described by Steedman in his book as 'obscurantist'. By failing even to give precise definitions of words such as 'value', and by heaping logical inconsistency upon terminological vagueness they could claim to be the inheritors of the true position of Marx. Two exemplars of this approach are Ben Fine and Laurence Harris. A repetition of their position, and a critique of it, would not be relevant to this work. The interested reader can consult the debate between Fine and Harris and myself in the *Socialist Register,* 1976 and 1977.

A second group have resorted to a quite different definition of the labour theory of value. Breaking from the tradition of Dobb, Meek and Sweezy they cease to *define* value as socially necessary embodied labour time. Quite often this is regarded as a break from the Ricardian influence on Marx. Usually greater, sometimes less, fidelity to the letter or spirit of Marx is claimed by this group. However this group have not, as yet, developed a coherent position, or interpretation of Marx, which has a clear alternative *definition of value.* Reeling back

86

from the Sraffa-based critique of the embodied labour definition and theory they have begun to take refuge in a notion of value which has more to do with real-world prices. This, in turn, creates problems because their standpoint, without adequate demarcation, can begin to resemble much of the neoclassical theory. Only the Marxist jargon shows the difference. An example of this approach is an article by Himmelweit and Mohun (1978). In so far as it moves towards a price-orientated definition of value (which we shall discuss in a later chapter) and away from the embodied labour definition, this approach is positive. In so far as it fosters imprecision, lacks clarity, and sustains the habits of thought of the Marxian Fundamentalists, it is a barrier to scientific advance.

The third group is by far the most rigorous. It would include the works of Armstrong, Glyn and Harrison (1978), Bowles and Gintis (1977), Rowthorn (1980) and Wright (1979). All the above, with different degrees of reluctance, still accept the embodied labour definition of value, and, at the same time, accept the formal veracity of Steedman's work and the Sraffa-based results. Furthermore, they are united by a wish to regard labour as the essential 'substance' of value, and exchange-value, under capitalism. The remarks in the previous chapter can be directed at their work.

One person in the latter group stands out, partly because his defence of the labour theory of value is more tenacious than the rest, partly because his defence is striking and superficially attractive, and partly because his work has raised some important questions which had not been developed and answered before. I refer to the work of Erik Olin Wright. (The (1977) work of Bowles and Gintis is also of interest, but it relates exclusively to the question of heterogeneous labour, which is not, at this point, our concern.) Because Wright's work raises some important questions it would be useful to discuss it here. Before that, however, we shall summarize Steedman's strongest argument against the labour theory of value, and then move on to Wright's work, which relates directly to this. We conclude with a more general discussion.

Steedman's redundancy argument

One of the implications of Sraffa's *Production of Commodities by Means of Commodities* is elaborated in Steedman's work. In the Sraffian scheme it is accepted that there are many determinants of the bundle of commodities representing the real wage and the technical (what Wright usefully calls the 'sociotechnical', to emphasize

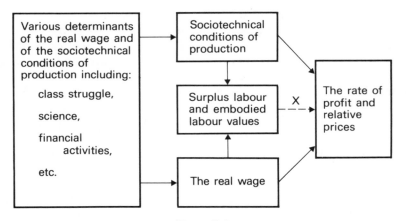

Figure 8.1
The Sraffian scheme and embodied labour redundancy

the social nature of technology) conditions of production. The class struggle, for example, may be important in determining the real wage; but once all these determinants have played their role, the sociotechnical conditions and the real wage alone determine the rate of profit in the system. The latter are the proximate causes of profits and relative prices. The class struggle can still play a crucial role in the dynamics of profit determination, but such causes have their effects on profits (and relative prices) by virtue of their effect on real wages and sociotechnical conditions only. This Sraffian account is illustrated in figure 8.1.

The Dobb—Meek—Sweezy tradition within Marxian value theory asserts that both surplus labour and embodied labour values are necessary to determine, amongst other things, the rate of profit and relative prices. This view is shown by the broken arrow 'X' in figure 8.1. (It must be noted that Meek abandoned this assertion before his death (Meek, 1973).) Steedman has pointed out that, as far as the determination of profits and relative prices are concerned, both surplus labour and the embodied labour values are *redundant.* This result should be clear from the examples in chapter 6 above, where the Sraffian approach was discussed. The sociotechnical conditions of production and the real wage are entirely sufficient to determine the rate of profit and relative prices. The embodied labour theory is not required. (This result complements our discussion in the preceding chapter which claimed that the labour theory was *illegitimate.*)

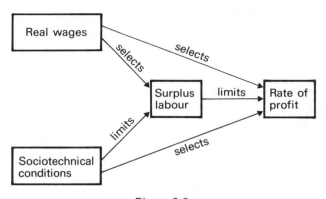

Figure 8.2
Wright's modified account of profit determination

Wright's modified labour theory

To simplify matters, we shall adopt Wright's approach of simply discussing the determinants of 'profits', excluding reference to relative
prices. However, by 'profits', as Wright himself makes clear, he really
means 'the rate of profit', and we shall retain this term here.

Wright's innovation is to introduce a complex and diversified
notion of causation. The core of his modified account of the labour
theory involves two different kinds of causation or 'modes of determination' as Wright calls them. The first is *'structural limitation'*. In
this type of causation a structure or element sets limits of variation
on another structure or element. Within these limits there is a variety
of possible outcomes, but the limits themselves are determinate. The
second mode of determination is *'selection'*. In this type of causation specific outcomes are selected from a range of structurally
limited possibilities. The second mode of determination, therefore,
establishes a specific outcome within the limits imposed by the first.

Wright then modifies the account of profit determination in
figure 6.4 above, to include his two notions of causality. Real wages
and sociotechnical conditions 'select' the profit level; but surplus
labour (i.e. the amount of socially necessary labour time embodied in
the net product; the amount of the social product, measured in
embodied labour terms, at the disposal of the capitalists for their
consumption or investment), places a 'structural limitation' on the
latter. In turn 'surplus labour' is 'selected' by the real wage and
'limited' by sociotechnical conditions. This gives the configuration in

figure 8.2. For simplicity, the various primary determinants of the real wage and sociotechnical conditions, appearing on the left-hand side of figure 8.1, are omitted.

In summary, therefore, Wright's model establishes a relationship between surplus labour, real wages, sociotechnical conditions and the rate of profit. Furthermore, according to Wright, surplus labour imposes the fundamental limits on the range of possible profits. With a given quantity of surplus labour there is an absolute ceiling on the possible quantity of profits. When surplus labour is zero, no profits at all are possible; as surplus labour increases, the possible maximum profit also increases monotonically. Within these limits, however, both the sociotechnical conditions of production and the real wage have a selection effect on profits.

In making the above assertion, Wright seems to be making a reference to the so-called 'fundamental Marxian theorem' of Morishima (see Morishima, 1974; Morishima and Catephores, 1978). According to this theorem, the rate of profit is positive if and only if surplus labour, as defined by Morishima, is positive. Wright recognizes the problem of ambiguity in the definition of embodied labour and surplus labour in joint production systems (which is discussed in chapter 9 below), and takes recourse in the Morishima definitions. The latter cannot yield negative values and negative surplus labour in any circumstances, unlike the definition highlighted by Steedman in a famous article (1975).

However, a passage in a book by Wright (1978, p. 133n.) gives a different impression. In this passage Wright asserts that a 100 per cent automated factory 'would clearly be a disaster for the capitalist class, since without labour in production there would be no surplus value [surplus labour—G.H.] and thus no profits'. This assertion is not based on Morishima, and it is wrong. Even a completely automated factory is likely to use raw materials and produced inputs from other firms. These firms could, themselves, employ labour. Hence these inputs will have labour embodied in them, and we can assume, on the basis of Morishima's definition or otherwise, that this embodied labour is positive. Real and money wages in the 100 per cent automated factory will be zero, so surplus labour will be positive. What would happen, however, if *all* factories and firms were 100 per cent automated? This is the same situation as that contrived by Mandel and discussed in chapter 7 above. In that chapter it was established that even under 100 per cent automation of the entire commodity-producing economy, the owners of the means of production would buy and sell their products from and to each other.

Positive demand, positive revenue and positive profits would all exist. There would not be, however, any surplus labour. This result does not contradict Morishima's fundamental Marxian theorem because in the latter Morishima assumes that the production of at least one basic good involves labour, and, therefore, he assumes that the economy is not 100 per cent automated. Wright's remark is *doubly* wrong. The 100 per cent automation of a factory does *not* imply zero surplus labour in that factory, and it is *not* true, in all cases, that zero surplus labour implies zero profits.

Leaving the criticism of Wright's book aside, we return to his 1979 article. In this Wright simply asserts that surplus labour is an upper and lower bound on profits, and he does not discuss automation. From this assertion he concludes that surplus labour provides an explanation of the range of profit levels in the economy. He then integrates his theory, summarized in figure 8.1, with an even more sophisticated account of causal relations within a capitalist economy. The latter model, however, remains at its core. We shall confine our discussion to this first, and basic, modification of the labour theory. Any fault found within the first modification will be reflected in Wright's more sophisticated account.

The arbitrariness of embodied labour

Our first criticism of Wright is anticipated in the previous chapter. In his model, surplus labour is identified as the limiting factor on profits; but, as Wright himself is aware, if *any* basic input (or 'factor of production') is held constant then it too will limit profits. For example, let us assume that energy is an input in the system. Energy will enter the production of most commodities and also, through home heating etc., into the production of labour-power itself. Every commodity, including labour-power, will have an amount of 'embodied energy'. The 'surplus energy' will be the net amount of energy coming from the energy sector into the rest of the economy. Profits are 'limited' in the same manner by surplus energy as they are by surplus labour. With tongue in cheek we can thus construct an 'energy theory of value'. Figure 8.1 can be modified with 'surplus energy' instead of 'surplus labour' in the central block. It is not seriously suggested that such a theory of value would have the same meaning or explanatory power as the labour theory, or that labour-power does not have special characteristics which are worthy of identification and must be understood to explain the inner workings of the capitalist system. Labour-power is important, central and unique. But we have to demonstrate its uniqueness and centrality, not assume it at the outset. At this stage the important point is to note that there is no *formal* problem if we proceed from any other basic input in the system and see it as placing a limit on profits. Wright's elaborate and elegant account does begin to look blinkered by an initial and unvalidated disposition towards the labour theory.

The argument in the preceding paragraph can be stated more rigorously with the Bródy (1970) proof which shows that labour as a source and measure of value is indiscernible from any other commodity, at least in the formal derivation of prices and profits. Any other 'source' can serve as well. The relative price system remains the same whether we start from labour or anything else. So too do profits remain the same if we start from 'surplus energy' instead of surplus labour.

In defence against the argument that any input could be chosen to supply the 'structural limitation' on profits, Wright gives special reasons for selecting labour and surplus labour. He asserts that the focus on the latter 'is itself derived from the class analysis of exploitation'. This seems to be putting the cart before the horse. Surely exploitation should be *derived* as a concept from an analysis such as the one proposed by Wright. Exploitation cannot be the initial basis of the surplus labour theory, otherwise we are assuming what we have to prove.

In fact, if we ask how classes themselves are defined, Wright's defence becomes completely circular when his response is discovered. According to Wright 'the dominant class is defined by those positions which appropriate surplus labour; the subordinate class by those positions which have their surplus labour appropriated' (Wright, 1979, p. 65). The argument is that we derive the importance of surplus labour by reference to the class analysis of exploitation. However, the class analysis of exploitation is itself derived from the notion of surplus labour. Wright goes round this circle more than once; the terms 'classes' and 'surplus labour' play leapfrog through the crucial passages of his article.

Calculation and causality

In his defence, however, Wright makes another point. Any basic commodity can serve as the basis for the *calculation* of profits or relative prices (and this is confirmed by Bródy's proof), but that does not mean that that element can be considered to be a *cause* in the determination of profits and relative prices. This point is substantial and valid, and requires extended discussion. It will be seen, however, that Wright's alternative account of the determination of profits lacks plausibility. It is valid to point out that to assemble a set of factors which are necessary to calculate profits is not the same thing as assembling a set of causes of the profit level. It is not valid, however, simply to posit a particular factor and claim that it is a cause. Wright has not *demonstrated* causality in his model.

Wright asserts that surplus labour *limits* profits; but to point out that a factor limits profits is not the same thing as to point out a *cause*, of any type, of the profit level or range of possible profit levels. Sraffa identifies a set of factors which are sufficient to *calculate* the precise level of profits. Wright identifies a factor (surplus labour) which is sufficient to *calculate* limits on profits. What is the difference? In the first place they are both calculations, not, at this stage, demonstrations of cause and effect. The difference worth noting is that Wright's calculation is simply a weaker and less precise version of the one provided by Sraffa; Sraffa's is sufficient to provide a precise answer whereas Wright's is not.

To reinforce the point that Wright has not shown a causal relation in his model we can reconsider the relationship he posits between surplus labour and profits. According to Wright, the former sets limits on the latter; surplus labour is the independent variable and profits is the dependent variable—dependent, that is, in the sense of being 'structurally limited' by surplus value. But why is one a cause of the other? We are given no reason. There is nothing to stop us, at this stage, making profits the independent variable and surplus labour the dependent variable. In other words, surplus labour is 'structurally limited' by profits, and profits are the 'proximate cause' of surplus labour. Wright's model can be changed, reversing the 'causality' between profits and surplus labour.

This is not to suggest, of course, that profits do, in fact, limit surplus labour. Counter-examples such as this are used to show that what is being assumed is what has to be proved: a mistake common to all proponents of the labour theory. The counter-examples show that other analysts, making the same mistake, can come to quite different conclusions regarding value and exploitation in the capitalist system.

Nested modes of determination

Before we move on from Wright's article, we shall make a few remarks on his idea of 'nested modes of determination', in which one factor, or set of factors, sets *limits* on a variable, and another factor, or set of factors, *selects* the precise outcome, which is, of course, within the limits provided by the former factors. In a more general sense this idea is discussed in a book by Wright (1978, pp. 15–26). In his article on the labour theory of value he makes specific use of this idea; surplus labour *limits* profits but sociotechnical conditions plus the real wage *select* the profit level.

This raises an obvious question: if selection is sufficient to determine the result, what then is the status of structural limitation? The level of profits that is selected will always be within the limits provided by surplus labour, because, *by definition,* the limits contain all the feasible profit rates for a given amount of surplus value. So surplus labour is a 'cause' which plays no role because the other causes act to determine the outcome.

Surplus labour will never actually bring itself to bear upon the result. The outcome selected is always, by definition, within the limits set down by surplus labour. Such limits, therefore, are entirely *redundant* in the determination of profits.

In general, it is difficult to envisage a causal role for *structural* limits if other factors, via the process of *selection,* are entirely sufficient to determine the outcome. It is like saying that the height of homo sapiens is *caused,* through 'structural limitation' by the thickness of the atmosphere. Certainly, humanoids could not survive on Earth if they were ten miles high! The invention of structural limits is arbitrary, for any real phenomenon, and it is wrong to simply assume that they have a causal role. Wright's whole methodology, with these 'nested modes of determination' is thrown in doubt.

Causality in the Sraffa system

Whilst Wright's account of profit determination has to be rejected, his discussion of causality has raised certain questions. In particular Wright has argued that the Sraffa system shows the factors which are necessary to calculate profits, it does not indicate causes. This issue is worthy of extended discussion.

At one level the Sraffa model is merely a mental construction, a 'thought experiment'. Read in this way it is certainly not devoid of meaning. For example, the prices that are derived in the system are the prices which are *logically* necessary to ensure an equalized profit rate. Prices and profits depend, *logically,* on sociotechnical conditions and the real wage, and factors which influence them, and nothing else. These formal results enable us to order and arrange data about the real world. They prevent us falling into the trap of logical inconsistency when beginning to analyse problems of value and distribution. It is at this formal level that logical problems have been identified, by means of the Sraffa system, in the neoclassical theory of distribution and the neoclassical aggregate production function. (For expository accounts of the problems see Harcourt, 1972; Hodgson, 1977b.)

In logic, however, there are no causes or effects, merely assumptions and conclusions. To demonstrate the falsity of such a formal system only two courses of action are possible; to challenge the initial assumptions or find a fault in the logic of the argument. A great deal of the misunderstanding about the Sraffa system is a failure to appreciate the way the model is being used, for most of the time, as a purely formal construction.

It is possible, however, to *interpret* the Sraffa system in various ways, and to posit statements about the real world. It must be made clear, and this is another frequent source of misunderstanding, that an infinite number of such interpretations are possible, even if only one of them is valid. The formal Sraffa system does not lead us automatically to a certain view of the production process, or, for example, to see the sphere of exchange as primary and the sphere of production as secondary. All these things can be, illegitimately or otherwise, *read in* to Sraffa's formal construction, but they are not there at the outset.

What follows is an interpretation of the Sraffa system, and it includes an ascription of causes and effects. From the above remarks, however, it will be clear that there is no reason why all adherents of the Sraffa system should automatically accept what is said. They may wish to put forward a modified, or distinct, interpretation.

It is not merely for the sake of convenience or uniformity that Sraffa, like many other value theorists including Marx, assumes an equalized rate of profit. An equalized, or general, rate of profit is appropriate to the Sraffa system because there are real forces in a capitalist economy which tend to bring rates of profit in different industries into line. These forces are the forces of competition. Marx, himself, makes this clear in several passages of his writings. For example: 'What competition between the different spheres of production brings about is the creation of the same general rate of profit in the different spheres' (Marx, 1969, p. 208). In another passage he writes that the formation of a general rate of profit, i.e. the equalization of the rate of profit, is an 'actual process' corresponding to 'real phenomena' (Marx, 1962, p. 151). It is not simply a mental equalization, or an initial assumption for theoretical convenience, it is an equalization which corresponds to processes in the real capitalist world. The argument for this is well known. Capital investment would flow to those industries with a higher rate of profit. This would cause the decline of industries with a lower profit rate. The only stable long-run position is where all the profit rates are more or less equal. Marx is quite aware of this argument and makes it abundantly clear in his works.

There is a real process behind the assumption of an equalized profit rate in the Sraffa system. However, Sraffa does not discuss the dynamics of this process. This is an omission in his work but it was made, perhaps, to focus attention on what he thought were the substantive issues. Partly as a consequence of this omission, causality in Sraffa has to be discussed in terms of comparative statics. This, of course, gives the exercise limited scope, but it is not without value. A full dynamic analysis will expose other causal factors, but, to repeat our earlier warning, such factors have to be *detected* not simply imputed into the model.

Let us assume that in a certain capitalist economy, at a certain point in time, the forces of competition have succeeded in bringing about an equalization of the rate of profit. Things change, but 10 years later the forces of competition triumph once more and a general rate of profit is formed again. However, it is quantitatively different from the rate of profit 10 years before. What factors have *caused* such a change in the rate of profit? Sraffian analysis shows that the proximate causes are the sociotechnical conditions and the real wage. There is no other proximate cause. It is not simply a question of calculation. These factors are *causes,* in the sense that we have described. (This account of profit determination will have to be modified with the introduction of money in the Sraffa system, and this is done in chapter 15 below.)

Marx, of course, held that embodied labour played a central role in the transformation of values into prices, and the formation of a general rate of profit. However, the causal role of labour, and surplus labour, is asserted rather than proved. Furthermore, as Steedman (1977) shows, labour and surplus labour cannot be regarded as causal factors in the same way and sense as the sociotechnical conditions and the real wage. Embodied labour values are not sufficient, for example, to determine prices or the general rate of profit: the technical structure of production also plays a role. Steedman shows that in some circumstances the attempt to calculate the rate of profit from embodied labour values will give an indirect answer, even if we add the necessary extra information. These results need to be re-examined in the light of the above remarks on causation. What is clear is that at the abstract level of analysis of Sraffa's *Production of Commodities by Means of Commodities,* or of Marx's chapter in *Capital* on the formation of a general rate of profit (volume 3, chapter 9), the Sraffian critique of the labour theory of value demonstrates that embodied labour values are redundant not only in the *calculation* of profits but also in their causal determination.

It may be suggested, in response, that there is a role for embodied labour and surplus labour outside the level of abstraction which is discussed above. I am aware of no rigorous theory of the capitalist system which includes such a role. The reader may recall Shaikh's 'vindication' of Marx's solution to the problem of transforming values into prices (Schwartz, 1977, pp. 106–39). Shaikh shows that embodied labour values can be used as a first approximation to prices, under certain conditions, and after successive adjustments in the light of differences in the *calculated* rates of profit these values can be gradually 'transformed', in an iterative manner, into prices. However, Shaikh does not succeed in showing that such a process occurs in the real world. Furthermore, there are an *infinite number* of 'first approximations' which can be used, in the same iterative process, to derive the same results. We could, conceivably, start with our old friend 'embodied energy', or even the number of letters in the name of the commodity when that name is translated into Serbo-Croat. Subject to certain conditions, all these 'first approximations' will lead us to the same end point. What matters in the iterative process is not the starting point but the process itself, and embodied labour plays no part in Shaikh's process. There is no evidence to show that this is anything more than a *calculation*; embodied labour values play no apparent role in the real capitalist world. (For further criticisms of Shaikh's 'vindication' see Lippi, 1979; Kurz, 1979. See also Morishima and Catephores, 1978, chs 6–7.)

Embodied labour and production

Quite often, the last resort of those who still wish to adhere to the concept of embodied labour is to assert that the concept is fundamental and essential because it direct attention to the labour process and social relations within production. Wright repeats this assertion. It is *nothing more* than an assertion. The concept of embodied labour value is neither necessary nor sufficient for an understanding of the social process of production. We shall show, in chapters 16–

18 of this work, that the concept of embodied labour value is *un-necessary* to an understanding of both exploitation and the social process of production. In fact the concept is more than unnecessary: it is an incumbrance to scientific thought. We turn, here, to an argument that the concept is *not sufficient* for such an adequate understanding of capitalist production.

Surplus labour, of embodied labour value, does not have immediate or automatic associations with a social process. At least in the first half of the twentieth century a technological–determinist version of Marxism was very common, if not in vogue. A Marxist of techno-logical–determinist hue would immediately focus on the technological determinants of surplus labour and embodied labour, not the social process of production. There is nothing attached to the concepts of surplus labour or embodied labour which lead us to the analytical haven of the labour process.

After all, we can calculate surplus labour or embodied labour only by reference to the economy as a whole. These are not to be detec-ted, either directly or indirectly, as phenomenal substances, within the firm. The association of terms like surplus labour and (embodied labour) value with production and the labour process is little more than prejudice or habit. Whilst our choice of categories does indeed influence our area and mode of investigation it is simply not demon-strated that embodied labour or surplus labour lead us in the desired direction.

A study of the history of Marxian economic analysis will support these remarks. Since the publication of the first volume of *Capital* in 1867 there has been much discussion of embodied labour values and surplus labour; but, despite the fact that large sections of volume 1 are devoted to the labour process there has been little discussion of it in the literature. The highly regarded reply by Hilferding to Bohm-Bawerk's criticism of Marx (see Sweezy, 1975) asserts the import-ance of embodied labour because it is a 'social' rather than a 'subjec-tive' category. There is no substantial discussion of the labour process in that work. In the two classics of Marxist economic theory to appear after 1940, Sweezy's *Theory of Capitalist Development* and Mandel's *Marxist Economic Theory*, there is nothing more than a scanty discussion of the labour process. In fact, most of the import-ant literature on the latter has appeared only after 1970, including Braverman's *Labor and Monopoly Capital.*

A century after the publication of the first volume of *Capital,* with Sraffa's theory of prices and independent studies of the labour pro-cess in capitalist society, we can discard the musty baggage of the labour theory of value.

CHAPTER 9

JOINT PRODUCTION AND EMBODIED LABOUR

Discovery commences with the awareness of anomaly.
THOMAS KUHN, *The Structure of Scientific Revolutions*

We do not wish to appear to be attacking a nut with a sledgehammer. Effective arguments have been given against the labour theory of value in previous chapters. That would appear to be that. However, there are some important formal results, interesting in themselves, but also damaging for the labour theory, which still have to be discussed. These results were influential in the abandonment of the labour theory by Ian Steedman and myself in 1973, and are discussed more fully in Hodgson (1974c). Here we have kept the exposition short and free of mathematics.

The different definitions of embodied labour

In the first chapter of his book *Marx's Economics* Morishima shows that there are two alternative approaches to the definition of embodied labour. The first starts from the definitional identity of the living labour employed, plus the labour embodied in the other inputs, with the total labour embodied in the output. Hence this approach is based on the 'labour costs' in each process, and it is, perhaps, the way in which most people think of 'embodied labour'. A second approach proceeds from the economic system as a whole, and the amount of labour required to produce an extra unit of a good in the net output is determined. However, both approaches give identical numerical results. In addition, both approaches rely on the determination of 'embodied labour' from the technical coefficients in the whole system by a method of simultaneous equations, when the number of goods equals the number of processes.

In the final chapter of the same book, Morishima constructs an entirely different definition of embodied labour. This considers the system as a whole, but it does not rely on the assumption that the number of goods is equal to the number of processes. An optimization problem is set up in which the question is asked: what is the minimum amount of socially necessary labour time required to produce a given good, or bundle of goods? Then the 'optimized embodied labour' in the good is found. This method is one of linear programming, rather than simultaneous equations.

Two points must be emphasized. First, each of these above definitions and approaches relies on the interrelations between the production processes in the system as a whole. In general it is not possible to determine the embodied labour in a particular good from one process alone. The amounts of 'embodied labour' are determined by the technology in the whole economy. Second, none of the approaches or definitions make any reference to prices, wages or profits. That information is not necessary to calculate the amounts of 'embodied labour'. In every case the amounts of 'embodied labour' are calculated from the given technology, including the amounts of socially necessary labour time employed. Hence the amounts of 'embodied labour' could be calculated in other modes of production, besides capitalism, as long as labour was homogeneous, or could be reduced, in some way, to a common standard. Technology may be different in different modes of production, but the respective amounts of embodied labour could still be calculated in each case. Hence the concept of 'embodied labour' is not socially specific to capitalism; it relates to the technical state of the productive forces, not to the relations of production.

To the reader who is used to thinking in terms of single-product systems, i.e. systems in which each process produces exactly one product, and there is no fixed capital remaining at the end of the production period, the above account of the different approaches to, and definitions of, embodied labour may seem to be much ado about nothing. In fact, in single-product systems, with no choice of techniques, all approaches and definitions give the same numerical results, as well as the more general identity of results from the two approaches in each case. In other words there is no ambiguity in the definition of embodied labour. In addition it can be shown that all the calculated embodied labour magnitudes will be positive as long as the system is feasible and productive.

Problems in joint product systems

However, more serious problems arise in joint product systems, i.e. when at least one process in the economy produces more than one good—an extra 'joint product'. Before we discuss these problems we must explain why joint products are *not* extreme and rare cases in real-world economies. For example, chemical industries, including petroleum refining and coal processing, have an overwhelming number of processes which produce useful by-products. In fact only rarely do the chemical reactions that are utilized produce just one substance. Coal is used to produce coal gas, coke, nylon, and other substances. From crude oil, petroleum, engine oils and paraffin are extracted. Modern competitive conditions have encouraged the use of by-products in some industries which otherwise would be regarded as waste. For example, wood chips and metal turnings are now utilized in vast amounts. Slag from coal mining, and even waste glass, to cite some extreme examples, are both used in road construction. Shoddy waste from the wool industry is now used as a fertilizer. Agriculture itself abounds in examples of joint production: e.g. wool and mutton from sheep, and wheat and straw from corn. It seems that single-product industries are the exception rather than the rule in many major areas of modern industry.

However, as Sraffa puts it: 'The interest of joint products does not lie so much in the familiar examples of wool and mutton, or wheat and straw, as in being the genus of which fixed capital is the leading species' (1960, p. 63). Sraffa has shown that, in general, fixed capital must be formally regarded as a kind of joint product, alongside the products which were intentionally created in production. Otherwise, neither value nor price depreciation can be correctly calculated for the fixed capital as it ages over time. Fixed instruments have existed ever since primitive man fashioned a stone axe which he did not dispose of after its first use in production. We must conclude, therefore, that single-product industries are extremely rare exceptions, far from being the rule, in the history of mankind. Capitalism, with its complex technology and vast accumulation of fixed capital, has reinforced the importance of joint-product analysis.

Consider the 'labour cost' approach to the calculation of embodied labour. In single-product processes we can focus the amounts of 'embodied labour' that are used up in production, plus the living labour employed, on a single product appearing in the output. With joint-product systems we cannot, quite obviously, do this. If one process produces two joint products then we can, perhaps, calculate the total living and embodied labour input. But how do we apportion this accreted labour time between the two produced products? Within the particular production process we have no means of knowing the amount of labour time that becomes embodied in each particular product. We can point to no actual procedure that apportions the labour time within the production process itself. Without further information we cannot determine the amounts of embodied labour from the conditions within the process.

One way out of the problem is to show or assume that other processes will be additionally utilized for every extra joint product that appears, so that the number of processes will be exactly equal to the total number of produced goods. Then it will be possible to calculate the 'embodied labour' in each good by setting up a number of equations. These will express the Marxian principle that the labour embodied in the inputs in each process, including the amount of socially necessary living labour employed, equals the labour embodied in the total output. No embodied labour is created outside production. The equations may then be solved simultaneously; ascribing a unique magnitude of 'embodied labour' to each good, so that the latter Marxian principle is not violated.

Negative embodied labour with joint production

Unfortunately, we have no reason to assume that the calculated 'embodied labour' results will be positive. Morishima, for instance, has shown that *negative* amounts of embodied labour can occur in joint production systems (Morishima, 1973, pp. 181–4). One particularly vulnerable type of commodity is fixed capital that has lasted more than one production period, i.e. 'old machines', and whose efficiency is waning. Steedman has constructed an example where the labour embodied in the surplus product is negative (Steedman, 1975). Under capitalist conditions this would mean that the whole of surplus value was negative, but Steedman has also shown that this is compatible with positive profits, and capitalists seeking to maximize their profits within the given technology.

Alternatively we can take refuge in a different definition of embodied labour (Morishima, 1974, pp. 616–17). This would be the minimum amount of socially necessary labour time required to produce a given commodity, regardless of what else may be produced as a joint product. This definition, which I call 'optimized embodied labour', ensures that all the results are positive. However, using it we abandon the implicit Marxian notion that embodied labour magnitudes are additive. It is no longer the case that the embodied labour in the whole is equal to the sum of the embodied labours in the parts. The optimized embodied labour in good A, plus the optimized embodied labour in good B, is generally *greater* than the optimized embodied labour in A and B considered together.

A third possible definition of embodied labour involves the imputation of 'labour costs' to each good when the *optimum* amount of embodied labour is being calculated in a given bundle of goods. Generally, however, this 'imputed embodied labour' will not be quantitatively independent of the actual bundle of goods that is chosen. The same good can have different amounts of 'imputed embodied labour' in different optimization situations. (Morishima has constructed the definition of imputed embodied labour, calling it 'optimized value', but he has incorrectly drawn the conclusion that the resulting magnitudes are dependent on 'demand' (Morishima, 1973, pp. 184–7). This does not follow, as the chosen bundle of goods need have no relation to 'demand' in the economy. Morishima has confused his theoretical object with the real world.)

We must, at least, conclude that in joint production situations the definition of embodied labour is highly ambiguous. We face the difficult choice of *either* accepting the possibility of negative embodied labour, *or* abandoning the principle of additivity with embodied labour magnitudes. Alternatively we can drop the concept of embodied labour altogether. *We have no other choice.*

CHAPTER 10

A NOTE ON SIMPLE COMMODITY
PRODUCTION

The truth is rarely pure, and never simple.
OSCAR WILDE

The notion of 'simple commodity production' is well established in
the Marxian literature. It refers to a real or imaginary mode of
production where all labourers possess their own means of production, and they produce commodities for a market. It is usually
argued that in such a mode of production prices will tend to be
proportional to quantities of embodied labour. The argument was
first constructed by Adam Smith, many years ago:

*In that early and rude state of society which precedes both the
accumulation of stock and the appropriation of land, the proportion
between the quantities of labour necessary for acquiring different objects
seem to be the only circumstance which can afford any rule for
exchanging them for one another. If among a nation of hunters, for
example, it usually costs twice the labour to kill a beaver which it does to
kill a deer, one beaver should naturally exchange for or be worth two deer.
It is natural that what is usually the produce of two days' or two hours'
labour, should be worth double of what is usually the produce of one
day's or one hour's labour* (Smith, 1970, p. 150).

Sweezy comments upon these lines as follows:

*It is easy to supply a proof of what Adam Smith took for granted. A
hunter by spending two hours of his time can have either one beaver or
two deer. Let us imagine now that one beaver exchanges for one deer 'on
the market'. Under the circumstances any one would be foolish to hunt
beaver. For in one hour it is possible to catch a deer and thence, by
exchange, to get a beaver, whereas to get a beaver directly would require
two hours. Consequently this situation is unstable and cannot last. The
supply of deer will expand, that of beaver contract until nothing but deer
is coming on the market and no takers can be found. Following this line of*

104

*reasoning it is possible to show by exclusion that only one exchange ratio,
namely one beaver for two deer, does constitute a stable solution. When
this ratio rules in the market, beaver hunters will have no incentive to shift
to deer hunting, and deer hunters will have no incentive to shift to beaver
hunting. This, therefore, is the equilibrium ratio of exchange. The value of
one beaver is two deer and* vice versa. *Adam Smith's proposition is thus
demonstrated to be correct* (Sweezy, 1968, p. 46).

On the whole, Adam Smith's proposition is accepted by most
Marxists and rejected by most non-Marxists. Usually non-Marxist
critics mess up their arguments by referring loosely to 'capital' in
simple commodity production. In response Marxists have a field-day
showing that in the strict sense 'capital' can only exist under capitalism, and not under simple commodity production. We shall attempt
a critique of the Smithian proposition which does not fall into the
errors of vulgar economics.

As Sweezy himself points out, the Smithian proposition will be
valid only under restrictive conditions:

*two implicit assumptions are necessary, namely, that hunters are prepared
to move freely from deer to beaver if by so doing they can improve their
position; and that there are no obstacles to such movement* (Sweezy,
1968, p. 46).

In our view such conditions would be extremely unlikely to apply
under simple commodity production. In contrast, under capitalism,
mobility of labour between industries is less frictional and promoted
by the very existence of a *labour market.* Under simple commodity
production, however, we must remember that the labourers are
united with their means of production, and there is no labour market.
To move from one industry to another a labourer would normally
have to sell one set of tools and buy another set. The second set of
means of production may be more or less expensive than the first. In
any case, labour mobility will be affected by the relative prices of the
means of production involved in each industry. In order to move
from an industry with cheap means of production to another with
dear means of production a labourer would, on the average, expect
to receive a higher rate of remuneration in the industry to which he
is moving.

Consider an example. One man works on the land for 10 hours, to
produce cabbages, using his spade and some fertilizer. The spade does
not depreciate physically. The fertilizer used has 1 hour of labour of

the same intensity embodied in it. A second man also works for 10 hours, at the same intensity as the man with a spade, in a bakery. Flour containing 1 hour's embodied labour of the same intensity is used up. In short, therefore, both men work for 10 hours, and in that period 1 hour of embodied labour is used up in each production process. Apart from the *fixed* means of production, i.e. the spade and the bakery respectively, both processes are identical in terms of the flow of labour time and the quantity and intensity of labour time performed. But now assume that the bakery is much more expensive than the spade, and that the flour and fertilizer have about the same price. Will the cabbages produced by the first man and the bread produced by the second command the same price on the market? It would be very unlikely. The bread would have to sell at a much higher price before there was labour mobility from cabbage-growing to baking, so that the new entrants to the industry could afford to purchase the bakery. In other words, it would be very unlikely, in equilibrium, for the two men to get the same monetary remuneration for their labour. The baker would get a higher payment.

The essence of the above argument can be summed up as follows: under simple commodity production the labourers are united by ownership, with their means of production. As a result there is no free and unconstrained labour mobility from industry to industry, and no labour market. Hence there is no force which brings the labourers' rates of remuneration into equality. Such equality is only possible with private ownership when the link between labour and its means of production is severed. This tallies with an argument, made by Morishima and Catephores (1978) and others that the orthodox Marxian notion of 'abstract labour' is only applicable to capitalism. Hence no homogeneous measure of labour-time is possible under simple commodity production. The category of abstract labour is a reflection, according to Marx, of a situation under capitalism where all forms of labour are united by the fact that they are exchanged on a market (see Colletti, 1972, pp. 79–84). Abstract labour, thus defined, has no material basis under simple commodity production.

It is also possible to refute the idea that prices are proportional to quantities of embodied labour under the early stages of capitalism, before the rate of profit was equalized between industries. In fact, by the fifteenth century a general rate of profit did exist. It was the rate of return on mercantile capital, as Engels pointed out when he edited *Capital* (Marx, 1962, p. 878). When industrial capital arrived on the scene it had to compete with the mercantile rate of profit. It appears, therefore, that a general rate of profit was in existence before a general labour market. As is well known, in a capitalist economy with dissimilar processes of production a necessary condition for prices to be proportional to quantities of embodied labour is that there is no equalized or general rate of profit. Consequently, it is highly unlikely that prices were ever in proportion to quantities of embodied labour. (For a further discussion of this issue see Morishima and Catephores, 1978, ch. 7.)

CHAPTER 11

LABOUR, VALUE AND PROPERTY

Man cannot live without some economic theology—without some rationalisation of the abstract and seemingly inchoate arrangements which provide him with his livelihood.

J. K. GALBRAITH, *American Capitalism*

If there was a meaningful way of calculating the total amount of labour time performed in both defence and criticism of every major theory, then the labour theory of value would possibly score highest. However, as the supporters of the labour theory know, labour expended is one thing; 'socially necessary' labour is another. We shall argue in this chapter that if the aim of the defence of the labour theory of value has been to promote the political aim of a socialist commonwealth, then its efforts have not, in all seriousness, been necessary. More than that, as Ellerman (1978) has pointed out, such defensive efforts have been *diversive*. What really lies behind the clash of ideologies held by socialists on the one hand, and supporters of capitalism on the other, are not, strictly speaking, two different theories of value, but two different *theories of property*. At the same time, however, most theories of value are infused with a theory of property, and there are connections between the two types of theory.

Capitalism and property

Capitalism, as we have seen, proclaimed the equality of all men under the law, in that everyone had the equal right to own property. (These rights were first applied to adult *men* only; men being regarded as the head of the household. Later women were given the entitlement to hold property in their own right.) Behind this, essentially, was a *humanist* view. In holding equal legal rights to property, a distinction was made between man and society, on the one hand, and the natural world on the other.

However, capitalist property rights were not communal but *private*. The right to own property was vested in *individuals*. As a

108

consequence, emergent capitalism had to both explain and justify an *unequal* distribution of wealth. Although individuals had equal rights to own property, the actual holdings of property were manifestly unequal.

An important attempt to make this justification is found in the seventeenth-century writings of John Locke. As C. B. Macpherson has recently pointed out, the abstract idea of 'labour' provided the universal human basis upon which individual property rights could, in theory, be founded:

Every man had a property in his own labour. And from the postulate that a man's labour was peculiarly, exclusively his own, all that was needed followed. The postulate reinforced the concept of property as exclusion. As his labour was his own, so was that with which he had mixed his labour, and that capital which he had accumulated by means of applying his labour. This was the principle that Locke made central to the liberal conception of property (Kamenka and Neale, 1975, p. 112).

Locke's argument, which we could call a 'labour theory of property', was prominent in classical liberal thought well into the nineteenth century. However, its survival did pose problems. The argument was likely to go unchallenged in a society of self-employed producers, relying, in the main, on their own labour to produce an output. However, when commerce developed to the extent that each self-employed producer used material inputs produced elsewhere, how could it be determined which part of the gross output should be the property of the immediate producer, and which part should be the property of the supplier of the material input? Or, less metaphorically, how much should the supplier be paid for his raw materials? With the rise of industrial capitalism, and the creation of a proletariat, the problems were compounded. The labour of the workers was combined with capital goods owned by the capitalist, to produce an output. Locke's view could be sustained only with difficulty, for example by arguing that the capitalist was performing a type of 'labour' himself.

A theory of value

To overcome these problems a comprehensive theory of *value* was required. Defenders of industrial capitalism had to show how costs, prices, wages and profits were determined, and defend a market mechanism which set these variables at the given level. Supporters of the capitalist system were thus forced to elaborate a theory of value and distribution. The whole history of classical, and later, neo-classical, economic thought shows a preoccupation with this problem. Such efforts, in part, could be seen as an implicit attempt to reconstruct a theory of individual property to succeed Locke.

It was not surprising that the first attempt to develop a systematic theory of value and distribution, in the writings of Adam Smith, started from the universal principle of labour. As is well known, Smith, Ricardo, and later Marx, developed the labour theory of value. Its main postulate was that *the value of the product was determined by labour* (in the case of Marx, 'socially necessary abstract labour'). At the same time, by these writers, a theory of distribution was evaluated; but Smith and Ricardo, in contrast to Marx, saw the market mechanism as the natural order of things, and saw their theory as a defence of private property and trade.

The connection between the different sides of the issue can be examined in a statement made by Smith in the *Wealth of Nations* to justify his labour theory of value: 'Labour was the first price—the original purchase-money that was paid for things.' Here Smith is using a metaphor, but an interesting one. The activity of labouring, which involves *production* of an output, is seen as an act of *exchange*. Someone is being 'paid', but who? The answer is clear, it is 'nature'. Production is an 'exchange with nature'. This phrase, meta-phorically or otherwise, is still used by neoclassical economists today (e.g. Hirshleifer, 1970, p. 27). This metaphor dissolves a distinction between nature and the human species: if an exchange can be made with nature then nature can hold property too. Man is no longer uniquely endowed with the right to property. An effect of this, which survives and prevails today in neoclassical thought, is to regard the laws governing the economy as similar to the laws governing nature. Furthermore, in the writings of most classical and neoclas-sical economists, this identification of society with nature leads most easily to the view that the existing capitalist society is the natural order of things.

At the same time, however, this naturalistic tendency subsumed the whole question that lay behind the theory of property: how could its existing distribution be justified? In short, the naturalistic outlook, combined with the labour theory of value, gave an answer to this question in *value theory* terms alone. An independent *theory of property* was left behind. This accounts for the lack of discussion of the *possessing agent,* as distinguished from his or her property, in the writings of Smith and Ricardo.

Utopian socialists and Marx

In contrast, the utopian socialists combined the labour theory of value with a different form of naturalism. Writers such as Proudhon in France and Hodgskin in Britain saw the existing order as *unnatural*. In the natural order there was no private ownership of the means of production, and no separate social classes. Capitalism was not consistent with natural law. This idea is clear in the following quotation from Hodgskin. How is it possible, this writer asked, to acknowledge 'as a natural phenomenon the present distribution of wealth; though it is in all its parts a palpable violation of that natural law which gives wealth to labour and labour only?' (Quoted in Rubin, 1979, p. 347.) The appropriation of the 'products of labour' by the owners of capital was, therefore, a defiance of natural law.

In retaining naturalism, however, and shifting its norm from the capitalist present to the socialist future, the utopian socialists abandoned the project of explaining the determination of value and distribution in a capitalist market economy. Their theories were predominantly normative in content.

Marx made by far the most important step by shifting political economy away from its naturalistic foundation. He made two contributions, above all, which placed political economy on a quite different theoretical basis and succeed, to this day, in demarcating his work from both classical and neoclassical economic theory. The first such contribution was summed up by his notion of a mode of production. In working with nature, human beings inevitably operated within a framework of social relations. These social relations determined both the manner in which production was motivated, and how the product was distributed between persons. Production, therefore, was a relation between persons, as well as with nature. This point is well established in Marxian literature and has been raised already in chapter 2 above.

The second contribution is less well explored. In the first volume of *Capital*, with in particular his distinction between labour and labour-power, Marx rejected both naturalistic and mechanistic theories of *production*. In both the classical and the neoclassical view, inputs such as 'labour' and 'capital' are mysteriously transformed into an output. Thus production is treated in a mechanistic fashion, as if human will and human conflict were not involved. Marx's long discussion of the process of production in *Capital* focuses on the elements of conflict between capitalist and worker, the progressive dynamism of capitalism in introducing new techniques, and implies, correctly, that the output of production is essentially *variable* in nature. Some of these themes are discussed in chapter 17.

Naturalism in Marx

However, traces of naturalism, and an associated mechanistic outlook, can still be found in *Capital.* One source of these was Marx's failure to develop a *theory of property.* In this respect his work resembled that of Smith and Ricardo. Like them, Marx inadvertently blocked his quest for an adequate theory of property by his adoption of the labour theory of value. Hodgskin and the Ricardian socialists had begun to develop a theory of property but only on the basis of naturalism. In rejecting the latter (correctly, of course) this route, for Marx, was blocked. Without a theory of property his opposition to capitalism had to find a different theoretical basis.

This basis was the elaborate set of attempts to demonstrate the 'inevitable downfall' of capitalism as proclaimed, in 1848, in the *Communist Manifesto.* The most elaborate and enduring of these was the famous 'law of the tendency of the rate of profit to fall' (see Hodgson, 1974a; Van Parijs, 1980; and many others). Such a theory saw inbuilt limits to the accumulation of capital, and was used as the 'scientific basis' for the advocacy of socialism. Capitalism, if left alone, would come to a natural end. Its eventual demise was predetermined. Such a theory, as I have argued elsewhere, downplays the role of human action both in determining the future course of capitalism and the construction of socialism. In this respect it has a *naturalistic* component.

In a very important study of Marx's labour theory of value, Lippi (1979) has shown that this theory has a naturalistic basis. In his famous 1868 letter to Kugelmann, Marx characterized the concept of value as a 'law of nature', assuming different *forms* only, in different societies. This is much more than a slip of the pen. Lippi shows that the following propositions run through the whole of Marx's theory of value:

The measurement of products by the quantity of labour necessary to produce them and the distribution of social labour . . . are general characteristics of human social life. Labour, . . . as real social cost, *is the 'immanent measure' of the product,* whatever the historical mode of production (Lippi, 1979, pp. xv–xvi, latter emphasis added).

This naturalistic conception of labour as the measure of value and real social cost, finds expression in the frequent Marxian metaphor that the working day is divided between the time that the worker 'works for the capitalist' (i.e. surplus labour) and the time the worker 'works for himself'. This expression brings in the hypothetical situation of the worker owning the existing capital goods and producing for himself, without the capitalist. Not only is the existing state of affairs judged by an ahistorical standard: 'But a man by himself cannot produce anything. The whole labour force is producing the whole output. ... The time that a man works for himself is a striking metaphor, not an analytical proposition' (Robinson, 1977, p. 54).

It is not possible to expunge completely the naturalistic traits in Marxian thought without the surgical removal of the labour theory of value. This, I believe, is demonstrated in Lippi's important study. In recent years, efforts to retain this theory have been made by many reputable writers, attempting to graft quantities of 'embodied labour' onto a Sraffa-type analysis. However, the first point to be made is that for the theoretical results of the Sraffa system, embodied labour is not required. Second, the whole exercise is a diversion from the real issues at hand: the attack on neoclassical theory and the construction of a radical analysis of property. We return to these themes and show, by implication, how diversionary the whole exercise of attempting to salvage the labour theory of value has become.

Neoclassical property theory

From the beginning, in neoclassical theory, there was an implicit theory of property. It was, effectively, a transformation of Locke's 'labour theory of property'. As we have seen, the latter amounted to the proposition that the individual had the right to the ownership of the product of his or her labour. We showed that this ran into problems of valuation, and prompted the development of the labour theory of value. This diversion into value theory was made necessary because of the attempt to justify *individual private ownership* in a complex interrelated system. A means had to be found to evaluate outputs and inputs (including labour) so as to justify the apportionment of *shares* of the product.

In the middle of the nineteenth century, with the beginnings of disaffection with the labour theory of value, two choices were open to the political economists of the time: *either* to abandon support for the principle of private ownership, and thus disregard many of the implicit tasks of value theory, *or* develop a new theory of value upon which to rest the justification of private property. Marx took the first option, but was hindered by his continuing adherence to the labour theory of value. The neoclassical school, in the 1870s and after, took the second option, constructing a theory of value based on marginal utility.

The relative ease of this transformation is shown as follows. From the *labour* theory of *individual property,* i.e.:

(LIP)   the individual has the right to own the product of his or her labour,

we get the *marginalist* theory of *individual property,* i.e.:

(MIP)   the individual has the right to own the marginal product of his or her input (labour, capital, land).

The explicit basis of this implied property theory was derived from the transformation of the labour theory of value, i.e.:

(LV)   the value of the product is determined by labour,

into the marginalist approach, i.e.:

(MV1) the value of the product is determined by marginal utility,

or, in later, more sophisticated, analyses, into

(MV2) the relative value of products is determined by a combination of marginal factors in general equilibrium.

By far the most effort, by radical writers, has been devoted to attacks on MV1 or MV2. Much less time has been addressed to a discussion and critique of MIP. One reason for this is that an adequate radical alternative to MIP does not exist.

For well-known reasons, in particular the evaluation of the competitive capitalist market as the natural state of affairs, the neoclassical approach retains a strong naturalism at its theoretical base. This naturalism is expressed in many ways, some mentioned above. Perhaps the most important is the neoclassical, naturalistic view of production. This is seen as a natural or automatic process in which inputs are transformed into outputs. This, in turn, sustains an implicit fiction of neoclassical theory: that the provision of an input gives a claim on a portion of the output, the latter being, in part, an *automatic result* of the former.

This fiction is as damaging as the one discussed above, and found in the orthodox Marxian literature, that the worker spends a part of the working day working for himself and part working for the capitalist. This division of the working day relies on a *fixed relationship* between *time taken* at work, and the *value and magnitude of output*. It may only be a metaphor, but it is one which has done considerable damage. It is reflected in the frequent assertion that the only capitalist solution to a crisis of profitability is for the capitalists to force down wages. The error is to assume that output and productivity are given. The very same error is found in these bourgeois writers who emphasize income restraint, rather than a restructuring of production, as a solution to capitalist crises. The error can be traced to the same mechanistic view of production.

The alternative

To escape from this mess, a number of theoretical innovations are required, some existing and simple, others incomplete. To indicate these innovations, we adopt Sweezy's (1968) distinction between qualitative value (the form of value) and quantitative value. In chapter 14 we redefine value as a monetary form of equilibrium price. This has no direct link with any form of embodied labour. The *form* of value, expressed in exchange, can be seen as the result of *private property*. This could be dubbed 'the property theory of value', or, more accurately, the 'property theory of the value-form'.

Turning to the quantitative determination of value, thus defined, our starting point is Sraffa's theory. This has to be enhanced, however, by the introduction of both money and a dynamic analysis of production. Steps toward this are made in chapters 15 and 17. With such an enhanced theory it would be possible to replace both the marginalist and the labour theories of value (MV1, MV2, and LV). In addition, a further move would be made away from naturalism, as a naturalistic theory of production is not comparable with a proper theory of money and a dynamic view of production.

However, a new theory of value would not be sufficient to provide a normative theory of property. The basis for this theory is found in Ellerman's (1978) development of Locke's labour theory of individual property, and earlier (1976) work by the present author. This is elaborated in chapters 16 and 18.

The thrust of this entire effort is summed up by Ellerman:

The Labour Theory

Neoclassical economists try to interpet a part of value theory as if it were a property theory. Marx made the opposite mistake of trying to develop property theory as if it were a value theory. But given the dominance of the value theoretic paradigm, the value theoretic treatment of the labour theory was like Voltaire's God; if it didn't exist, someone would have to invent it. Marx played that historical role. It is only after Marx has completed his prodigious effort that latter-day radical economists can 'stand on the shoulders of the giant' and see that the labour theoretic analysis and critique of capitalist production can only be successfully carried out by completely reconstructing the 'labour theory of value', from the ground up, as the labour theory of property (Ellerman, 1978, p. 19).

The development of *this* labour theory of property is quite different from that found in Locke. It is in their normative assertions that the contrast is most clear. Instead of proclaiming the right to *individual* property, the modern theory is constructed with the following proposition in mind: that the working class *as a whole* has the right to *collective* ownership of the *social* product. Hence there is no *immediate* problem of *value* in this theory; it stands alone. Yet, as we shall see, a great deal of positive analysis is required to sustain it, and to break free of the fetters of preceding systems of thought.

We can condense the stand that is taken in this present work into two, respectively positive and normative, propositions; (SV) and (LSP). The first is the 'Sraffian', 'structural' and 'social' theory of value which we attempt to develop:

(SV)   The value of commodities is a social result of the structure of sociotechnical and monetary conditions, predominated by the sphere of production.

(LSP)   The working class as a whole has a right to collective ownership of the social product.

It should be already clear, and this is confirmed below, that this is little more than standing 'on the shoulders of the giant'.

PART III
MONEY

CHAPTER 12

MONEY AND EXCHANGE

Money is the God among commodities.
MARX, *Grundrisse*

We are now at a stage where money can be introduced. Needless to say, some of the propositions in former chapters will have to be modified or rejected, but others will retain their validity. Money is the subject of the next four chapters.

Capitalism is generalized commodity production. The commodity category covers not only the majority of produced goods and services, but also two important other items. The first is labour-power, which, unlike the situation in most other modes of production, is a commodity under capitalism. The further analysis of this special commodity is left to later chapters. The second is money. This, by its nature, is always produced for exchange, so it is always a commodity, no matter in which mode of production it may be found.

A monetary economy contrasted with barter

The obvious starting point of a discussion of money is a basic distinction between a monetary and a barter economy. Clower has expressed this very clearly, and what follows in the next few paragraphs is taken from his work (Clower, 1967). Both a barter economy and a monetary economy contain a large number of goods produced for exchange. The distinguishing feature of a barter economy is that each commodity can be traded for any other commodity. In a pure barter economy no particular exchange relation between two commodities is excluded: anything can be exchanged for anything else.

This is illustrated in figure 12.1. An 'X' shows that exchange is possible between the two commodities in question. A monetary economy, however, is distinguished by the fact that some exchange relations are excluded, by custom, convenience, or law. Two dissimilar commodities cannot be exchanged for each other unless one of them is money. This is illustrated in figure 12.2, where the first

	Commodity 1	Commodity 2	Commodity 3	Commodity 4
Commodity 1	X	X	X	X
Commodity 2	X	X	X	X
Commodity 3	X	X	X	X
Commodity 4	X	X	X	X

Figure 12.1
Exchange relations in a barter economy

commodity is designated as money. A '0' shows that no exchange is possible. It is not immediately obvious that a monetary economy is marked by the *restriction* of exchange relations, rather than by their liberalization. To emphasize this point, Clower writes:

It then follows that a barter economy is one in which all commodities are money commodities. *It may seem paradoxical at first sight; but if one ponders the matter it becomes clear that the peculiar feature of a money as contrasted with a barter economy is precisely that* some *commodities in a money economy* cannot *be traded directly for all other commodities; i.e. some exchanges necessarily involve intermediate monetary transactions* (Clower, 1967, p. 5).

Whilst this quotation will serve to make a point it must be noted that the statement that 'a barter economy is one in which all commodities are money commodities' would not be true if money proper had more characteristics than the ordinary commodity. We shall suggest that the latter is the case below.

The inefficiency of barter

It is well known that, compared to a monetary economy, a barter system is an inefficient method of exchange. For exchange to take place under barter the two parties both must have the desire to possess the other person's commodity. In other words, barter requires a double coincidence of wants. Clearly, what is a desirable com-

	Money	Commodity 2	Commodity 3	Commodity 4
Money	X	X	X	X
Commodity 2	X	X	O	O
Commodity 3	X	O	X	O
Commodity 4	X	O	O	X

Figure 12.2
Exchange relations in a monetary economy

modity for one individual is not necessarily a desirable commodity for another, and such a double coincidence of wants will be difficult to obtain.

Furthermore, there is an information problem. A party who wishes to barter a commodity has to communicate at least three pieces of information to potential buyers: first, what is being offered; second, what is desired in exchange for it; and third, the desired exchange value for the one commodity in terms of the other. In contrast, in a money economy we require only the first piece of information plus a price.

In addition a problem can arise in a barter economy if one of the commodities in the exchange is not divisible. It may be desired to exchange two-thirds a live hen for a spade. But two-thirds a live hen is a dead hen, and one and a half spades are as useful as one.

Regarding exchange-values, without money there is a multiplicity of ways in which they can be expressed. If there are n types of commodity in the economy then any single commodity will have $n - 1$ expressions of exchange value, that is in terms of the remaining $n - 1$ commodities in the economy. So, in all, for all n commodities it can be shown that there will be $n(n-1)/2$ possible exchange-value relations. In contrast, in a monetary economy with n commodities plus money there are only n possible exchange-value relations. For example, in an economy with 100 non-money commodities there will be 4950 exchange-value relations under barter, and only 100 exchange-value relations after the introduction of money.

By common usage of the term, the price of a commodity is its

exchange-value expressed in terms of money. Strictly speaking, therefore, the term 'price' should not be applied to a barter economy, but
to avoid clumsiness of language it is sometimes necessary to break
this rule. The price of money, if that phrase has any meaning, is
clearly unity.

Supply and demand again

We make no apology for repeating a point made in chapter 5: in a
barter economy supply and demand are indistinguishable, and as
separate concepts they have no meaning in those circumstances. This
truth, basic and obvious as it is, has to be repeated because it is
absent from all the major textbooks in economic theory. The
explanation for its absence may be that it has not been well understood since James Mill first propounded it in his *Commerce Defended*
(1808), or that it has been confused with Say's Law (Mill himself did
not make it clear that it applies to a barter economy only), or that its
repetition may have proved embarrassing for neoclassicism. I suspect
that it has been a combination of all three reasons that accounts for
its absence.

To make things clear once more: a demand consists of both a will
to purchase and an effective means of purchasing. In a barter economy the means of purchasing cannot be money proper so it must be
another commodity, an equivalent. This equivalent is the instrument
of demand. The magnitude of demand is measured by the exchange-
value of the equivalent. Yet the equivalent is a good *supplied.* A
supply consists of a will to sell an object and the desire to obtain
another good in return. The latter is a good *demanded.* Both supply
and demand each consist of an element of supply and an element of
demand. A commodity which is demanded is always, at the same
time, an instrument of supply. A commodity which is supplied is
always, at the same time, an instrument of demand. In a barter economy supply and demand are not only identical, they are meaningless
and misleading terms.

In a money economy demand and supply *can* be distinguished
from each other. They each have an independent and significant
meaning. Demand is the willingness to buy a commodity expressed
by the bringing of *money* to the market. The magnitude of demand
is measured by the amount of *money* that is presented. Supply is the
willingness to sell a commodity expressed by the demand for *money*
in return. It is measured by that amount of money. The intrusion of
money tears apart the acts of purchase and sale. By its status as the

exclusive means of exchange it enables the phenomena of supply and demand to be distinguished, and it endows them with meaning.

However, the concepts of supply and demand cannot be applied, independently, to money itself. This should be obvious on reflection from what we have said above. The only way in which a 'demand for money' can manifest itself is through the *supply* of another commodity. A 'demand for money' *is* a conventional supply of another commodity. Furthermore, the actual 'money supply' is nothing else but the aggregate demand for all other commodities. A text which is exceptional in that it makes the latter point clear is Blaug's *Economic Theory in Retrospect* (1968, pp. 145ff.).

Walras' Law

As we have shown above, in a barter economy the terms demand and supply are identical (and effectively meaningless) even for an individual trader. It is a mere tautology, the learning of which should bring no great surprises, to state, therefore, that in the economy as a whole total demand must equal total supply, and that excess demand or supply must be zero. There is simply no point in furnishing a mathematical proof of this proposition!

What happens when we move from a barter to a monetary economy? Let us first make a simplifying assumption (which we shall later reject as invalid). We shall assume that money functions simply as a medium of exchange and unit of account. The total price of all goods demanded is, by definition, equal to a certain sum of this money. As money is merely a medium of exchange and unit of account in this case, then the latter sum of money, which is 'supplied' by this total demand, must all be taken up or 'demanded', otherwise the money would be more than a medium of exchange and unit of account. The money is 'demanded', by definition, through the supply of other commodities. The total supply must be exactly equal to the amount of money in 'demand', again by definition. Hence the total price of all goods supplied must be equal to the total price of all goods in demand. This identity is sometimes known as Walras' Law. It simply states the *logical* impossibility of an excess supply, or an excess demand, of commodities in an economy where money functions simply as a medium of exchange and unit of account. Given those assumptions it is true, by definition of supply and demand.

We must note that there is considerable confusion in the literature on the use of terms such as 'Walras' Law', 'Say's Law' and 'Say's Identity'. Our usage of the term 'Walras' Law' is identical to that of

Blaug (1968), Henderson and Quandt (1971), and many others, except that they do not make it clear that the Law is meaningless or empty when applied to a barter economy. Unfortunately, Clower (1965) uses the term 'Walras' Law' in a different sense. He presents it as a falsifiable proposition, similar to what we have called 'Say's Law' below, rather than an identity which follows from a certain clearly stated premise. The fact that the premise does not correspond to the real world does not alter the distinctive character of the proposition.

The social character of money

It has been emphasized above that exchange is a social act, within a specific set of social and legal relations. In a money economy these social relations sanctify money as the universal medium of exchange. However, money does not arise merely because all individuals in society find the use of money convenient, to avoid the tedium and inefficiency of barter. Money does not arise from a mere aggregation of individual inconveniences. Money bears the stamp, both literally and figuratively, of a system of social relations. It is no accident that the head of a monarch or president appears on the cash money of most nations. The social character of money is discussed extensively by Simmel (1978) who makes it clear that money does not become universally acceptable as a medium of exchange as a consequence of individual choice. It acquires this quality as a result of *social* development. The evolution of money as a social institution resembles the growth of a moral code or a legal system (see Laidler and Rowe, 1980).

A Marxian analysis of money springs from the dual features of exchange-value and use-value, which all commodities possess. However, starting from the social and objective conception of use-value described in chapter 3 we shall see that the use-value of money is unique amongst commodities.

The use-value of money

Marx wrote: 'The money commodity acquires . . . a formal use-value, arising out of its specific social function' (1976, p. 184). We can describe the use-value of money as follows. It is a description which is not dissimilar to the functions of money listed in the orthodox textbooks:

(1) Money can be readily exchanged for all other commodities, a feature which it alone possesses in a money economy; it is the universal medium of exchange.

(2) Money is the unit of account through which all exchange-values become expressed in money terms, i.e. as prices.

(3) Money is the means by which a claim on a portion of all other use-values, i.e. the wealth of society, can be made; and as money can be possessed by any citizen in a capitalist economy, it is, therefore, the *'general material representative of wealth'* (Marx, 1973, p. 221). All commodities, as use-values, are a *particular* store of wealth, but this is wealth in relation to the owner, and not, necessarily, wealth in relation to all. Following from its exclusive, socially sanctioned, quality of being exchangeable for all other commodities, money alone is the general material representative of wealth. Given this ready and universal exchangeability, it is thus highly convenient to store wealth in the form of money.

(4) The fourth function follows directly from the third. An exchange economy is always, by its very decentralized and unplanned nature, plagued by uncertainty. Both prices and use-values are continuously changing over time. In general, therefore, with certain exceptions, it is *less risky* to store wealth in the form of money. On the whole the use-value of money is constant, and its price, if that has meaning, is always unity. Money is, therefore, *a means of dealing with an uncertain future.*

To summarize, the use-value of money is based on the following characteristics: first, it is the universal medium of exchange; second, it is the unit of account; third, it is the general material representative of wealth; and fourth, it is a means of dealing with an uncertain future.

It is clear from the above that the use-value of money is remarkably different from the use-value of any run-of-the-mill commodity. The use-value of money does not arise from its physical nature, nor from any characteristics ascribed to it by individuals, but from the socially derived and sanctioned position of money as an unique commodity. Marx makes a similar point, when he writes:

Money,. . . . *as a* merely social result, *does not at all presuppose an
individual relation to its owner; possession of it is not the development of
any particular essential aspect of his individuality; but rather possession of
what lacks individuality, since this social [relation] exists at the same time*

as a sensuous, external object which can be mechanically seized, and lost
in the same manner. Its relation to the individual thus appears as a purely
accidental one; while this relation to a thing having no connection with his
individuality gives him, at the same time, by virtue of the thing's character,
a general power over society (Marx, 1973, p. 222).

In another work, Marx again makes the point that the use-value of
money is social and universal, rather than specific and individual:

The commodity which has been set apart as the universal equivalent is now
an object which satisfies a universal need arising from the exchange process
itself, and has the same use-value for everybody—that of being carrier of
exchange-value or a universal medium of exchange. Thus the contradiction
inherent in the commodity as such, namely that of being a particular use-
value and simultaneously universal equivalent, and hence a use-value for
everybody or a universal use-value, has been solved in the case of this one
commodity (Marx, 1971, p. 48).

Hence the use-value of money, it being unique among commodities,
is directly linked to its role in exchange and exchange-value. Other
commodities, contrary to neoclassical fable, have no such connection
between their use-value and exchange-value.

Marx argued that an objective social function of money is to forge
strong links between the subjectively perceived mass of use-values,
the individuals in the economy, and the social system itself. Once
again let us quote Marx's penetrating views on the nature of money:

The reciprocal and all-sided dependence of individuals who are indifferent
to one another forms their social connection. This social bond is expressed
in exchange-value, *by means of which alone each individual's own activity*
or his product becomes an activity and a product for him; he must
produce a general product—exchange-value, *or, the latter isolated for itself*
and individualized, money. *On the other side, the power which each*
individual exercises over the activity of others or over social wealth exists
in him as the owner of exchange-values, *of money. The individual carries*
his social power, as well as his bond with society, in his pocket (Marx,
1973, pp. 156–7).

Prices and exchange-values

Like all other commodities, the exchange-value of money consists of
the set of ratios in which it will exchange for all other commodities.
It is, therefore, in the case of money, nothing but the set of prices of
all other commodities. However, prices are more than exchange-

values. Being expressed in terms of money, with its recognizable, social and universal character, prices have a special status above exchange-values.

With the introduction of money, as we have seen, the acts of purchase and sale are torn apart. All exchange-values are expressed in the single monetary unit of account, as prices. Money achieves a despotic status among commodities. It acts as the medium and measure of all things. It excludes all goods which do not succumb to its measure and power. It becomes the guiding and illuminating light of the economy. Money is not just a thing under capitalism; it is an impersonal power and a social institution.

It is in the character of institutions that they have the power to illuminate reality in a one-sided and distorting manner. It is the same with money. Its social despotism gives rise to a belief in, and a practical acknowledgement of, its despotic powers. One consequence of this is extremely important. As we have seen, money has a special and universal use-value. Its functions of unit of account and measure of wealth, all give money the apparent attributes of stability and conformity. This apparent attribute is seemingly underlined by the fact that the price of money is unity. It appears to economic agents, in the daily ritual of buying and selling, that money, alone among commodities, is stable and secure. Consciously or unconsciously, this apparent stability is related to a supposition that the supply and demand for money must be equilibrium; for that is a necessary condition for stability of price among all commodities. For example, the price increase of a particular commodity would tend to be regarded as an indication of the excess demand for that commodity, rather than an indication of the excess supply of money, even if the latter is, in fact, the case. In conclusion, therefore, the social status of money gives it licence to make the sometimes unwarranted claim that its own market has a conformity of demand and supply. Under capitalism, monotheism is the rule; money is that single God, and to it is attached the usual monotheistic claim of infallibility.

It is only when the functions of money are being undermined, such as in an inflationary situation, that the supply and demand of money cease to act as if, in the eyes of buyers and sellers, they were in conformity.

Inflation and money illusion

The effective, practically endorsed, despotism of money is the source of 'money illusion', i.e. the propensity among economic agents automatically to regard changes in money prices as general changes in exchange-values, whatever the other circumstances. People suffering from money illusion feel richer if their income rises in money terms, even if prices are rising at the same rate. In reality it is not an individual illusion, for it has an objective basis in social relations and material reality. It is founded on the institutional role of money and the resultant perception of the conformity of its supply and demand. The general consequence is to regard price increases as the result of changes in the supply and demand of other commodities. The 'illusion' is social and real.

In cases of rampant price inflation, however, the use-value of money is undermined. Its powers as a stable store of wealth, hedge against uncertainty, and inter-temporal unit of account are diminished. The social foundation of a secure money system is eroded. The despotism of money is eclipsed. Due to its significant and persistent devaluation in these circumstances, money no longer supports the perception that its supply and demand are in balance. Strong social forces batter down the buttresses of 'money illusion'. Buyers and sellers cease to regard money as a stable unit, and they tend to compare prices in relation to each other, rather than exclusively in relation to money. Prices begin to function as exchange-values. The usefulness of money as a fabric of the market is diminished. A tendency to hold wealth in the form of non-money commodities is encouraged. The result of inflation is to relapse into chaos and disequilibrium; and eventually, in hyperinflationary circumstances, money fades out of use, and there is a reversion to barter.

In a negative sense, therefore, the phenomenon of inflation endorses our analysis of money. Inflation is an enervating cancerous growth on the social basis of the use-value of money. The perniciousness of this cancer, and the mortal danger it represents for the money economy, is a confirmation of the power of money in a non-inflationary situation. Furthermore, as inflation erodes the use-value of money this shows that the latter is founded on a social rather than either an individual or a physical basis.

The object of this book is to examine capitalism. Inflation, however, represents capitalism in crisis rather than in health. Also inflation arises in particular and concrete circumstances, so it would be beyond the scope of this work to analyse that phenomenon. This is not to underestimate its importance, for it is only by surveying the power of money at the zenith of its reign that the severity of its possible fall can be estimated.

Say's Law and the paradox of money

Implicitly or explicitly, some economists assert that the supply and demand for money are, in fact, always in balance, and not only in the perceptions of buyers and sellers. It would follow, by Walras' Law, that any excess supply of one non-money commodity must be matched by the excess demand for another. Money itself cannot be in excess demand, according to our initial assumption. In these circumstances, with the rather rash initial assumption, we can derive the proposition that an aggregate excess demand is impossible. With our assumption that the supply and demand for money are exactly equal, and money acting as a mere medium of exchange and unit of account, every demand of a non-money good will be matched by a corresponding supply of another non-money good. The total supply of non-money goods will equal the total demand for them.

We have defined Walras' Law as the proposition that if money were simply a medium of exchange and unit of account then an excess demand or supply of commodities would be impossible. Walras's Law is a piece of logic, following on from the definitions of such terms as 'supply' and 'demand'. It is not refutable by any piece of empirical evidence. It is true by definition.

In the paragraph before last we discussed a quite different proposition. Some assert that the supply and demand for money always are in balance in the real world. Following on from this it can be argued that an excess supply or excess demand for commodities is impossible. This proposition, which can be refuted by an appeal to empirical evidence, is known as Say's Law in much of the literature. (Blaug and others use the term 'Say's Identity', but in my view this is confusing. What is at hand is not an identity but a falsifiable proposition. My use of the term 'Say's Law' is, I believe, in accord with the most frequent use of the term in the writings of Keynes and Marx.)

Say's Law is false. Its initial assumption does not correspond with the picture of money in the real world, nor with the necessary characteristics of our theoretical object: the capitalist mode of production.

If Say's Law were true then there would be important real-world consequences. For example, involuntary unemployment, i.e. an excess supply of labour-power, must be matched by a corresponding excess demand for other commodities. This, it is argued, is a disequilibrium situation. The prices of the commodities, due to the fact that they are in excess demand, will rise. Producers will expand their production, in search of the higher profits made feasible by the raising of prices. Consequently, more labour-power will be hired. Involuntary unemployment will be reduced. This process will continue until involuntary unemployment is brought down to zero.

If the supply and demand for money are not equal then the above argument is clearly false. A lot, therefore, depends on the truth or falsity of this initial proposition. We shall now discuss why it is not the case that the demand for money will, in general, be equal to the supply.

It has been argued above that in a secure monetary economy people tend to regard money as being the only commodity for which supply and demand are always in balance. But that does not mean that in reality they are in balance. A perception of reality is not the same as reality itself. Individuals behave as if the illusion was real; but that does not make it real. Yet the illusion, despite its non-correspondence with reality, acts itself as a real social force. Such is the paradox of money. Say's Law is false as economic doctrine, yet in a peculiar and limited sense it is true.

The excess demand for money

We have noted that the real basis of the false idea of Say's Law is the actual despotic power of money in a monetary economy. This despotic power, in a secure monetary economy, gives rise to the illusion that the total demand and total supply of money are equal in the economy as a whole. The basis of Say's Law is this illusion.

However, individuals tend to behave in a different way. Only rarely is each individual's demand for money exactly equal to his supply of it onto the market, so it would be an exceptional fluke if the aggregate money supply was equal to the total demand for it. People perceive aggregate behaviour as one thing, but they often act in such a way that if their behaviour was reflected through the economy as a whole this aggregate would be different from the one they perceive.

In a secure money economy it is likely that individuals will have an excess demand for money, and there will be an excess demand for money in the economy as a whole. Money, as we have seen when we discussed its use-value, functions as the universal store of wealth. This attribute leads to the use of money as a store, and the hoarding of money for that purpose. The propensity to exchange goods for money will, therefore, be stronger than the propensity to exchange money for goods. An excess demand for money will result.

If there is such an excess demand for money then Say's Law is clearly invalidated. The attribute of money as a universal store of wealth contradicts the Law. As we shall see below, the rejection of Say's Law is important in the writings of both Marx and Keynes.

However, Say's Law would be invalidated even if there were an excess supply of money. This excess supply must be matched by an aggregate excess demand for other commodities, contradicting the Law. These circumstances are likely to be associated with inflation.

The above discussion of the excess demand (or excess supply) of money has been abstracted from production. Essentially, we have discussed short-term changes in supply, abstracting from adjustments resulting from changes in production. This could give credence to the view that Say's Law still applied in the long run, and excess demand is eventually corrected by relevant adjustments in the production of commodities. Specifically, the excess demand for money would be corrected by increased production of that commodity, and the economy would move happily onto full employment equilibrium.

Such a view, that Say's Law asserts itself through adjustments in production, is not realistic. Money is a peculiar commodity, often produced under special conditions. If money takes the form of gold, then it is highly precious and produced after high mining and exploration costs have been incurred. An excess demand for gold cannot easily be met by increased production. In the modern capitalist economy token and credit money replaces gold. Token money is produced by the state. *It is not produced under capitalist conditions.* The excess demand for money does not result in increased production of money through the pursuit of profit by the state. The creation of token money depends on *state policy,* and it does not necessarily respond to the conditions of supply and demand in the market. Credit money is produced by (private or public) banking institutions. Such institutions may respond to market conditions but they may be restricted in their powers to create money by state regulations. Once again, in the production of money the market does not readily lead to the appropriate adjustments. An excess demand for money does not automatically lead to an increased production of that commodity. Say's Law is once again invalidated.

A further problem exists if we consider an excess supply of money. Neither cash nor token money is physically consumed. In addition they do not depreciate rapidly. If there were an excess supply of money, and even if production of money was reduced, then the excess supply of money would have to be matched by increased production of other commodities. If the economy is at full employment then this may not be possible. The resulting inflation is a manifest refutation of Say's Law.

We may conclude that deviations from full employment equilibrium are not short-run aberrations. They are more the rule than the exception. The market does not automatically create full employment. This long-run violation of Say's Law is not emphasized in Clower's work because that author puts emphasis on the conditions of exchange in abstraction from production. It is the modern, radical, Keynesians, such as Davidson (1974, 1977) who have emphasized the 'zero elasticity of production of money', which, in layman's language, is simply the old adage that 'money does not grow on trees'. Keynes, himself, however, gave emphasis to this point in the *General Theory*:

Unemployment develops, that is to say, because people want the moon—
men cannot be employed when the object of desire (i.e. money) is
something which cannot be produced and the demand for which cannot be
readily choked off (1936, p. 235).

In a sense, this is a vindication of our earlier pronouncement, derived from the Marxian tradition, that conditions of exchange cannot be analysed adequately outside of the conditions of production. It is precisely these constraints on the *production* of money which enable it to function as a store of value.

CHAPTER 13

MONEY IN ECONOMIC THOUGHT

The history of science is no different from social history here: there are
those in both 'who have learnt nothing and forgotten nothing', especially
when they have seen the show from the front row.

LOUIS ALTHUSSER, *Reading Capital*

In this chapter we shall briefly survey the different approaches to
money in the history of economic thought. With the exception of
one particular school we shall deal with these approaches in chrono-
logical order. It will be seen, however, that the theory of money has
far from developed in a linear fashion, and much modern doctrine
marks a major retreat from previously established frontiers of theoretical understanding.

Classical economics, Say's Law and Marx's Critique

Ricardo gave tacit approval of Say's Law. In the tradition of Locke,
Hume and Smith, the monetary and non-monetary aspects of the
economy were rigidly separated. Relative prices were seen to be
determined in the so-called 'real', or non-money sphere. Money was
simply a *numéraire*; it intervened merely to determine the absolute
level of prices. Money was a 'veil'; merely a lubricant in the system, a
medium of exchange. According to classical economists, relative
prices were determined by the amount of labour embodied in commodities and money had no effect on the matter (see Mini, 1974,
pp. 38–9, 99–101).

Following from this, Ricardo denied the possibility of general
overproduction: 'there can never, for any length of time, be a surplus
of any commodity' (Ricardo, 1971, p. 292n). His view of money is
typified as follows: 'Productions are always bought by productions,
or by services; money is only the medium by which the exchange is
effected' (1971, p. 292).

Marx broke from the classical view of money. He particularly
lambasted Ricardo in the following important passage:

133

*Money is not only 'the medium by which the exchange is effected', but
at the same time the medium by which the exchange of product with
product is divided into two acts, which are independent of each other and
separate in time and space* (Marx, 1968, p. 504).

He then goes on to make the observation that money is likely to be
in excess demand in a capitalist economy in certain circumstances:

*At a given moment, the supply of all commodities can be greater than the
demand for all commodities, since the demand for the* general commodity,
*money, exchange-value, is greater than the demand for all particular
commodities, in other words the motive to turn the commodity into
money, to realise its exchange-value, prevails over the motive to transform
the commodity again into use-value* (Marx, 1969, p. 505).

In turn, this leads to the possibility of economic crisis:

The difficulty of transforming the commodity . . . *into its opposite,
money, . . . lies in the fact that . . . the person who has effected a sale, who
therefore has commodities in the form of money, is not compelled to buy
again at once. . . . In barter this contradiction does not exist: no one can
be a seller without being a buyer or a buyer without being a seller. . . .
The difficulty of converting the commodity into money, of selling it, only
arises from the fact that the commodity must be turned into money but
the money need not be immediately turned into commodity, and
therefore* sale *and* purchase *can be separated. We have said that this* form
contains the possibility *of crisis. . . . Sale and purchase may fall apart.
They thus represent potential* crisis *and their coincidence always a critical
factor for the commodity* (Marx, 1969, p. 509).

(Note that certain references to 'individual labour' and 'general social
labour' have been removed from the above passage. In the original
they represent an irrelevant and unwarranted juxtaposition of Marx's
theory of money with his erroneous labour theory of value. In the
above lines we have carried out an easy but necessary surgical operation.)

Marx's analysis of money is a remarkable break from the belittling
treatment of money in the writings of the classical economists. It is
clear additional evidence that Marx's economic thought is essentially
distinct from that of Smith and Ricardo, despite the important
threads of continuity between the three economists (such as the
labour theory of value).

Money and prices in Marx

We shall argue that, despite Marx's insights into the nature of money, the labour theory of value constricts the development and impact of his monetary theory. Furthermore, the juxtaposition of this theory with the labour theory of value leads to certain inconsistencies. Consider the dual relation of prices and resource allocation. Marx makes it clear that money can have a disequilibrating effect, leading to crisis and recession with overproduction and unemployed resources. Hence it is admitted that money can alter the scale of output and the equilibrium pattern of resource allocation; but what about prices? Marx thought in terms of a monetary system based on gold, hence the *absolute* level of prices was determined by the 'value' or 'cost of production' of gold (see Marx, 1971, pp. 159–87). Marx criticized Ricardo for suspecting that an increase in the number of banknotes could lead to a general increase in prices in a gold-based money system. However, he shared with Ricardo and Smith the view that *relative* prices were determined by the respective amounts of labour embodied in commodities, and *money had no effect on relative prices*. This is in strange contrast to his account of how money affects relative resource allocation.

In the next chapter we shall show that monetary conditions affect relative as well as absolute prices. But at this stage it is necessary to discuss further the relation between Marx's labour theory of value and his theory of money. Money, according to Marx, is not only the general material representative of wealth but also the form of appearance of all the products of the different labouring activities which go on in capitalist production. In other words, it is the universal nature of money which brings all different labouring activities in relation to each other (see Marx, 1976, p. 187). On this point Marx developed a valid and important insight into the nature of capitalism.

However, Marx takes a further step. He asserts that money is the measure of the labour embodied in commodities:

Because all commodities, as values, are objectified human labour, and therefore in themselves commensurable, their values can be communally measured in one and the same specific commodity, and this commodity can be converted into the common measure of their values, that is into money. Money as the measure of value is the necessary form of appearance of the measure of value which is immanent in commodities, namely labour-time (Marx, 1976, p. 188).

This questionable and perhaps ambiguous assertion is tied up with Marx's theory of abstract labour. Marx argues that 'abstract labour' is the essence that unites all the different forms of concrete labour under capitalism. Furthermore, this category 'abstract labour' is not merely a mental abstraction, but is created daily in the reality of exchange itself (see Marx, 1976, pp. 166–7; the same point has been emphasized by Colletti, 1972, pp. 82–8). We have already prefigured the objections to this formulation. The assertion that merely because all commodities are being exchanged for money then all the different forms of labour within them, and specifically labour, not anything else, are being *equated* has little to support it. Without the labour theory of value, which we have rejected above, Marx's formulation of the concept 'abstract labour' cannot be supported.

Despite being theoretically misconceived, the specific unity of the labour theory of value with a theory of money in Marx's work is, however, aesthetically attractive. Marx asserts, correctly, that both money and the existence of labour-power as a commodity are necessary aspects of the capitalist system. In the *Grundrisse* he states that without money capitalism could not exist (Marx, 1973, p. 253) and without wage-labour there is no money (ibid., p. 223). In short, for Marx, heterogeneous labour is homogenized through monetary exchange and objectified in money.

In retrospect things are not as simple, nor as aesthetically pleasing. First, money *can* exist without wage-labour. There is no theoretical reason why we should assume otherwise. In pre-capitalist modes of production wage-labour was not prominent, yet money often played a more significant role. Labour is not the unique 'substance' of commodities. The idea that money, as a homogeneous entity, must, of necessity, be the expression of some other homogeneous substance, i.e. 'abstract labour', is both antiquated and unfounded.

Money in neoclassical theory

We have discussed the classical and the Marxian approach to money. It is now the turn of the neoclassicals. In fact, the neoclassical 'revolution' in economic theory in the 1870s was, in terms of monetary theory, a return to the classical conception of money. Needless to say, the major advances made by Marx in monetary theory were neither understood nor incorporated. Perhaps it is in this respect, and in no other, that the misleading term 'neoclassical economics' is justified. (Keynes highlighted the same element of continuity between the classical and post-1870 economics with his use of the term 'classical economics' for both (Keynes, 1936, p. 3n.).)

A central element in the neoclassical theory of value is the deriva-

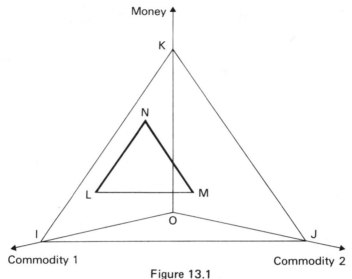

Figure 13.1
Budget constraints in a monetary economy

tion of an equilibrium position, by means of the combination of consumer preferences expressed in a utility function, with a budget constraint provided by the level of real income. A necessary assumption within this body of theory is that individuals may freely exchange commodity units until they reach the point where utility is maximized. This type of analysis admits as feasible all exchanges of commodity for commodity. But, as Clower puts it:

In sharp contrast, choice alternatives in a money economy must be so
defined as to satisfy the requirement that money be offered or demanded
as one of the commodities entering into every trade. Analytically, what
this entails is a clear separation between goods demanded for purchase
(offers to sell money) and goods offered for sale (offers to buy money)
(Clower, 1967, p. 7).

Clower's point is clearly reminiscent of Marx. It is also a devastating indictment of the bulk of the formalistic apparatus of neoclassical theory.

Let us illustrate this point. We shall assume a three-commodity economy in which one of the three commodities is money. What we propose is an extension of the budget constraint to this three-commodity world. This entails a three-dimensional model. It is pictured, in two dimensions of course, in figure 13.1. The point L

lies in the plane IJK. L represents an initial endowment of commodities, comprising amounts of Commodity 1, Commodity 2, and
money. The three points L, M and N all lie in the same plane, IJK.
Clearly, each of the three points represents a different endowment of
commodities. The line LN is parallel to IK and MN is parallel to JK.

Prices are such that IJK represents the set of endowments which
can be directly or indirectly traded for L. It is the usual budget constraint, in three dimensions. The endowment M is preferred to any
other on that plane, so the owner desires to trade and move from L
to M. However, a direct trade is not possible. An amount of Commodity 1 must be traded for money first, then that money must be
used to buy an amount of Commodity 2, reaching the point M. A
trade of Commodity 1 for money is a movement in a vertical plane
parallel to IOK, so given the budget constraint the trade moves us
from L to N. A trade of money for Commodity 2 is a movement in a
vertical plane parallel to OJK. So this trade moves us from N to M.
As this is a monetary economy a direct route from L to M is not
possible, so a zigzag movement such as L to N to M, each straight line
in the zigzag being in a vertical plane, is required.

Clearly there is no guarantee that an endowment represented by
the point such as N will be preferred to the initial endowment L.
Hence the trade LN will be undertaken only if the owner is sufficiently certain that the future trade NM can be accomplished. In an
uncertain world it is possible that the trade LN will not be undertaken and the owner will remain at L, despite the fact that it is
known that M is preferred.

We can see that a monetary economy cannot include the type of
continuously maximizing marginal movements along a budget constraint that are found in neoclassical analysis. Such marginal movements are possible only if every commodity can, in principle, be
directly exchanged for any other. This will occur in a barter economy only, where money does not exist. Neoclassical equilibrium
analysis is, therefore, 'formally equivalent to the classical conception
of a barter economy' (Clower, 1967, p. 9).

Money proper, i.e. money that is more than simply a medium of
exchange and unit of account, does not exist in neoclassical theory.
Most of that theory is, therefore, irrelevant to an understanding of a
capitalist economy with money.

When an attempt is made to smuggle money into neoclassical
general equilibrium analysis (an attempt that is bound to be unsuccessful) a general uneasiness can be detected. Sometimes money is
banished from that neoclassical holy of holies, the consumer's utility

function, and holdings of money are related simply to a proportion of other commodity endowments (see, for example, Henderson and Quandt, 1971, p. 174). This removes the use-value of money from the picture; it is simply then a function of other use-values. Money becomes a passive, rather than an active, element. It is not real money; it is simply a ghostly medium of exchange.

The 'monetarists'

It would appear to be paradoxical, therefore, that in recent years several orthodox neoclassical economists have become the high priests of a new creed: 'monetarism'. Milton Friedman is the most famous 'monetarist', and he is well known for his advocacy of the market mechanism and his general hostility to public enterprise and control. His political stance, therefore, is perfectly consistent with most of the neoclassical economists of the past.

In part, the monetarist school was a reaction to a post-war version of economic theory (sometimes misleadingly referred to as 'Keynesian') which regarded money as 'unimportant' in the determination of, amongst other things, the absolute price level. An overpowering amount of evidence has been marshalled to support the monetarists' arguments; but this is not the place to examine this evidence in depth. We simply wish to make the point that 'monetarism' is not necessarily associated with an adequate analysis of money.

A glimpse at the historical origins of monetarist thought is instructive. The original, more crude, quantity theory of money related the absolute price level rigidly and directly to the quantity of money in circulation. This crude quantity theory was advocated by, amongst others, Locke, Hume and Ricardo. They incorrectly regarded money as outside the 'real' basis of the economy. Money was merely a medium of exchange: a 'veil'. It intervened only to determine the absolute price level; if the quantity of money increased, so too would prices. Hence, in classical theory, money was 'unimportant' in the sense that it was peripheral, unrelated to production, and non-'real'. Yet money was 'important' with regard to the absolute price level.

Saying that money is 'important' does not mean that the nature of money is understood. There are several indications, in the writings of the monetarists, that such understanding is in limited supply. In a careful study of Friedman's work, Davidson (1974) gives support to this conclusion. For example, in the theoretical framework of Friedman and the other neoclassical monetarists, the essence of uncertainty, in the real economic world, is omitted. 'Uncertainty' is instead reduced to a probabilistic calculus, where economic agents can act 'as if' they possess perfect knowledge of the future. This is not uncertainty in the sense of Knight or Keynes, which, in the words of the latter, is uncertainty over events about which we cannot form 'any calculable probability whatever'.

Second, the monetarists effectively adopt Say's Law and they adhere to Walrasian general equilibrium analysis which, as we have shown in this present work, and has been admitted by major proponents of general equilibrium analysis such as Hahn, *does not include money*. As Davidson has pointed out, it is somewhat of a contradiction to fetishize both Walrasian general equilibrium analysis and the rate of growth of the quantity of money. If the Walrasian equations have a relation to the real world then 'the quantity of money is indeed nugatory' (1974, p. 99).

Third, the monetarists do not pay adequate regard to the social and institutional framework of the modern economy. They discuss the supply of money without discussion of the peculiar conditions of its production. They discuss the market without recognition of the social relations, i.e. private ownership of the means of production, contract law, etc., that form the basis of the functions of money in the modern economy. This neglect of social relations and institutions derives both from the adopted and spurious universality of neoclassical analysis, and the failure to note that many of these institutions either exist, or take their particular form, precisely because of the existence of uncertainty in the non-probabilistic sense.

Inflation, the real object of analysis of the monetarists, is a social phenomenon. It results from social forces in a monetary economy, and takes different forms at different stages of development of that economy. Hence the hyperinflation of the Weimar Republic in Germany in the 1920s did not result from the same forces, and did not have the same transmission mechanisms, as inflation in contemporary Britain or the United States. It may be possible to show, on the basis of evidence, that in all cases, at all times, there is a connection between inflation and the supply of money. However, that is only little more than a truism, and much less of a theoretical explanation of inflation. Monetarist arguments are devoid of an analysis of economic phenomena in terms of specific social relations. In particular, monetarism has failed to explain the social forces that lie behind, and determine, the level of the money supply. A necessary prelude to that explanation is an analysis of capitalist production and exchange. For that reason 'monetarism' will fail as long as it is shackled to the neoclassical paradigm.

Keynes and the 'Keynesians'

Keynes' writings on economic theory, brilliant as they are, suffer from two major weaknesses. First, they are marred by an inability to make a *complete* break from neoclassical habits of thought. Implicit in Keynes' theoretical writing is a degree of antipathy to neoclassical individualism, a rejection of impractical formalism, and a denial of the passive fatalism of the neoclassicals in regard to economic policy. However, like Marx, Keynes was afflicted with an outdated and in-adequate theory of value. In the case of Marx the affliction was the labour theory of value. In the case of Keynes it was neoclassical marginalism. Second, Keynes did not find the time before his death to popularize his theories, or to refute the crude versions of his work that had appeared. (He was, however, able to refute some formalistic interpretations of his work; see, for example, Moggridge, 1976, pp. 165–7.) It has taken extensive recent scholarship to begin to unearth the body of Keynes' thought from the layers of obscuring 'Keynesianism' (see, in particular, Leijonhufvud, 1968).

In his own summary of *The General Theory of Employment, Interest and Money,* Keynes emphasizes a number of points which contrast with the basic so-called 'Keynesian' tool-kit (Keynes, 1937). Keynes makes a number of points in this article. First, in a capitalist economy the future is inherently uncertain to the extent that there is 'no scientific basis on which to form any calculable probability what-ever'. Second, practical involvement in the world compels us to form expectations of the future and to act upon them. Third, as a conse-quence of the fallible nature of all expectations they are liable to be volatile and unstable, with important economic consequences. Fourth, the desire to hold money is also based on such fallible and volatile expectations. Fifth, such a change in the demand for money is likely to affect the rate of interest, consequently the volume of investment will also 'fluctuate wildly from time to time'. Sixth, the self-righting mechanisms in the economy which could compensate for a fall in the level of investment arise 'at a much later stage and in an uncertain degree'. Seventh, 'the level of output and employment as a whole depends upon the amount of investment'. Eighth, 'More comprehensively, aggregate output depends on the propensity to hoard, on the policy of the monetary authority as it affects the quantity of money, on the state of confidence concerning the prospective yield of capital assets, on the propensity to spend, and on the social factors which influence the level of the money wage'. In short, therefore, Keynes' main aim was to offer a 'theory of why output and employment are so liable to fluctuation'.

Keynes and Marx

The resemblance of Keynes' statements to those of Marx, cited earlier, is striking. It is a pity, therefore, that Keynes never came to grips with Marx's economic thought. In some respects, however, Keynes' theory of money is slightly in advance of that of Marx. (Although in most other theoretical areas the superiority is reversed.) First, the concept of indeterminacy finds a central place in Keynes' writing, whereas Marx was unable to make a complete break from deterministic Newtonian and Darwinian influences in economic theory. (Witness, for example, Marx's attempts to show that the demise of the capitalist system was 'inevitable'. Such an error is exhibited in his unsuccessful attempt to construct a theory of the tendency of the rate of profit to fall.) This tinge of determinism in Marx's economics contrasts with the vociferous anti-determinism in most of his political writings.

Second, although Marx's analysis of money was constructed in part with the outdated tools of the labour theory of value he recognized no need to adapt his (erroneous) theory of value to explain relative prices in a monetary environment. In other words, his theories of value and money were only partially united. In contrast, Keynes wrote: 'The division of economics between the theory of value and distribution on the one hand and the theory of money on the other hand is, I think, a false division' (Keynes, 1936, p. 293). However, Keynes had his own theoretical burden, namely the neoclassical theory of value. He was not able to drop that burden in his lifetime.

In addition, Keynes' presentation of monetary theory is often at variance to that of Marx. For example, Keynes makes great play of the term 'liquidity preference'. This indicates that Keynes regarded the holding of money as an individual propensity rather than a socially determined act. Marx, in contrast, would lean towards the latter view. However, in many instances Keynes' utilization of the term is merely a matter of terminology. It is possible, therefore, to interpret much of Keynes' monetary theory in terms which are perfectly harmonious with Marx.

Keynes shares with Marx a complete rejection of Say's Law. He traces the influence of that law in the works of Marshall, Pigou, and others. Particularly he finds its presence in the Marshallian proposition that an act of individual saving automatically leads to a corresponding act of investment:

Those who think in this way are deceived, nevertheless, by an optical illusion, which makes two essentially different activities appear to be the same. They are fallaciously supposing that there is a nexus which unites decisions to abstain from present consumption with decisions to provide for future consumption; whereas the motives which determine the latter are not linked in any simple way with the motives which determine the former (Keynes, 1936, p. 21).

As Clower (1968, p. 278) points out, most later writers have argued that either this portion of Keynes' indictment of orthodoxy is wrong, or the proposition which Keynes attacks is not the one which he thought he was attacking. Clower argues, convincingly, that these later writers were misguided. The refutation of Say's Law remains a central and valid feature of the work of both Marx and Keynes.

CHAPTER 14

VALUE AND MONETARY EQUILIBRIUM

But the market is the best judge of value; for by the concourse of buyers
and sellers the quantity of wares and the occasion for them are best
known; things are just worth so much as they can be sold for, according to
the old rule, valet quantum potest.

NICHOLAS BARBON, *Discourse of Trade,* 1690

In this chapter we shall discuss the existence of an economic equilibrium in a monetary economy, drawing upon recent work in this field. Finally we shall pose a definition of value different from the one used by most Marxists.

Neo-Keynesian equilibrium analysis

Important recent work has shown that a 'non-Walrasian' equilibrium can exist in a monetary economy. In other words it has been shown that it is possible for the economy to be in equilibrium whilst there is an excess demand for money, and an excess supply of other commodities. In such circumstances Say's Law, as we have defined it, is clearly invalidated. We refer to the work of Younes (1975) and Benassy (1975).

Benassy provides an example which illustrates the impact of money in the formation of an economic equilibrium. We shall discuss it here, in an altered and simplified form. Like Benassy, we shall use the concept of utility; but we shall remove it at a later stage. Consider an economy in which there is one capitalist and one worker. The daily production process has just been completed, and the capitalist owns two produced loaves of bread. The worker owns no bread at this stage, but he is able and willing to hire his labour-power for up to 10 hours the next day. Both capitalist and worker have £10 in cash money. They have no other assets.

The capitalist wishes to sell some bread to the worker and hire some of his labour-power for the next day. The worker wishes to hire out some of that labour-power and buy some bread. However, the

144

exchange environment is uncertain, and to deal with future contingencies both worker and capitalist are not willing to spend all their money at any stage; they both wish to continue to hold some money as a hedge against uncertainty.

Assume, for the sake of simplicity, that both capitalist and worker get an independent and equal amount of utility from possessing one loaf of bread, £10 in cash, and controlling 5 hours of labour-power. They both obtain *less* additional utility from owning an additional loaf of bread, an extra £10 in cash, or controlling an extra 5 hours of labour-power. We shall also make the assumption that the given initial market price of bread is £12 a loaf, and the wage rate is £2.50 an hour.

The worker wishes to buy bread, but at these prices the utility gained from buying five-sixths of a loaf with his £10 would be less than the utility lost by losing that £10 in cash money. The capitalist wishes to hire labour-power but the utility gained from having the use of 4 hours' labour would be less than the utility lost in parting from the £10 to pay for it. It is true, of course, that both the capitalist and the worker will each get some money back if, after buying, they then sell their available assets to the other party. The problem is that the initial transaction cannot take place. No fluid circulation of commodities takes place, and, in the words of Keynes, instead there is a 'sticky mess'.

Will prices be forced down so that the market can function? Although some trading will be possible, Benassy shows that even with price flexibility the economy will not, in general, reach a position where either excess demand or excess supply are zero. We can appreciate this point intuitively. Excess demand or supply will only be zero at the 'Walrasian' equilibrium point where both the capitalist and the worker each own one loaf of bread, £10 in cash, and each have the disposal of 5 hours of labour time. Prices at this point must be £10 a loaf and £2 for an hour of labour-time. With these prices and the above allocation of resources each party will have no incentive to trade any further, and thus there will be no excess demand or supply in the economy. However, in order to reach this 'Walrasian' equilibrium point the price of bread must be £10 and the wage rate £2 *throughout the whole period of trading.* Unless the initial trade is at these prices one party will lose out, and be unable to express a full demand for a particular commodity in cash terms, and this particular commodity will end up in excess supply.

The key point that is illustrated with this example is that the market, in a monetary economy, is constricted and 'sticky'. Money is the only commodity that can be exchanged for other commodities and it is the only commodity in which demand and supply can be expressed. The inherent demand for money, however, restricts the use of money as a conveyor of such information. Both the capitalist and the worker want certain commodities, and are willing to sell others, but the necessary information cannot be signalled. If they did not have to rely on monetary exchange they could negotiate with each other and probably reach the 'Walrasian' position, or something near it, through barter in a situation of near-perfect information. The result in a monetary economy, with imperfect information, is the achievement of a 'non-Walrasian' equilibrium. In our example in this equilibrium there is an excess supply of bread and an excess supply of labour, i.e. the worker is involuntarily employed for part of the time. The economy is stuck in a position of overproduction and un-employment. Furthermore, relative and absolute prices are different from those in the 'Walrasian' position.

On reflection it should be clear that, in the above example, if the propensity to hoard money of the worker and the capitalist were reduced then the determined equilibrium position would move towards the 'Walrasian' barter-equilibrium. If the traders used money as a medium of exchange and unit of account only, and showed no desire to hold money as a hedge against uncertainty, then fluid trading would go on. However, the desire to hold money in the con-text of uncertainty, along with an exchange environment which rules out any trade which excludes money, prevent the attainment of the 'Walrasian' equilibrium position.

On the basis of the Neo-Keynesian analysis we have shown that a barter-equilibrium is a limiting case of a monetary equilibrium. This result is of importance because it shows that the general equilibrium analysis of a non-money commodity economy has some relevance to the analysis of a monetary and capitalist economy. In particular, this legitimizes the use of Sraffian analysis. It is not, however, permissible to adopt the conventional general equilibrium analysis for the reasons we mentioned earlier in chapters 3 and 4.

Despite the importance of the Neo-Keynesian equilibrium analysis. and the valid conclusions which can be drawn from it, it does have some conceptual weaknesses. First, it is centred on exchange, exclud-ing the sphere of production. Second, following on from this, exchange is seen as the means to the sole end of consumption and utility maximization. Other motives for exchange are excluded.

Nevertheless, there are tactical advantages, for polemical purposes, in showing the limitations of the neoclassical analysis whilst retaining

the concept of utility. It is sometimes better to attack on one or two
fronts, instead of them all at the same time.

Neo-Marxian revisions

We shall add a few remarks which should indicate the way in which
the Neo-Keynesian analysis could be recast in a Neo-Marxian mould.

According to our conception, production and exchange are not
stages on a one-way street which leads from factors of production to
consumption and utility maximization. Rather it is more like a
circular and repetitive process. Each of the agents within the economy has an objective, or objectives, but not utility maximization.
Alternatively, the objectives could be profit maximization, the
survival and procreation of possessing agents, or the maximization of
some index of consumption. In realistic circumstances persons will
aim to achieve a combination of two or more of these objectives.

The moment of exchange will be combined with, and dominated
by, the moment of production, on the lines that we discussed in
chapter 4. This factor will add to the uncertainty of the market.
Despite attempts by the capitalists to regulate and regularize production it is always, by its nature, not completely determinate and
predictable. This is particularly the case because labour-power is
utilized in production, and the extraction of real living labour from
labour-power always involves a degree of struggle and potential
resistance by the worker. This point will be raised again in a later
chapter.

Having made these revisions it is clear that none of the important
conclusions reached by the Neo-Keynesians are undermined: in fact
they are reinforced. There is even less reason to assume that a full
employment equilibrium will be attained. There is an even greater
role to be played by uncertainty and indeterminacy.

The formalization of this Neo-Marxian approach would be difficult, and lies outside the scope of this work. It must be regarded as a
project for future research. However, even now it is evident that
research into that matter is clearly a step in a realistic direction,
which will bring us closer to an understanding of the real capitalist
world.

The notion of shifting equilibrium

It may be suggested that the situation in a monetary economy is
simply chaotic; but this is an overstatement. Equilibrium exists in a
monetary economy, but it is of a different nature to that in a barter

economy. Keynes calls the type of equilibrium which embraces money and uncertainty a 'shifting equilibrium', meaning by the latter an equilibrium 'in which changing views about the future are capable of influencing the present situation' (Keynes, 1936, p. 293). Keynes' distinction between shifting and stationary equilibrium is discussed further in Kregel (1976).

If expectations of the future were constant for short periods, giving rise to a constant propensity to hoard money, then the 'shifting' equilibrium would remain stationary. However, it would not of course be the 'Walrasian' stationary equilibrium. Furthermore, the economy would eventually face changed assessments of an uncertain future, so the economy would be continually 'groping' towards new shifting equilibria. These gropings are neither totally anarchic or indeterminate nor totally determinate and calculable. Shifting equilibrium is not permanent or stable, but it is asserted continually through the apparent chaos.

Sraffa's analysis and money

We have already discussed the theory of value developed by Sraffa (1960). We have also noted that money is effectively absent from the Sraffa system. If it exists it is only an arbitrary *numéraire*. It is always possible to *designate* one good in the Sraffa model as money, and make this chosen good the price *numéraire*. However, apart from having the ascribed status of being the unit of account, such a money commodity is indistinguishable from other goods in the system. Its status as the money commodity is not inherent in its economic role or position. It is true that the designated commodity could, for example, function as the medium of exchange, but that feature is not marked out in any way in the theoretical model. The absence of such a feature means, in effect, that *any* commodity could serve as the medium of exchange. This contradicts the fact that money is the *only* commodity which can be traded for others.

This does not, in any way, undermine the devastating role of the work of the Sraffa school in demolishing the neoclassical theory of distribution, nor the general importance of Sraffa's work. It is also opportune to repeat the previous observation that Marx's formal theory of relative prices takes no account of the effect of money on such relative prices. Hence part of Marx's theory is placed in a similar quandary to Sraffa's analysis.

This difficulty regarding the Sraffa system can, in our opinion, be resolved. First, it must be recognized that the analysis of the long-run stationary state is a limiting and special case of shifting equilibrium analysis. So even if Sraffa's analysis applies only to the long-run stationary state it is still of major interest, and within certain limits has an important validity. Second, it is possible to introduce money into the Sraffa system. An attempt to do this is made in the next chapter.

Marx's definition of value

Before we turn to our proposed redefinition of the concept of value we shall discuss the utilization of the word in Marx's writings.

The word 'value' is not clearly defined in *Capital*. Often Marx will state what 'value' is, but he is rarely clear as to whether such a statement is a matter of definition or an *analysis* of value in terms of some other substance. Assume we have never heard of the word 'steam' before. One person explains to us that steam is water. This statement is true and informative. But if we take it as the *definition* of steam then we are sorely misinformed. Without a clear and explicit definition we can never capture the essential meaning of the word. The same problem arises with the word 'value' in Marx's writings.

Two major and well-known theorists, namely Dobb (1940, 1973) and Sweezy (1968) have assumed that the word 'value' is *defined* as a socially necessary embodied labour-time in Marx's works. However, they do not cite one explicit definition, in these terms, from *Capital* or any other of Marx's economic writings. As far as this present author is aware, no such clear definition exists.

More recently, Steedman has insisted that: 'By the value of a commodity, Marx meant the quantity of labour socially necessary for the production of that commodity' (1977, pp. 39–40). In an attempt to verify this interpretation, Steedman quotes no less than 18 passages from Marx (pp. 208–10). The reader is encouraged to inspect these. He or she will note the following. First the words 'define', 'defined', or 'definition' do not appear once in these 18 quotations. Second, none of them is clearly a *definition* of value. Clauses such as 'labour is the substance of value' or 'value is nothing else but labour-time' abound, but these are not definitions. It is like saying 'water is the substance of steam' and 'steam is nothing else but water'. We are still not informed what value or steam are. Steedman's case is not, in my view, proved.

In fact there are passages in Marx, not quoted by Steedman, which give a contrary impression to the definition of value in terms of labour-time. In the celebrated first chapter of *Capital* Marx briefly mentions a 'discovery' made by the classical economists; an erroneous 'discovery' which Marx, himself, took almost for granted:

The belated scientific discovery that the products of labour, in so far as
they are values, are merely the material expressions of the human labour
expended to produce them, marks an epoch in the history of mankind's
development (Marx, 1976, p. 167).

If 'value' was *defined* as socially necessary embodied labour-time, then it hardly would be a 'scientific discovery' marking 'an epoch in the history of mankind's development' to find out that 'values are merely the material expressions of human labour'! The definition of value in terms of embodied labour makes a nonsense of the above passage. It clearly indicates that Marx could have had something else in mind.

It is clear that *either* Marx was inconsistent in his use of the word value, *or* Dobb, Steedman and Sweezy are wrong in their interpretation of Marx's use of the word. There is no other way out. Perhaps, on balance, Marx was simply inconsistent; but this, if it were true, should warn us to be cautious when citing Marx's authority on such questions of definition.

We simply want to add that it is *possible,* in certain passages of Marx's works, that he had a different definition of value in mind. There are a few passages in *Capital* which give the impression that Marx sometimes thought that value was defined in terms of money or prices in some way. For example: 'Money is merely the form in which the value of commodities appears in the process of circulation' (Marx, 1972, pp. 161–2). Despite some remarks in a footnote which contradict our alternative interpretation (Marx, 1976, p. 269n.) at least one passage in *Capital* is consistent with a definition of value as *equilibrium price,* expressed in terms of money units: 'the exchange, or sale, of commodities at their value is the rational state of affairs, i.e. the natural law of their equilibrium' (Marx, 1962, p. 184). Alternatively, the latter quotation could also be compatible with a definition of value as socially necessary embodied labour-time. In that case, it would be inconsistent with Marx's demonstration, in the third volume of *Capital,* that prices are permanently out of proportion with the amounts of labour embodied in commodities under capitalist production (ibid., ch. 9).

We certainly should not be too dogmatic when quoting Marx. It does seem that Marx could have been inconsistent, on a number of counts. We do not wish to commit ourselves to one interpretation or another; we shall leave that to the Marxologists. We simply wish to demonstrate that our alternative definition of value is not as heretical as it may seem at first.

A Neo-Marxian definition of value

In this work 'value' is defined as equilibrium price, expressed in money units. Clearly, value can only exist in a commodity economy with money. It is important to emphasize that this definition is not made on the basis of an appeal to the authority of Marx. Such authority may or may not exist. Unlike *Capital,* in this work the 'substance' of value is not seen as labour-time, whatever that identification might mean. It is important to note that the word value is used in the sense of equilibrium price in the majority of orthodox literature, a significant part of Marxian literature, Sraffa's work, and the major part of economic writing for the last 200 years. Our definition, therefore, is not without precedent.

This definition allows us to examine such issues as 'the labour theory of value' with some insertion of meaning and a reduction of confusion. Furthermore, it allows us to utilize such powerful categories as 'surplus value', albeit in a slightly different sense. Most, if not all, empirical work by Marxists on the magnitude of surplus value has implicitly or explicitly assumed that 'value' is quantitatively equal to equilibrium price. In addition, a prominent theorist such as Mandel, in the glossary in one of his major works, defines 'surplus value' in the following manner: 'the monetary form assumed by the social surplus product in a commodity producing society' (Mandel, 1976, pp. 587–8). Our definition is precisely the same.

Finally, the definition of value as equilibrium price, expressed in money terms, is consistent with Marx's insistence that 'value' is a category that pertains to commodity-producing societies only. The definition of value as embodied labour-time relates value to no particular form of society, and that is another good reason for rejecting that definition.

We shall now discuss the position of this definition of value in the expositional structure of this work. It should then be clear why the definition is introduced at this late stage.

Value and equilibrium

The demonstration of the existence of an equilibrium in a monetary economy is an important step in the analysis of capitalism. Without such a demonstration the theory of value degenerates into empty indeterminacy. We have not discussed this equilibrium in much detail, or demonstrated its stability; but given the complexity of the subject it would be far beyond the scope of this work to attempt to do these things.

In this work, key concepts have been defined as the appropriate stage of analysis is reached. Exchange-value, i.e. the ratio in which commodities exchange, refers particularly to a barter economy, in or out of equilibrium. Prices exist in a money economy and they are the monetary expression of exchange-values, in or out of an equilibrium situation. The concept of price, therefore, reflects the functions of money as a unit of account and medium of exchange. Value is defined as equilibrium price, in a monetary economy. As this equilibrium is 'shifting', value additionally reflects the function of money as a hedge against the uncertain conditions which influence that shifting equilibrium. Most non-Marxian economists have made no clear distinction between value and price. Marx did, but his concept of value is different from ours.

Having forged a link between monetary and value theory, bringing money into our general theory of value we can now discuss the question: what determines value? In a quantitative sense, the determination of value can only be investigated by a 'non-Walrasian' general equilibrium analysis, such as those carried out by Benassy and Younes, or that found in the next chapter. From analyses such as these it is clear that no simple set of factors or elements enter into the quantitative determination of value. It will depend upon consumer preferences, use-values, expectations of the future, and social and technological relations. This answer may appear eclectic, but these elements can be related and formalized in a rigorous mathematical way.

Formal general equilibrium analysis, in a monetary economy, indicates the relative impact of the above-listed elements in the quantitative determination of value. However, it is still necessary to ask what lies behind these variables, and determines them. Clearly, a number of contrasting interpretations are possible, including a particular ideological one which would interpret 'consumer preferences' and 'expectations' in an individualistic rather than a social way. We have already argued that exchange, commodities, and money are founded on specific social relations not inherited from nature but built by man. Our analysis, therefore, would deny the individualistic interpretation of the determining variables.

The latter point is clarified and extended if we consider the qualitative determination of value. Value, as a social relation, is based on a social system with a number of specific elements. First, there must be the appropriate legal system and property relations for commodity trading. Second, money must exist and be socially recognized as such. Value, therefore, is clearly based on a specific set of social relations, without which it would not exist. Having asserted the possibility of a quantitative determination of value, the qualitative aspect will occupy more of our attention.

The key significance of values, as compared to prices, is that they reflect general social conditions and relations, in production as well as exchange. Prices, on the other hand, seem to be merely accidental reflections of market conditions, of fluctuations in supply and demand. Values are not of that character. They have a solidity which not only reflects social conditions but also itself provides an economic force. Economic agents act on the assumption of certain equilibrium conditions; to assume otherwise, i.e. chaos, would make economic decision-making a farcical impossibility. Value not only exists in the real world, it is also a notion necessary for economic agents to adopt, albeit often implicitly, in order to make meaningful observations and decisions about the real capitalist world.

CHAPTER 15

MONEY AND THE SRAFFA SYSTEM

A monetary economy . . . is essentially one in which changing views about the future are capable of influencing the quantity of employment and not merely its direction.

J. M. KEYNES, *The General Theory of Employment, Interest and Money*

It has already been shown that the Sraffa system, as traditionally conceived, does not include money. It is the purpose of this chapter to outline a way of including certain types of money into the system. This will permit a further evaluation of the shifting equilibrium state, discussed above.

In this chapter, use is made of the term 'liquidity preference'. This is partly for ease of exposition, and partly because it is a term with which the reader will be familiar. However, it is not meant to be interpreted as an asocial, individualistic or psychologistic concept, as it is in some writing. The very word 'preference' could be taken to indicate such an interpretation. The absence of a suitable alternative term in the literature is regrettable.

We shall assume that, for the purpose of this chapter, there are just two types of money—account money and cash money in the form of gold coin. These two types of money perform slightly different roles, and have different effects. If money is held in the form of cash, i.e. gold, then clearly the holder does not receive any interest payment. On the other hand, if cash money is deposited in a bank then the holder parts with some of the liquidity associated with the possession of cash, and this degree of liquidity is transferred to the banker. For this benefit the bank often pays interest. The importance of this distinction between interest-bearing account money and 'sterile' cash money will be elaborated below.

Another important distinction between cash and account money is that the former is physically produced, and has a tangible physical form, whereas the latter has not. Account money is simply numbers in books, or, in the modern era, data in computer memory-banks.

154

The physical form of cash money is necessary, otherwise it could not be fully liquid, nor fulfil its complete function as cash. This physical feature of cash money makes possible the application of Sraffa-type analysis to the phenomenon.

A simple economy

To explain the approach we shall use the example of a simple economy. A more general version of the analysis can be found elsewhere (Hodgson, 1981b) but the nature of the generalization, to those familiar with matrices, should be fairly obvious, and need not concern us here.

In the economy there are the following commodities: 'machines', 'corn' and labour-power. Money will be added later. One machine may be used, with one unit of labour, to produce two machines in a given time period. Alternatively, in the same time, the one machine and the one unit of labour may be combined with one unit of corn to produce two units of harvested corn at the end of the period. This gives the following schema:

	INPUTS				OUTPUTS	
	Machines	Corn	Labour		Machines	Corn
Machine industry:	1	0	1	→	2	0
Corn industry:	1	1	1	→	1	2

Constant returns to scale are assumed, so that the elements in any of the above rows may be multiplied by a positive scalar number to give any appropriate scale of output. Note also, in this simple example, the machines are 'as good as new' at the end of the period.

We shall define w as the wage per unit of labour-time, p_1 as the price of a machine and p_2 as the price of corn. The units of these three variables are, as yet, unspecified. We may proceed, in the usual way, from the identity

$$\text{Costs} + \text{Profit} = \text{Revenue}.$$

This gives the following equations:

Machine industry: $(p_1 + w)(1 + r) = 2p_1$
Corn industry: $(p_1 + p_2 + w)(1 + r) = p_1 + 2p_2$ (15.1)

where r is the rate of profit, assumed to be equal in both industries.

Eliminating w from the latter two equations the following may be derived:

$$p_1/p_2 = 1 - r.$$

Hence the relative price of the two commodities, machines and corn, is a simple function of the rate of profit. In fact, in this case, the function is linear, but more generally it will be a curve.

The introduction of money

We may begin to introduce money in the system. It is assumed that there is a liquidity preference for cash money in each industry. This money is held to deal with unforeseen emergencies, etc., and will depend on the degree of uncertainty. We shall assume that the liquidity preference in each case is a variable. There are m_1 units of cash money (gold) held in the machine industry and m_2 units in the corn industry. For simplicity, there are no gold stocks in the gold industry.

This cash money, or gold, is *produced* in a third industry within the system, under capitalist conditions like the first two industries. In the gold industry one machine is used with one unit of labour to mine one unit of gold in the given time-period. The schema is modified as follows:

	INPUTS					OUTPUTS		
	Machines	Corn	Gold	Labour		Machines	Corn	Gold
Machine industry:	1	0	m_1	1	→	2	0	m_1
Corn industry:	1	1	m_2	1	→	1	2	m_2
Gold industry:	1	0	0	1	→	1	0	1

We now come to another important feature of the model that distinguishes it from the conventional Sraffa system. Cash money is produced in this model so it may be asked: to where does it go? The other industries do not use up gold, they simply *hold on* to a quantity, per unit of labour performed. So if the economy was at a stationary level then no more cash money would need to be produced and the gold industry would go out of business. In contrast, in the usual Sraffa system it does not matter if the economy is expanding or not. An important feature of this shifting equilibrium model is that total employment and output must be assumed to be expanding over time. As a result there is a need for more and more cash money in the system, at least as long as m_1 and m_2 do not decline. This ensures that the gold industry will stay in business. Hence, in contrast to Sraffa's model, the actual level of output and employment are, to some extent, involved in the specification of the shifting equilibrium model, which includes money. However, the fact that the economy is expanding does not mean, in itself, that price, wage and profit relations are necessarily affected in a different way from the conventional Sraffa system.

It may be argued that it is illegitimate to include money in such a system, particularly in the form of an input and an output in the process of production. To argue against this point it must be asserted again that money is a necessary part of the capitalist system. This assertion, however, is clearly not enough. It may be argued that money, although necessary to the system, is not like technology, and that the latter can be considered independently of the economic system. In response, it can be said that whilst technology has a degree of autonomy it is dubious that it can be separated from the social relations of production. The production process always bears the stamp of the social relations that pervade the whole economy, particularly in the case of the application of labour itself. So the first counter-argument is that money, like technology, is not independent of the type of economic and social system involved (see Rowthorn, 1974, pp. 76–7; Lukács, 1972, pp. 136–9).

The reader may still not be convinced that it is legitimate to include money in the tables of inputs and outputs. We have already asserted that cash money, in the model, is a physically produced commodity. From this point additional arguments can be given. The work of von Neumann (1945) and Sraffa (1960) includes a way of treating fixed capital in the process of production. With this, fixed capital appears not only as a required input in various processes but also as a 'produced' output in the table of outputs. Quite often, in these models, the fixed capital endures a physical change in the production process, being worn, or run-in, but that is not necessarily the case. Hence, like money in our model, a physical metamorphosis of fixed capital can be excluded. Neither, in these models, is the fixed capital, altered or not, the intended aim of production. Yet it is still regarded as a product and an input. In addition it seems that it is *necessary* to treat fixed capital in this way in order to derive an adequate theory of the depreciation of fixed capital (see Steedman, 1977, ch. 10). Hence the work of von Neumann and Sraffa with fixed capital can be cited as a precedent for the inclusion of money.

It should be noted, in passing, that the introduction of money does not affect the amount of labour-time embodied in a machine or a unit of corn. This should be fairly obvious because money is not actually used in the production of those commodities. A small consequence of this point will be noted later below.

Account money and the rate of interest

In the above, only the physical aspects of the economy have been elaborated. It has been convenient to leave the discussion of non-physical account money until now. The monetary and financial system must be considered in more detail. We have assumed that the gold industry, run on capitalist lines, produces cash money. In general this gold is then traded for labour-power, and with other capitalists for inputs to produce more gold and make further profits. In our simple example the other inputs would be machines. Consequently, cash money finds its way into the other sectors of the economy. Due to economic expansion, greater cash money is required to match greater demands for liquidity.

It is assumed, for simplicity, that the function of banking is carried out by the industrial capitalists themselves. Cash money is lent and borrowed between capitalists, and accounts are kept of debts and credits. Interest is paid on *this* money, which is not cash money, and we shall call it *account money*. Cash money, unlike account money, is not interest-bearing.

We shall assume that the rate of interest is uniform, on all account money, debts or credits, and it is denoted by i. If the system commenced at some date in the past with no borrowing and lending, and no account money, then a debt, when it appeared, would be balanced by an equal credit, and as a result of the uniform interest rate the sum of all debts would be equal to the sum of all credits. This should be obvious because one person's debt is always someone else's credit.

We shall assume that no physical or labour inputs are required to administrate the banking system. Account money is not *produced* in the production system, like cash money. Also, we repeat, it has no physical presence. Account money cannot be considered as an input or an output in the production system.

The account money that is held in each industry is defined as m_{a_1}, m_{a_2} and m_{a_3}, in the machine, corn and gold industry respectively. Overdrafts are represented by negative quantities. Unlike the coefficients in tables of physical inputs and outputs, coefficients representing quantities of account money can be negative.

We can now turn to a further calculation of prices and profits. Both wages and prices can now be given a suitable *numéraire*: they are measured in terms of money. Amounts of account money gain interest at a rate i, and as a result they are multiplied by a factor of $(1 + i)$ for every unit time-period. (This is analogous to the standard practice of augmenting the price of capital invested by profits, *via* multiplication by the factor $(1 + r)$.)

Price and profit equations

The accounts for each industry can now be presented in full, including interest, account money, and cash. We have:

Machine industry:

$$(p_1 + w + m_1 + m_{a_1})(1 + r) = 2p_1 + m_1 + m_{a_1}(1 + i)$$

Corn industry:

$$(p_1 + p_2 + w + m_2 + m_{a_2})(1 + r) = p_1 + 2p_2 + m_2 + m_{a_2}(1 + i)$$

Gold industry:

$$(p_1 + w + m_{a_3})(1 + r) = p_1 + 1 + m_{a_3}(1 + i) \qquad (15.2)$$

It is useful to compare the above equations with equations (15.1). First of all, amounts of cash money or account money have been added on the left-hand side of each equation, as if they were a 'cost'. These amounts of money are included in the total outlay of capital and form a part of that total outlay when the rate of profit is computed. In addition, the amounts of *cash* money, m_1 and m_2, appear on the right-hand side of the equations, indicating that their value has been preserved and is still at the disposal of the capitalist concerned. The amounts of *account* money, m_{a_1}, m_{a_2} and m_{a_3}, also appear on the right-hand side, but augmented by the rate of interest, indicating, for example, that wealth in the industry has increased if both the account money and the rate of interest are positive. The third equation has not got a predecessor, but it simply represents the accounts of the gold industry, presented on the same basis.

We have a fourth equation, which follows from the fact that the sum of all account money credits (or debts) is zero:

$$m_{a_1} + m_{a_2} + m_{a_3} = 0$$

We proceed as before by first eliminating w from the first two equations. The following equation is derived:

$$p_1 - p_2 (1 - r) = (m_1 - m_2)r + (m_{a_1} - m_{a_2})(r - i)$$

It is clear that the former ratio between the prices of machines and corn, in the non-money Sraffa system discussed above, no longer pertains. This former ratio (i.e. $p_1/p_2 = 1 - r$) applies if and only if the right-hand side of the above equation is zero. In general, therefore, liquidity preference for money, both in the cash and account form, will affect relative prices. Although this model is based on limited and special assumptions, there is good reason to assume that relative prices are similarly affected in the real capitalist world.

It is interesting to note a number of features of the model. First, if the rate of interest is equal to the rate of profit ($i = r$) then *account* money does not affect relative prices. In fact it drops out of the picture entirely, even in a generalized matrix model. Second, if the amount of debt (credit) in the machine and corn industries is equal then the rate of interest does not affect prices. Third, if *total* money assets, including cash money, are equal in those two industries, then relative prices are as in the non-money system if the rate of interest is zero.

The wage–profit frontier

Proceeding further with the algebra, it is possible to eliminate p_1 from the first and third equations (15.2). We get:

$$w = \frac{1 - r - m_1 r^2 - (m_{a_1} r + m_{a_3}(1 - r))(r - i)}{1 + r}$$

This is the Sraffian wage–profit frontier in the monetized system. If, for example, m_1 is zero and the rates of profit and interest are equal then the monetized wage–profit frontier reduces to:

$$w = \frac{1 - r}{1 + r}$$

This is the wage–profit frontier in the normal non-money Sraffa system. It can be easily derived by eliminating p_1 and by measuring the wage in terms of corn (i.e. setting $p_2 = 1$) in Equations (15.1) (which are the equations set up before money was introduced in our model).

The effect of the introduction of money is to distort the wage–profit frontier. A number of circumstances reduce this distortion to zero. In particular, in our model, if m_1, m_{a_1} and m_{a_3} are all zero

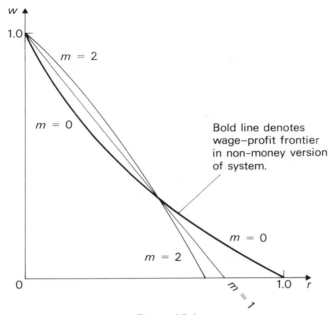

Figure 15.1
Distortions of the wage—profit frontier

then the wage—profit frontier is identical to that in the non-money system. In general, therefore, liquidity preferences can distort the wage—profit frontier, but if all money holdings, both cash and account money, are zero, then it is clear that no distortion is present.

From inspection of the wage profit frontier in the monetized system it can be seen that the distortion is not necessarily in one direction. However, if the rates of profit and interest are equal, or if m_{a_1} and m_{a_3} are both non-negative, then the wage—profit frontier will be distorted towards the origin, i.e. either the wage, or the rate of profit, will be reduced, or both, as a result of the introduction of money. Nevertheless, it is quite easy to construct examples where the wage—profit frontier, or at least a segment of it, moves away from the origin, and both wages and the rate of profit can be increased. We construct an example of wage—profit frontier distortion below, and one in which the latter phenomenon takes place.

Assume that $m_1 = -m_{a_1} = -m_{a_3} = m$, and that $r = 2i$. We get

$$w = \frac{1 - r + \frac{1}{2}mr\,(1 - 2r)}{1 + r}$$

The frontier is plotted, for different values of m, in figure 15.1.

It is clear, therefore, that in the monetized Sraffa system, relative prices, profits and wages can all be affected by the key monetary variables. These variables, in turn, are dependent on liquidity preference and the general state of capitalist expectations. Hence wages, prices and profits are affected by expectations of the future.

This point has a number of important consequences. First, it is another reason to reject a purely technical explanation of relative prices. Although such an interpretation is not found in Sraffa's work it has been adopted by some of his followers. The introduction of money shows that such a purely technical explanation is impossible. Relative prices are affected by expectations, and the latter are not derived from technology, they are projections into a highly uncertain future. Second, the introduction of money gives a further argument against the labour theory of value, even in its most sophisticated version. In a monetized system relative prices cannot be computed on the basis of embodied labour values alone: the transformation of values into prices does not work. Additional, monetary, information is required.

The model and the real capitalist world

It is obvious, however, that our model is highly simplified. It is more a 'thought experiment' than an accurate description of reality. In what way can it be applied to the real capitalist world?

A central feature of the above model is that cash money (we have called it gold) is *produced* within the system. The model applies even if most money transactions are carried out with account money: as long as this account money is *based* on gold then the model will be relevant. It could be said, therefore, that the model could be made to apply, with appropriate modifications, to much of the history of capitalism. Even up to 1971 the United States dollar was based on the value of a given quantity of gold. However, in the twentieth century, gold has rarely been used as a medium of exchange. Direct exchangeability with gold has not been legal or possible in most countries on a day-to-day basis.

What happens when the currency is no longer based on any precious metal, and assumes the form of notes or coin? These will not be produced by firms operating under capitalist conditions; their production will be undertaken by the state. The 'rate of profit' on the 'production' of this currency will bear no relation to the general rate of profit in the economy as a whole. The above model will not apply without modification.

However, it is possible to modify the model. The equation which derives from the accounts in the gold industry above is replaced by another equation which does not refer to the production of money at all. However, we must still assume that cash money is being produced by the state and it is finding its way into the private sector. This could result from state purchases of commodities from the private sector, but these need not be specified in detail.

We can assume, for example, that in the economy the real wage is constant, i.e. whatever the value of money wages the same commodities are purchased by each worker. This constant real wage could result either from a government-imposed incomes policy, which indexed money wages to the price of the goods purchased by the workers, or from successful efforts by the workers to raise money wages just in line with prices as a result of trade union action. This gives an equation to replace the one lost by the deletion of the accounts of the gold industry. In the equation, w is a weighted sum of other prices.

Let us return to our simple example and illustrate this. Assume that the real wage is half a unit of corn. Thus:

$$p_2 = 2w.$$

This replaces the third equation (15.2). Solving for p_1 and w we get:

$$w = \frac{m_1 r^2 + m_2 r(1-r) + m_{a1} r(r-i) + m_{a2}(1-r)(r-i)}{1 - 5r + 2r^2}$$

This gives the magnitude, in terms of money, of the real wage. Clearly, it is dependent on the monetary variables. Also:

$$p_1 = \frac{m_1 r(1-3r) + m_{a1}(1-3r)(r-i) + m_2 r(1+r) + m_{a2}(1+r)(r-i)}{1 - 5r + 2r^2}$$

It should be noted that whilst it is quite common to fix the real wage in a Sraffa model, the above approach is unique because it includes monetary variables.

Another assumption that could be made about wages, thus also 'closing' the model, is that there is a wage freeze, i.e. *money* wages, not real wages, are fixed, by enforcement by the government. Assume that w takes a given money value. We get:

$$p_1 = \frac{w(1 + r) + m_1 r + m_{a1}(r - i)}{1 - r}$$

$$p_2 = \frac{w(1 + r) + m_1 r^2 + m_{a1} r(r - i) + m_2 r(1 - r) + m_{a2}(1 - r)(r - i)}{(1 - r)^2}$$

Once again, prices depend on monetary variables. However, in the last two examples, with the state replacing the gold industry, the sum of m_{a1} and m_{a2} need not be zero. If it were positive, for example, then the state would have a debt to the private sector.

Conclusion

In this chapter an approach has been developed which integrates the theory of value and distribution in Sraffa's work with monetary theory. It should be emphasized, however, that the modified model, unlike the orthodox Sraffian system, no longer represents the long-run stationary state. It is more akin to the notion of shifting equilibrium defined and discussed by Keynes. In this shifting equilibrium, relative prices, absolute prices, wages and profits are dependent on monetary variables. The latter, in turn, are dependent on expectations of the future. As the future is inherently uncertain, prices, wages and profits depend upon assumptions, on the part of the capitalist, which have no complete rational foundation. At the same time, however, prices, wages and profits are related to each other, and some elements of determinacy assert themselves through the apparent chaos.

The latter models, in which the real wage was fixed in some way, could be extended and have an application to the study of different types of incomes policy in capitalist economies, and their effects on prices and profits.

PART IV
CAPITALIST PRODUCTION

CHAPTER 16

ABSTRACT AND HETEROGENEOUS LABOUR

We have already seen how the political economist establishes the unity of labour and capital in a variety of ways: Capital is accumulated labour. . . . The machine is capital directly equated with labour. . . . The worker is capital. . . . Wages belong to the costs of capital. . . . In relation to the worker, labour is the reproduction of his life-capital. . . . In relation to the capitalist, labour is an aspect of his capital's activity. Finally, the political economist postulates the original unity of capital and labour as the unity of the capitalist and the worker; this is the original state of paradise. The way in which these two aspects, as two persons, leap at each other's throats is for the political economist an accidental *event, and hence only to be explained by reference to external factors.*

KARL MARX, *Economic and Philosophic Manuscripts of 1844*

The near simultaneous destruction of both the aggregative neo-classical theory of distribution and the labour theory of value, both, in part, resulting from the work of Sraffa, has brought a number of economic, even philosophical, problems to the fore. It is necessary, first of all, to explain briefly how we have arrived at this particular theoretical conjuncture.

Before the destruction of the twin tenets of the labour theory of value, and the theory of distribution based on the neoclassical aggregate production function, both neoclassical economists and mainstream Marxists had 'labour' as a manifestly heterogeneous but essentially homogeneous substance. In neoclassical theory, both 'capital' and 'land' had the same paradoxical quality. Together, all three formed the famous 'Holy Trinity' of factors of production: 'capital', 'labour' and 'land'. Each, in its turn, had its respective reward: profit, wages, rent. In Marx's writings it was different of course. Both capital and labour were seen as respectively 'dead' and 'living' labour, the former being past labour, stored up, or embodied, in capital goods. But, in Marx, all such labour, whilst manifestly heterogeneous, was an expression of some 'common substance'. This substance was called 'abstract labour'.

After Sraffa, however, all this is in ruins. The aggregate neoclassical production function, and the theory of distribution upon which it is based, has been shown to be untenable and even logically inconsistent (Harcourt, 1972). The same fate has befallen the orthodox Marxian labour theory of value (Steedman, 1977).

The consequent reaction of neoclassical economics to this attack on one of its tenets is well known. It has taken refuge in a *dis*aggregated production function, and general equilibrium analysis. Before, the output (O) was seen as a result of inputs of factors of production, both capital (K) and labour (L) in a simple model:

$$O = f(K, L)$$

Now, in the disaggregated analysis, there are a number of types of capital (K_1, K_2, ... K_m) and a number of types of labour (L_1, L_2, ... L_n) and the following production function:

$$O = f(K_1, K_2, ... K_m, L_1, L_2, ... L_n)$$

Both labour and capital are heterogeneous. Instead of two, there are $m + n$ factors of production. Each one of these, be it called 'capital' or 'labour', is as good as another. Any clear distinction between labour and capital is dissolved.

Only one slight difference appears in this analysis. Capital, in each firm, and aggregated in terms of its price, commands a uniform profit rate (r) across the economy. In contrast, there is no uniform wage-rate. Even this difference is illusory, however. The essential distinction is not between labour and capital in the model but between a good or service which requires advanced *money capital* and one which does not. The items requiring advanced money capital will be augmented by the profit-rate, the others will not. Even labour-power, if it has to be paid in advance of the receipt of revenue from the sale of output, will 'command' a profit-rate. Essentially, in the model, there is no difference between a wage and a price. Everything, including the different types of labour, is reduced to 'capital'.

One of the triumphs of the Sraffa-based critique of the neoclassical aggregate production function was to proclaim that capital was not homogeneous. The neoclassical response has been to point out that labour is not homogeneous either. Everyone, of course, was aware of this fact, but not of its consequences. The heterogeneity of *both* capital and labour threatened to dissolve any distinction between these two 'substances'.

The problem, to some extent, is masked by some well-known results which appear in Sraffa's work. For example, the wage-rate(s) is (are) always an *inverse function* of the rate of profit, in contrast to other prices which can, in certain circumstances, increase if the profit-rate increases. The special feature of the wage results from a fact which is not made explicit in the Sraffa or neoclassical models: *labour-power is not produced under capitalist conditions; it is not itself produced for profit.* In a Sraffa model wages will always be a 'deduction' from profits, because no profits are being made in the household sector. This point was made in chapter 6 above, and it will be discussed later below.

The problem, to repeat, is that there is no adequate distinction between 'labour' and 'capital'. This problem has become more acute with the dissolution of the aggregative models. For neoclassical economics, however, the problem does not appear to exist. As long ago as the first decade of this century, neoclassical economists began to reduce all labour to a form of capital: 'human capital'. The logical basis of this was made clear by Fisher (1906). This work was drawn to the attention of Marshall who, with characteristic intuition, still persevered in a distinction between labour and capital. Since that time, however, the 'human capital' approach has gained considerable ground.

A removal of an essential distinction between 'labour' and 'capital' need not concern the neoclassical economists because, in their view, elements of 'labour' and 'capital' are rewarded on the same basis: marginal productivity. And they are not disposed to criticize this perceived state of affairs. The removal of the distinction should, for obvious reasons, concern radicals and Marxists.

For subscribers to the labour theory of value there is no problem because, in their view, labour alone is the source of all value. In this case, labour and machines are clearly distinguishable. The problem of heterogeneous *concrete* labour is overcome with Marx's notion of 'abstract labour'. According to this notion, it is the exchange of different commodities with the 'common substance' of *money* on the market which 'equates' the different types of labour within commodities (see Marx, 1976, pp. 166–7; Colletti, 1972, pp. 78–88). Clearly, this view is not tenable without the labour theory of value. Labour is, indeed, a special substance, but there is no reason to assume that it *alone* finds its expression in monetary value. Without the labour theory of value the problem remains.

However, as we shall see below, Marx helps us provide much of the answer to the problem. In particular, embedded in his notion of 'abstract labour' is a description of a common quality of human labour which is reinforced by the capitalist labour market. We shall discuss this later.

We should make it clear that our purpose, initially at least, is to discuss the distinction, strictly speaking, between human labour and labour-power on the one hand and capital goods on the other. Capital itself (as a social relation) is discussed in the next chapter.

Human consciousness

It is tempting first to approach the problem from a psychological or physiological point of view. What unique attributes of human beings are expressed in the activity of labour? Marx, in distinguishing the human architect from the non-human bee, laid stress on the fact that the human is endowed with consciousness and intent:

what distinguishes the worst architect from the best of bees is that the architect builds the cell in his mind before he constructs it in wax. At the end of every labour process, a result emerges which had already been conceived by the worker at the beginning, hence already existing ideally. Man not only effects a change of form in the materials of nature; he also realizes his own purpose in those materials. And this is a purpose he is conscious of, it determines the mode of his activity with the rigidity of a law, and he must subordinate his will to it. This subordination is no mere momentary act. Apart from the exertion of the working organs, a purposeful will is required for the entire duration of the work (Marx, 1976, p. 284).

What, in Marx's view expressed above, is true for a bee must also be true, or more true, for a machine. Human labour is demarcated from capital goods by the possession of consciousness. However, this point does not have prominence, elsewhere, in Marx's writing. Furthermore, from a more modern view, there are a whole host of controversies and problems surrounding the issue of human consciousness.

Psychology has created a refuge from this problem. It is behaviourism. This prominent tendency in psychological theory, exemplified by the works of B. F. Skinner and others, denies the reality of such human attributes as consciousness and intent. The passion for the quantifiable and observable in science has led to the dismissal of such words from the scientists' vocabulary: 'Merely to mention these pariah words in scientific discourse is to risk immediate loss of attention and audience' (Matson, 1964, p. 174).

In recent years, however, the behaviourist view has been under-mined, by Matson, Koestler (1967) and others. In particular, Koestler does not rehabilitate the notion of consciousness to then fall into the associated trap of Cartesian dualism, i.e. a simple dualism between mind and matter. He proposes that there is a *hierarchy of levels* of consciousness. This hierarchy is extended and complex in man, less so in other animals.

It is impossible to go over the details of this debate between psychologists. It may be, ultimately, that the concept of conscious-ness cannot be given adequate scientific verification. Even so, there are many notions in science, such as cause and effect, which likewise cannot be endorsed by scientific proof, at least in empiricist terms. It was Kant, of course, who suggested that such concepts, whilst being *a priori* rather than *a posteriori,* are nevertheless *essential* to human understanding. Perhaps the notions of consciousness and intent have a similar status. Perhaps, for social science, these concepts are essen-tial.

However, leaving the general methodological questions aside, it is clear *that for capitalism* such notions are essential. The core of the legal system in capitalist society is *contract law.* It is necessary, for this system of law, to demarcate between contracts which have the *conscious* agreement of the parties concerned and those which do not. Furthermore, in the legal system as a whole, the notions of *intent* and *responsibility* are crucial. For example, the legal responsi-bility for a crime, according to modern law, is assigned to the person or persons who intentionally committed the act. The task of a jury in a court of law is to discover the legally responsible person whose intentional actions gave rise to the crime. The legal imputation of guilt rests on the person who intentionally pulled the trigger of the gun which led to the death of another. It does not rest on the mech-anism of the gun itself, nor the person who manufactured the gun. And if the accused can be shown to have *unintentionally* pulled the trigger then there is no legal imputation of guilt for murder. The con-cepts of consciousness, intent, and responsibility for actions, are essential to modern law. The legal system, therefore, demarcates intentional human actions from the functions of a machine.

Applied to labour and labour-power, we get the following proposi-tions. Under capitalism, labour-power is hired under a system of contract. Capitalism, therefore, imputes consciousness to labour-power. In addition, the activity of work requires a degree of inten-tional activity on behalf of the worker, as Marx pointed out above.

Versatility

A second crucial difference between human labour and capital goods is that the latter are built and designed for restricted purposes, whereas human beings, whilst not being intentionally designed, have a much wider range of creative powers. Human beings are broadly versatile, each individual having the potential to carry out a large number of tasks. What is important, furthermore, is that each individual has the potential, with appropriate training, to carry out a similar range of work. Whilst we each live in a different environment, and differ, to some degree, in our mental and physical character, all human beings are biologically similar. Even in combination with human labour a spade cannot be used to carry water, write letters, cut wood and make conversation. However, most people, with the appropriate implements and training, can perform all these tasks.

It could be said that human labour has a *natural* versatility, which would show, to some extent, in all modes of production. What is clear, however, is that the common range of versatile labour is re-inforced and extended by capitalism. This is a prominent theme of Marx's *Capital*. After first making the common physiological nature of labour clear:

> *however varied the useful kinds of labour, or productive activities, it is a physiological fact that they are functions of the human organism, and that each such function, whatever may be its nature or its form, is essentially the expenditure of human brain, nerves, muscles and sense organs* (Marx, 1976, p. 164).

Marx later goes on to assert that modern industry is continually transforming

> *the functions of the worker . . . and incessantly throws masses of capital and of workers from one branch of production to another. Thus large-scale industry, by its very nature, necessitates variation of labour, fluidity of functions, and mobility of the worker in all directions. . . . variation of labour imposes itself after the manner of an overpowering natural law . . .* (ibid., pp. 617–18).

Does capitalism have a tendency to create versatile machinery, as well as reinforcing the versatility of labour? There is no doubt that machinery has become progressively more complex. Furthermore, there is the development of automation and the use of the relatively versatile computer. These developments are significant but it is clear that a stock of versatile capital goods is not the outcome, nor a purpose, of capitalist production. On the whole capital goods are produced for a specific purpose, or range of purposes. It would be wasteful to create a mass of highly versatile machinery. Even the computer itself, after it burst onto the market in a most versatile arrangement (its initial production being viable on that general basis only) has assumed more specialized forms. The use of 'robots' in production is spreading rapidly, but they have always been highly dissimilar and specialized in their functions.

Like most species, human beings are the product of millions of years of collective evolution and adaptation. Each person, from a gap as small as 10 generations, can inherit the genes of up to 1024 others. However, unlike other species, human beings have very complex languages, elaborate means of communication, and sophisticated social arrangements to produce their needs. On top of that, the modern individual is enmeshed in the world market, increasingly mobile, and part of an increasingly homogenized world culture. Machines, in contrast, have not evolved, nor adapted themselves to their environment. They have been produced, *by man,* for a specialized function, or a narrow range of functions. The machine is an appendage to man, rather than *vice-versa.* Capitalism, as a social system, does not require the increasing versatility of the machine. In elaborating a complex division of labour it creates specialisms from both labour and machine, but demands mobility of only the former. Wherever possible it reduces production to a *mechanical* function, shedding labour which then has to find different work, but creating the *special* machine. Even domesticated animals, where possible, are replaced by machines. The object of this mechanization of production, from the point of view of the capitalist, is to increase output and thereby profits. The muscle of man is replaced by the specialized and more advanced muscle of motor-power, the mind and memory of man, wherever possible, is replaced by the electronic computer or electronic device of specialized function. In this tendency the difference between man and machine is reinforced.

Skills and their production

We shall now develop a simple model to illustrate the development of human skills. This will clarify the conception of versatility and enable further comment on the idea of abstract labour. Let us assume, for simplicity, that human labour requires just two different skills, and each person has acquired a measure of each of these

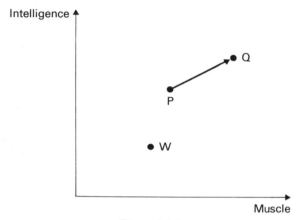

Figure 16.1
Skills, work and experience

skills, but this can vary from person to person. Let us call these two skills 'muscle' and 'intelligence'. These will each be measured on a positive, linear, scale. At a certain point in time an individual will have a measure of each of these two skills. These measures can be represented by cartesian coordinates as in figure 16.1, initially at point P. Then the individual undergoes an experience which *transforms* his or her skills. This experience could be education or training, or, at an earlier age, educative development within the family. Significantly, some such training would generally occur during the process of work itself, in the familiar pattern of 'learning by doing'. All such experiences, which improve one or more skills, whether in the home, educational institutions, or at work itself, we shall call training experiences. One such experience has the effect of moving the individual to new skill coordinates, represented by Q. It could be reasonably assumed that *all* persons with skill coordinates P will be transformed, by the *same* experience, to Q, but that persons with *different* skill coordinates will not necessarily develop in the same direction. (The assumption that a single training experience has the same effect on persons with the same skill coordinates would enable such a single training experience to be described by a square matrix: in our simple case a 'two-by-two' matrix.)

These training experiences affect a person's *potential*, not his or her *actual* performance. Work will require the exercise of a person's skills up to or below that person's capacity. In general it will be below this capacity. A person at P or Q in figure 16.1 could be exercising skills at only level W. In Marxian terminology, training experiences directly affect labour-power, not labour itself. The fact that an individual will often be working at below his or her potential means that if a less skilled person were to perform the task then that person could do it in the same time, with the same quantity and quality of output. *Versatility* would be a measure of the number or categories of task that a person could perform with a given skill-level coordinates. The higher these skill levels the more versatile, on the whole, the person would be.

Potential labour-power and performed labour

It should be clear that the above two-dimensional analysis can, in principle, be extended to any finite number of dimensions. Within modern capitalism different types of work are frequently being analysed in terms of their component skills. Work-study experts frequently employ this 'factor analysis'. The named skills usually include such items as responsibility, manual dexterity, decision-making abilities, and tolerance of danger at work. Furthermore this factor analysis is often the basis for calculating wage payments, after each skill level is given a more or less arbitrary weighting. There is evidence that this method of determining wages is very widespread in modern capitalism (Lupton and Bowey, 1974).

In any case, it should be clear that, under capitalism, wage payments will be made more on the basis of *performed,* and not *potential,* skills. It is interesting to note that most attempts to explain different wage-levels, on the basis of differences in education, training, etc., do not make the latter distinction. This is the error committed by the 'human capital' school. By reducing labour-power to 'capital' the distinctions between *performed* labour, the labour-power hired out to the capitalist, and the *potential* labour-power, are ignored. Labour is treated as a machine. On reflection, however, it should be quite clear that the determinants of potential labour-power, education in particular, will bear no close relation to contracted labour-power or labour performed. Differences of education, it would be expected, would not offer an adequate explanation of differences in wages.

The above discussion should clarify the distinction we have already made between human beings on the one hand and animals and machines on the other. We shall briefly elaborate on this. A non-domestic animal has skills honed down by the combined action of evolution and environment. Whilst an animal will often be performing (running, hunting, fighting, etc.) below its potential, to survive it will occasionally be called upon to use most or all of its powers. The process of evolution will not often lead to the sustained or general existence of powers which are superfluous to survival. If such super-fluous powers were in existence, the genes to which they owed their origin would have no precedence in the next generation. These genes would be just as easily diluted as becoming the objects of natural selection. This is not so with man. Man has some degree of conscious control of his immediate environment, and his skills are determined by socialization, training and education, not by natural selection.

A machine, on the other hand, is the product of human imagination. It is produced, within a certain type of economic system, for a more-or-less limited purpose. The machine will often work at less than full efficiency, but often, at some point, full efficiency will be required. This is because the production of a machine with super-fluous capacity or powers is unlikely in an economic system, such as capitalism, which is constrained by costs, or scarcity of materials. The only non-accidental excess capacity which comes to mind is that which would be built in to deal with unforeseen demands on the machine. For example, the size of a computer memory-bank may be extended by a certain margin to deal with such unforeseen demands on its capacity. However, in general, the differences between the potential and realized powers of the machine will be much less than those between potential labour-power and performed labour.

This amounts, once again, to the statement that human beings are more versatile than machines or animals. With their given potential, animals and machines can perform only a limited number of tasks.

We must note, in passing, that our statement that human beings often work below their potential may lead to the retort that humans, unlike animals or machines, are not 'exploited'. This remark, how-ever, would follow from just one meaning of the latter word: the sense of 'using-up' or 'utilizing'. The contention that capitalism is an exploitative system, examined below, follows from a different, but common alternative, meaning of the word.

Agents of possession

We now come to a third difference between capital goods and labour-power. It is simple, but of great significance. It relates, strictly, to a capitalist mode of production, where both capital goods, and labour-power, can be privately owned by individuals. Each 'factor', in this system, has a relationship with an individual owner. Unlike capital goods, however, labour and labour-power are linked, inseparably, to the original possessor of that labour-power. More exactly, when the worker hires his or her labour-power for a given amount of time, this worker remains with the labour-power, and the activity of labouring, in the workplace. In contrast, the owner of a capital good can engage in other activities, at some distance from the workplace, whilst his or her capital is set to work for the reward of its owner.

Clearly, under capitalism, workers are not slaves. The latter are continuously *owned* by their masters. The sale of labour-power under capitalism is not a permanent sale; it is for a specified period of time. At the end of that time the capitalist has no rights over the worker. The selling of labour-power, therefore, is more akin to the *hiring* of a machine, etc., rather than an outright sale. This distinction is maintained in modern parlance: we talk of a worker being *hired,* of *hired* hands, etc. Thus we may say that the worker keeps *possession* of his or her labour-power even though it is being hired out to a capitalist.

In earlier chapters we defined the *possessing agent* as one who has the legal right to own and hire or sell property, including his or her labour-power. The key difference between the property of labour-power, on the one hand, and capital goods on the other, is that *labour-power remains united with its possessing agent.* (This point, surprisingly, is made by Marshall in his *Principles,* 1920, p. 471; without discussion of all the implications, however.) It is our third distinction between 'labour' and 'capital', applying to capitalism.

The production of labour-power

A final, crucial, distinction between labour-power and capital goods, under a capitalist system, is that in general *labour-power is not produced under capitalist conditions.* The production and reproduction of labour-power under such conditions is impossible, *by virtue of the nature of capitalism itself.* If human beings (i.e. labour-power) were produced under capitalist conditions (i.e. for a profit) and sold on the market, then they would not be wage-earners, they would be slaves. The system *would not be capitalism*: it would be slavery. Workers would have no choice as to their employer, and they, themselves, would not possess their labour-power. Under slavery it is possible for labour-power to become a commodity i.e. it is possible for slaves to be reared and sold on the market. But in that case labour-power is *sold,* not *hired,* and the owner of labour-power is not the slave himself.

Under capitalism, labour-power is a commodity. But it is a commodity of a very special kind. It is hired on the market, not sold. And it is not wholly or intentionally *produced for hire*; it is produced for a complex of reasons, most of them unrelated to the calculus of profit and loss; and it is not produced by a capitalist firm. Considerations such as these have led some theorists to declare that labour-power is not a commodity. This, of course, depends on a narrow definition of the word commodity (i.e. something *intentionally produced* for sale or hire on the market) which excludes labour-power. We choose to retain a broader definition (i.e. a commodity is a good or service sold or hired on the market). Whilst the statement that labour-power is a commodity is by no means sufficient to define capitalism (it is also necessary to emphasize, in particular, that the workers do not own the means of production) our definition of 'commodity' is useful to emphasize a key difference between capitalism and simple commodity production. With the latter there is no market for labour-power, whereas, under capitalism, this market has a crucial role.

Let us trace the production of labour-power in a little more detail. The initial stages of human development take place, traditionally, within the family. None of these (childbirth, child-rearing, and socialization within the family) takes place under strictly capitalist conditions. The family may utilize goods or services from elsewhere which are hired or sold on the market (the services of a private midwife, food and clothing for the child, etc.). But none of these is utilized for the production of profit within the home: *the child is not sold* on the market. This initial stage produces not only labour-power, but also, when the child acquires legal rights, a *possessing agent* is produced.

A second stage could be defined to include schooling, and other forms of education and training. These can take place in either state-funded or private institutions. Clearly in the case of state-funded institutions, financed out of taxation, education does not operate on the basis of financial profit and loss: educational services are not produced for sale on the market—they are not *marketed,* to use the modern term. This is different, of course, in the case of private educational institutions, where educational services are marketed for a fee. But these educational institutions, public or private, produce *educational services,* they do not produce labour-power, as they do not have the resulting educated labour-power in their possession. In short, therefore, the production of educated labour-power is not the object of capitalist production, although it may take place within capitalist production relations.

Similar considerations would apply to apprentices who acquire certain skills through training provided by the capitalist firm by which they are employed. In general, the firm does not end up as having this trained labour-power in its possession. However, the apprentice may contract with the firm to stay in its employment for a minimum term after training. However, this is really the extended hire of labour-power which is going to undergo a process of training and transformation during that period of hire. The apprentice is not *sold*. This fact creates a problem for capitalism. From the point of view of the firm there are clear advantages in having trained, rather than untrained, labour-power in its employment. However, if the firm undertakes to apprentice and train some of its workers, then it cannot guarantee, precisely because labour-power is hired rather than sold to the firm, that the trained personnel will remain in its employment. The firm could spend a great deal of money on training and then find that the workers leave to go elsewhere. This gives the *individual* capitalist a disincentive to train his workforce, despite the fact that such training would be in the interests of capital in general. This point was made by Marshall (1920, p. 470) but he did not recognize that the problem arises from capitalist relations of production, not production in general.

As we noted above, many workers will acquire skills simply through the process of work itself, i.e. 'learning by doing'. The production of this labour-power of enlarged potential is clearly not the object of capitalist production, even if it takes place within the heartland of capitalist production itself. At capitalism's core, the sphere of production, there are processes going on, such as this, which are not *directly* regulated by the processes of capitalism.

In conclusion, therefore, we may conclude that the production of labour-power within capitalism is not, and cannot be, the object of capitalist production. However, as we shall elaborate in later chapters, the process of production of labour-power is affected, even dominated, by capitalist social relations. The production of labour-power nestles on an island within a capitalist sea, and the island, although buffeted, cannot be entirely invaded by the sea without negating the nature of capitalism itself. Capitalism, whilst being *generalized commodity production,* cannot *generalize to the limit* without accomplishing its dissolution. Capitalist production cannot conquer all.

Consequently, the family and the state are crucial to the production of labour-power within capitalism. Capitalism *depends* upon these forms, whilst at the same time the family and the state are dependent on the products of capitalist production. The complex articulation of these spheres, in particular the family and capitalist production, has been an object of study and debate in recent years. (One of the best studies of the issue is Himmelweit and Mohun, 1977. See also Humphries, 1977, and Beneria, 1979.)

Some implications

It has already been noted that the difference between the potential labour-power of human beings and their hired labour-power has a consequence for the theory of relative wages. Wage payments are not made on the basis of potential labour-power, but on the basis of hired labour-power or performed labour. We can reinforce this point by adding that the production of potential or hired labour-power is not the object of capitalist production. In other words, training experiences are not the singular objects of capitalist production relations. In contrast, the production of hired and potential labour-power takes place within the household and educational institutions. To a great extent it is unregulated, unquantified and spontaneous. It is not a direct part of the cash nexus. For these reasons, the production of labour-power cannot be reduced to a common set of 'socially necessary' costs. The lack of complete penetration by the market mechanism in this sphere, and the lack of an alternative, generalized, mechanism of regulation, means precisely this: we cannot determine the general cost of production of labour-power, other than by taking an *ex post* 'average' of existing conditions. In a very real sense the cost of production of labour-power is relatively unaffected by market forces, and this invalidates the orthodox Marxian (e.g. Roncaglia, 1974), and neoclassical, approaches to the theory of both relative and absolute wages.

This is not meant to be a dismissal of all attempts to construct such a theory. In one sense it is a confirmation of Marx, who talks of a 'historical and moral element' (Marx, 1976, p. 275) in the determination of wages. In another sense it contradicts Marx in his attempt to deduce 'abstract labour' from the manifest exchange-value of commodities. According to Marx, exchange-value depends on socially necessary labour, including the socially necessary labour in the production of labour-power itself. For reasons discussed above, it is difficult to give a meaning to 'socially necessary labour' in the case of the production of labour-power. It is not regulated, completely and directly, by the capitalist market. This difficulty is not recognized in the formal attempts of Roncaglia (1974), Rowthorn (1980) and others to 'reduce' skilled to unskilled labour. Such attempts assume that each form of skilled labour has a determinate cost of production.

Sraffa and the non-capitalist household

We have noted already that the issue in this chapter has a relationship with an aspect of the Sraffa system. We can elaborate on this here. In general the price of a commodity is formed as follows:

[costs of production (in price terms) of commodity]
x (1 + profit rate) = [price of commodity]

This equation generates the set of basic equations, for all the industries involved, in the Sraffa system. In contrast, for the production of the commodity labour-power, assuming that the workers do not save, we have the following:

[price of real wage] = [wage]

The profit-rate does not appear. (This issue has been discussed already in chapter 6.) Also the term on the left-hand side, i.e. the price of the commodities consumed by the workers, is not, as we have argued, the 'cost of production' of labour-power. In part, this was recognized in Sraffa with his brief but misleading designation of part of the real wage as a 'surplus': we shall not adopt this terminology here (see Sraffa, 1960, pp. 9–10).

The first set of n equations, relating to the n industries in the economy, are sufficient to determine the normal Sraffian equations which relate prices, wages and the rate of profit, and to generate the wage–profit frontier. The wage appears as an element of cost in the term on the left-hand side. Imagine, for a moment, that labour-power was produced under capitalist conditions. Then we would have the following (impossible) formulation:

[cost of production of labour-power] x (1 + profit rate) = ['wage']

Strictly, we should have 'price of labour' instead of wages. This term will enter the n equations for the other industries in the system. (The 'labour industry' would be the $n+1$th industry in this impossible system.) As a consequence the rate of profit will enter into the determination of the wage. In principle there will be no difference between the labour industry and any other industry. And just as some industries can have a product whose price goes up as the rate of profit increases, so too can the 'wage' increase if the rate of profit goes up. However, this positive correlation between wages and the rate of profit is possible only because the rate of profit has entered into the sphere of production of labour-power itself. In the real capitalist world this cannot occur. In most cases, at constant technology, wages will fall if the rate of profit increases. This is an implication of the fact that labour-power is not produced under capitalist conditions.

Some conclusions

We may summarize four qualities which, under capitalism, distinguish labour-power from capital goods:

(1) labour-power is endowed with consciousness, and labour is an intentional activity;
(2) labour-power has a degree of versatility exceeding that of working machines and animals;
(3) labour-power, unlike capital goods, cannot be separated from its possessing agent;
(4) labour-power is not, and cannot, itself be produced under capitalist conditions.

Not only do these qualities distinguish labour-power from other commodities, but also they define the common element between the various sorts of concrete labour (heterogeneous labour) in the system. The four qualities both distinguish and unite labour-power. We have indicated that the existence of such common qualities (particularly explicit are (1) and (2)) is recognized in Marx, and would seem to have some connection with his notion of abstract labour. On the other hand, the complete orthodox Marxian definition and conception of abstract labour is not acceptable. It is tempting to redefine abstract labour in terms of the four common qualities above. (This is done in the glossary of this work.)

An important consequence of the discussion in this chapter is that, as a result of the common qualities, it is possible to speak of the workers as a *social class*. Without the specification of these qualities it would be more difficult to regard all workers as belonging to a single class, as groups of them would be performing quite different tasks, for different wages. However, the four common qualities are necessary, but they are certainly not sufficient, to define the category of working class. Having deduced the 'abstract' qualities of labour-power it is also necessary to state that the working class lives by the sale of its labour-power. Other considerations, such as those explored by Wright (1978) may also apply.

With the concept of class it is feasible to discuss and evaluate the *exploitation of that class* by another. This is a central theme of a later chapter.

CHAPTER 17

PRODUCTION UNDER CAPITALIST CONDITIONS

Just as the commodity itself is a unity formed of use-value and value, so the process of production must be a unity, composed of the labour process and the process of creating value.

KARL MARX, *Capital*, vol. 1, ch. 7

In aim, and to some degree in content, this chapter is similar to the seventh chapter of the first volume of *Capital*, entitled 'The labour process and the valorization process'. In our account, however, the labour theory of value is absent. That does not mean that the commodity labour-power does not play a crucial role.

The plan of this present chapter is as follows. We shall start from the neoclassical 'black-box' view of production, which treats the production process in a mechanistic and asocial manner. From this we can proceed to make some remarks about production in general. Capitalist relations of production are discussed specifically at the next stage, when we come to set out, in outline, the preconditions for the capitalist production process. Then follows a number of comments on these preconditions, which deal with some points of controversy. In all, the treatment of the subject is a little sketchy here, as an adequate treatment would deserve a book on its own. Our account can be usefully supplemented by a critical re-reading of parts 3–5 of volume 1 of *Capital*, from which many of the ideas in this present chapter are derived.

The black-box view of production

The view of production in the neoclassical textbooks, and in other writings, is of an automatic and mechanical conversion of inputs, such as different types of labour and capital, into an output. This has a number of misleading implications, which must be discussed here. This view of production, which we shall call the black-box view, is epitomized by the neoclassical production function (both in aggregated and disaggregated form). With this theoretical device, which obscures at least as much as it reveals, production is treated as an asocial or naturalistic process in which inputs are mysteriously converted into an output.

It must be noted, however, that the black-box view of production is also found elsewhere. It finds an expression, for example, in a popular view held both by right-wing politicians and some Marxists, that an increase in profits must, of necessity, involve a reduction of wages. Such a view regards output as *given,* for a given set of inputs.

It is possible that a similar criticism could be levelled against the Sraffa model in which there are fixed input and output coefficients. It is certainly true that the model can be regarded as a complex 'black box'. However, this conception is not built in to Sraffa's model, and it would be wrong to claim that it must necessarily be interpreted in this way. First, the model is simply a 'snapshot' view of the production of commodities, and it does not deal with dynamic relations over time. Second, there is no reason, as Steedman (1977) has pointed out, that the Sraffa model cannot be extended to deal with some key dynamic elements in the labour process.

For neoclassical theory, the implications of the black-box view are crucial. The first such implication is to regard production as an automatic and 'passive' process. In contrast, in the neoclassical paradigm, consumption, taking place in the hallowed sphere of the household, is an 'active' process, resulting from the exercise of discrimination and *choice.* The individual, in expressing his or her 'preferences' is, therefore, the active and predominant element in the system as a whole. This alleged difference between production and consumption in much neoclassical writing is the true source of the mistaken view of 'consumer sovereignty' (see Mini, 1974, pp. 275–6). Other criticisms of this view, however, have concentrated on different aspects of the system, e.g. oligopoly, uncertainty, etc., implying that the consumer *would* be sovereign under a market system of perfect competition and knowledge. Once the relation of the notion of consumer sovereignty to the black-box view of production is understood, it can be seen that the critique of this notion can be extended to all types of capitalist market.

The second implication of the black-box view of production also has diverse consequences. If output is regarded as an automatic consequence of given inputs then it is possible to construct a functional relationship between the quantity of output and the input quantities. With this functional relationship variations of output are seen as the mechanical result of different input provisions: a certain increase in labour-power employed gives rise to a certain, corresponding, increase in net output, for example. With such direct relationships between inputs and *net* output it is possible to see input quantities, or functions of them, as *causally responsible* for *shares* in net output. This is precisely what is done in the neoclassical theory of distribution, developed by J. B. Clark: 'a workman leaves the mill, carrying his pay in his pocket . . . before he leaves the mill he is the rightful owner of a part of the wealth that the day's industry has brought forth' (Clark, 1899, p. 8), and echoed by M. Friedman: 'Given a reasonable approximation to competitive conditions, it is argued, marginal productivity theory shows that each man gets what he produces' (Friedman, 1962, p. 196). In such accounts of production and distribution, the notion of causal responsibility of marginal inputs for marginal outputs is associated with a theory of *property*: the *owner* of an input has a corresponding *claim,* it is believed, on a *share* of the produced output. This has been described by Ellerman as the 'pie-shares' view (Ellerman, 1978).

This pie-shares view is not absent from orthodox Marxism. Here it is held that past or present labour is causally responsible for the entire output. Whilst, as we shall see below, there is some substance in this view, certain misinterpretations are possible. It is not the case, for example, that labour is alone causally responsible for the *value* of the output, as has been already made clear. Second, different types of causality have to be distinguished. For if causality is interpreted in a physical sense there are clearly *other* physical causes of output, other than labour, e.g. electrical power, used in production. The substance of the view of labour as causally responsible for output, as we shall see, is found precisely by escaping from the black-box conception of the production process which highlights physical causes alone.

Production as such

In the above-mentioned chapter from *Capital,* Marx distinguishes from the labour process as such, and the labour process under commodity-producing and capitalist conditions. His notion of the labour process in general is made clear in the following passage:

The labour process, as we have just presented it in its simple and abstract elements, is purposeful activity aimed at the production of use-values. It is an appropriation of what exists in nature for the requirements of man. It is the universal condition for the metabolic interaction between man and nature, the everlasting nature-imposed condition of human existence, and

*it is therefore independent of every form of that existence, or rather it is
common to all forms of society in which human beings live* (Marx, 1976,
p. 290).

As Marx shows, it is possible to discuss the preconditions of production in general, without regard to the type of human society
involved. First it must be made clear that in this context the fruits of
nature which do not involve human labour, are not regarded as the
results of *production*. Production is, *in this context,* an interaction
between purposeful human beings and their natural environment. We
may set out the *general preconditions* of such production as follows:

(1)   intentional human activity;
(2)   relevant technical knowledge;
(3)   instruments of production (i.e. tools, power sources, etc.);
(4)   object of work (i.e. materials to be transformed into the pro-
      duct, or, in the case of a good *or* service, object or recipient of
      productive activity).

In the first precondition, above, a distinction is made between intentional (or purposeful), and unintentional, human activity. Neither
the waste products of the human body, nor, necessarily, footprints in
the snow, are objects of production. All these are not necessarily
intentional products of human activity.

This emphasis on intentional human activity, and the implied
notion of human consciousness, leads us to the view that the process
of production cannot be regarded as an entirely causal process in the
physical sense. Involving, as it does, human intentions, production is
both *teleological* and causal. The black-box view does not embrace
the teleological nature of human productive activity. Production is,
on the one hand, teleological and goal-directed, on the other hand it
relies on technology and the forces of nature. In production, physical
causality and teleology are entwined. This entwining of causal means
and teleological ends is, according to Colletti, 'the secret and key to
historical materialism' (1972, p. 67). Lukács is also noted for his
emphasis on the teleological element in human progress (see, for
example, Lukács, 1972).

In production as such it is clear that the teleological element is
embodied in human labour alone. This justifies the description of the
process of production as the *labour process,* emphasizing, at the outset, a crucial asymmetry between intentional labour and non-inten-
tional instruments of production.

However, although intent and consciousness are sufficient to begin to define production as such, the word acquires a forceful meaning in relation to *social* reality only. In particular, as we shall see, *capitalist* society gives production a narrow or precise meaning: capitalist production, even within capitalism itself, becomes a subset of production as such. We now turn to a discussion of production under capitalist conditions.

Production under capitalist conditions

At first we shall augment the four general preconditions of production as such. We have three *macro-preconditions,* seven *micro-preconditions* and three *micro-* and *macro-postconditions,* the precise meanings of these terms being described below. The following are the conditions for capitalist production:

(a) *Macro-preconditions*
  (1) Division of labour in society (see chapter 4 above).
  (2) Commodity-relations in society (see chapter 4 above).
  (3) A 'free' working class ('the free worker . . . must be free in the double sense that as a free individual he can dispose of his labour-power as his own commodity, and that, on the other hand, he has no other commodity for sale, i.e. . . . he is free of all the objects needed for the realization of his labour-power' (Marx, 1976, pp. 272–3)).

(b) *Micro-preconditions*
  (4) The capitalist firm, as a legal entity.
  (5) Instruments of production (i.e. capital goods) hired or owned by the firm.
  (6) Relevant technical knowledge in the hands of the firm.
  (7) Object of work (i.e. materials to be transformed, etc.).
  (8) The expectation, on behalf of the controlling capitalists in the firm, of future profits.
  (9) The hiring of labour-power by the firm, of relevant skills.
  (10) The performance of labour, under the direction of the firm.

(c) *Micro-postconditions*
  (11) The sale of the product on the market by the firm.
  (12) The realization of positive profits by the firm.

(d)   Macro-postcondition

> (13)   A positive surplus product (i.e. the residue of the total product, after the real wage and capital replacements are deducted, consisting of at least one commodity).

We define a macro-condition (pre- or post-) as one which is required for the economy as a whole, or at least a major part of it. A micro-condition relates to the firm only. Some firms may satisfy the micro-conditions, others may not. Only the former will engage in capitalist production. A precondition is a condition which is necessary for production to take place. A postcondition is a condition which is necessary for production to be repeated indefinitely. For example, if a firm fails to sell its product, or make a profit, then it may continue in production, but not so indefinitely. The postconditions are not necessary for production to take place, but they are necessary for it to be continued indefinitely.

It can be seen that the four general preconditions of production are embedded in the above 13 conditions of capitalist production. We may note, in passing, that simple commodity production requires only (1), (2), (5), (6), (7), (10) and (11) out of the 13.

The capitalist and manager

The role of the capitalist as an owner or part-owner of the firm is essential to *capitalist* production, but it is not essential to production in general. Ownership does not produce anything. If, in contrast, the capitalist or manager play a productive role in bringing together labour-power and instruments of production, and coordinating work itself, they are then performing a special form of labour. These tasks do not derive, necessarily, from the status of owner; other people could be *employed* to perform these tasks.

Another source of misunderstanding is the role of capitalist expectations (condition (8)). Like private ownership of the means of production, the expectation of profit is essential to production under *capitalist* conditions. As these expectations are made with regard to an uncertain future then a large element of *risk* is involved. Thus the taking of risk by capitalists is regarded as an activity essential for production, and profit is regarded as the due reward for such risk. Apart from the fact that workers take risks (see Jonsson, 1978), sometimes risking life, health and limb in the process of production, a similar sort of confusion is involved in the latter view. The confusion is between what is necessary for production under capitalist conditions and what is necessary for production as such.

The agency of production

The distinction between the activity of production in itself, i.e. the labour process, and the conditions of capitalist production, is made repeatedly by Marx. One such passage is quoted here:

> the sale and purchase of labour-power . . . presupposes that the means of production and subsistence have become autonomous objects confronting the worker, i.e. it presupposes the personification of the means of production and subsistence which, as purchasers, negotiate a contract with the workers as vendors. When we leave this process which is enacted in the market-place, in the sphere of circulation, and proceed directly to the immediate process of production, we find that it is primarily a labour process. In the labour process the worker enters as worker into a normal active relationship with the means of production determined by the nature and purpose of the work itself. He takes possession of the means of production and handles them simply as the means and materials of his work. The autonomous nature of these means of production, the way they hold fast to their independence and display a mind of their own, their separation from labour—all this is now abolished in practice (Marx, 1976, pp. 1006–7).

It is axiomatic to the radical critique of capitalist society, and, indeed, for the science of 'historical materialism' itself, that *labour*, broadly defined, is the *agency of production*, i.e. the active, social and *human* element in the process of production as such. In contrast, despite appearances to the contrary, the *ownership* of the means of production is not an agency within the sphere of production.

It can now be seen that the determination of *value*, defined either as embodied labour or in price terms, is not essential to this point. Capital goods can contribute to the value of the product but they are not active agents in the process of production, neither, necessarily, are their owners. The classical economists started with labour and the division of labour, giving part recognition to labour as the active agency, but this was supplemented and somewhat obscured by the labour theory of *value*. This red herring has diverted almost the whole of the Marxian tradition, from Marx onwards, from what can now be seen as the essential point; a point, we must emphasize, which is embedded at intervals in Marx's writing. To repeat, the essential point is this: it is labour, not 'capital' which is agency of production as such. This point is implied in the use of the term 'labour process' to describe production.

We note, in passing, that the distinction between production as such, i.e. the labour process, and the conditions of capitalist production, is rooted in the distinction between use-value (as defined in chapter 4 above, not in terms of utility) and exchange-value (or *value* as defined in chapter 14). The labour process, production-in-general, is the creation of use-values, but production under capitalist conditions is, additionally, the creation of exchange-value and the accretion of value. It would seem that the distinction between use-value and exchange-value, found in the classical economists as well as in Marx, but rejected in the neoclassical tradition, is the essential starting point of the radical political economy of capitalist society.

The nature of the firm

We now move on to a different point. As we have seen, one of the conditions of capitalist production is the existence of the firm. It is appropriate to ask what conditions, in turn, give rise to the establishment of the firm within commodity-producing society. The Marxian tradition has not given an adequate answer to this question. The best answer is found elsewhere, in the famous and seminal paper by R. H. Coase (1937). Unusually, this paper bears traces of the influence of not only marginalism and the neoclassicals, but also Keynes, and the Marxian tradition through Dobb. To some extent it stands between traditions in economic theory, but its primary influence has been upon orthodoxy.

Coase asks the question why the price mechanism does not allocate resources *within the firm* itself. With only very few exceptions the allocation of resources within the firm is not accomplished through the price mechanism but by the manager or entrepreneur:

> *Outside the firm, price movements direct production, which is coordinated through a series of exchange transactions on the market. Within a firm, these market transactions are eliminated and in place of the complicated market structure with exchange transactions is substituted the entrepreneur-coordinator, who directs production* (p. 388).

This, of course, Marx recognized, in his statement that the division of labour was present within 'every factory, but the workers do not bring about this division by exchanging their individual products' (1976, p. 132). The same point was repeated by Dobb and could possibly have influenced Coase; but it was the latter who asked why this occurred and gave a reasonable answer to the question.

Coase's answer is as follows:

The main reason why it is profitable to establish a firm would seem to be
that there is a cost of using the price mechanism. The most obvious cost of
'organizing' production through the price mechanism is that of discovering
what the relevant prices are. . . . It is true that contracts are not
eliminated when there is a firm but they are greatly reduced. A factor of
production (or the owner thereof) does not have to make a series of
contracts with the factors with whom he is cooperating within the firm, as
would be necessary, of course, if this cooperation were as a direct result of
the working of the price mechanism. For this series of contracts is
substituted one. At this stage, it is important to note the character of the
contract into which a factor enters that is employed within a firm. The
contract is one whereby the factor, for a certain remuneration (which may
be fixed or fluctuating), agrees to obey the directions of the entrepreneur
within certain limits (pp. 390–1).

Clearly, the only 'factor' which is *necessarily* contracted in this
way is labour. Other factors could, in principle, be owned by the
firm. In this case a contract would not be required. Labour-power, in
contrast, cannot be owned by the firm. It can only be hired for a
period of time. To *own* labour-power is to own a slave. Coase does
not make this distinction between labour-power and other 'factors'
clear, but he does insist that *limits* to the powers of the entrepreneur
must exist. A contract without such limits would be, according to
Coase 'voluntary slavery', and according to a cited authority 'void
and unenforceable'. Later in the same article, Coase again gives
labour specific mention, emphasizing the fact that the employer, or
his agents, have control, within limits, of the type of work performed.

Coase's paper explains, in part, *why the labour process is not*
regulated within the capitalist firm by the mechanism of the market.
This mechanism is cumbersome and costly within this sphere. Marx's
conceptual distinction between the labour process and the process of
capitalist production is reinforced, in reality, by the practical failure
of the market mechanism to regulate the labour process.

At one point in his article, however, when dealing critically with
an alternative view which emphasizes the role of uncertainty, Coase
almost throws out the baby with the bathwater. The result is that
Coase does not give adequate emphasis to imperfect knowledge and
uncertainty. Perhaps this facilitates the marginalist approach to be
found within the paper. What is clear, however, is that uncertainty is
a necessary condition for the rise of the firm. If there were no uncertainty, then there would be no 'cost of using the price mechanism'
or of 'discovering what the relevant prices are'. We have already made

the point that uncertainty is a feature of all feasible market economies. This, with the existence of a 'free' labour force, gives rise to the firm.

The employment contract

In the above-cited conditions of capitalist production a distinction has been made between labour and labour-power. The paper by Coase, and another by H. A. Simon (1951), are relevant to this distinction. Before the connection is made clear, however, we must note frequent assertions, in recent years, that the distinction between labour and labour-power has no relevance and meaning. One unfortunate example is found in an otherwise illuminating paper by Steedman (1979). Steedman argues that in hiring his or her *labour-power* the worker is making a (legally enforcible) promise of *future labour*. Thus the distinction is of no usefulness in economic theory.

It certainly does not clinch the argument, but it is worth saying, that for Marx the distinction between labour and labour-power was essential to the theoretical structure of *Capital* and to the critique of classical political economy:

> *Instead of* labour, *Ricardo should have discussed labour-*power. *But had he done so,* capital *would also have been revealed as the material conditions of labour, confronting the labourer as power that had acquired an independent existence and capital would at once have been revealed as a* definite social relationship (Marx, 1969, p. 400).

It need hardly be said, but a quotation, even from Marx, does not necessarily prove a case. I believe that an adequate reply to the modern conflation of labour and labour-power cannot be constructed out of quotations from Marx. (It would be preferable and easier if it could.) Such a reply should draw from the famous paper by the semi-marginalist Coase, and a less well known paper by Simon.

Without making acknowledgement to Coase, and 14 years afterwards, Simon repeats some of the themes of the former's paper and places them in a more rigorous framework. Simon opens with a clear statement of the case he is to attack:

> *In traditional economic theory employees . . . enter into the system in two sharply distinct roles. Initially, they are owners of a factor of production (their own labour) which they sell for a definite price. Having done so, they become completely passive factors of production employed by the*

*entrepreneur in such a way to maximize his profit. This view of viewing
the employment contract and the management of labour involves a very
high order of abstraction–such a high order, in fact, as to leave out of
account the most striking empirical facts of the situation as we observe it
in the real world. In particular, it abstracts away the most obvious
peculiarities of the employment contract, those which distinguish it from
other kinds of contracts; and ignores the most significant features of the
administrative process, i.e., the process of actually managing the factors of
production, including labour* (Simon, 1951, p. 293).

Simon then proceeds to define the concept of authority and to
examine the nature of the employment contract. The employment
contract is seen to differ 'fundamentally from a sales contract–the
kind of contract that is assumed in ordinary formulations of price
theory'. In the sales contract a 'completely specified commodity' is
exchanged for a specific sum of money. In contrast, in the employment contract, Simon points out that the worker agrees to work in
several possible ways, and allows his or her employer to select which
particular way he or she is to work. The worker agrees to accept the
authority of the employer, and allows this person to choose which
work is to be performed (from a mutually agreed set of possible
patterns of work, performed at different rates, levels of accuracy,
etc.) in return for a specified wage.

With use of a formal model, Simon shows the precise conditions in
which an employment contract, rather than a sales contract, will be
negotiated between capitalist and worker. Translated into everyday
language, Simon shows that, on the one hand, the worker will agree
to an employment contract if he or she is relatively indifferent as to
which of the possible patterns of work the employer decides to
select. On the other hand, the capitalist will negotiate a higher wage
than that which pertains in a sales contract, if he or she is uncertain
as to which precise pattern of work is to be performed. In other
words, in the face of uncertainty, the capitalist will pay a higher
wage for the privilege of postponing the precise specification of the
pattern of work to be performed. It can be concluded, therefore,
that the existence of *uncertainty* is one of the reasons for the selection of an employment contract.

Changing market conditions outside the firm, changing size of the
workforce, changing level of output, changing organization of labour
at the point of production, changing technology and work methods,
and changing skills on behalf of the workforce, these, and others,
require changes in the patterns of work. All these changes are ex-

tremely difficult to predict. Thus they would justify a preference, on behalf of management, of an employment contract rather than a sales contract. (However, according to Marglin (1974) there are other historical reasons for the imposition of an employment contract, in particular the need for capital to assert authority and discipline over the workforce.)

Even piece-work is an employment contract rather than a sales contract. Unlike the worker who is paid by the hour, the piece-worker is paid by the quantity of output. However, he or she is not under a sales contract simply to produce a specified output. The worker is still under the authority of the employer, and management can still often play a part in regulating the pace and methods of work. For example, management may insist that the work is done according to certain methods in order to reduce waste of raw materials, or to ensure a higher quality of output. The fact that the authority of management is rendered, to some degree, superfluous under piece-work, and workers prefer under this system to be left to do things in their own way, makes piece-work a marginal and special form of the employment contract.

Labour and labour-power

The hiring of labour-power by the worker is not, therefore, a contract to perform a specific activity. The actual pattern of work to be performed by the worker is not known at the time of making the contract. All that is known is the set of possible patterns of work; and this set, quite often, is vaguely defined. Even if the set were to be defined with precision, however, the future activity of work at the point of production is *uncertain* in many respects. Furthermore, in making the contract of employment the worker agrees, within limits, to accept the authority of the employer, allowing management to decide, *in the future,* what, precisely, is to be done at work.

It can be seen, therefore, that Simon's analysis sustains the distinction between labour and labour-power. In addition it illuminates the role of uncertainty in the hiring of labour-power and the performance of labour, and helps clarify why the employer retains authority over the worker in production. Indeed, if the distinction between labour-power and labour did not, in fact, exist, then it is hard to see why managerial authority is preserved. Instead of the battalion of foremen, supervisors, personnel managers and managing directors, we could anticipate a platoon of inspectors of the quantity and quality of output, and an army of lawyers to dispute or preserve each letter of the contract. This, in fact, is not the case. Marx was right to insist that one of the characteristics of production under capitalist conditions is 'the worker works under the control of the capitalist' (1976, p. 291).

In addition, Marx makes a significant distinction between what he calls variable and constant capital. Although his definition of these terms is not always clear, and often 'variable capital' is used to describe the wages paid to the worker, most often it means the worker's labour-power. We shall retain the latter definition here. This is done because the word 'variable' encapsulates an essential feature of labour-power, under an employment contract, which does not apply to capital goods, which are under a sales contract. The utilization of labour-power is both *uncertain* and *variable*. This point does not seem to be widely appreciated. An intelligent exception is Rowthorn, who clarifies the issue, but without making reference to Simon's work:

> *By calling labour-power 'variable' capital, Marx established a conceptual connection between the creation of surplus-value and the despotic nature of the capitalist production process. The surplus-value created by workers in this process is not determined simply by the means of consumption needed to sustain them, but also by the amount and intensity of the labour they are compelled to perform. By increasing the amount or intensity of labour his workers perform, the individual capitalist is able to . . .* vary *the amount of surplus-value his workers create. Thus, the term 'variable' draws attention to the fact that the surplus-value actually created varies according to the relative power of the combatants within the production process* (Rowthorn, 1974, p. 87; 1980, p. 45).

Although Rowthorn still insists, in the above article, on viewing the whole thing through the spectacles of the labour theory of value, his discussion of variable capital makes important sense, especially if surplus value is defined in the terms of this book. In this way, in addition, we can regard the *value of* variable capital as, quite simply, the *money wage*.

Rowthorn's study has drawn attention to the dominance of the capitalist over the labourer in the process of production. It is important to make clear, however, that the capitalist dominates the pattern of work *within limits*. Although the capitalist may use all sorts of threats and sanctions against the worker, and the worker may have no alternative employment or source of income, in principle the employment contract is *voluntary*, and the powers of coercion are limited. If this were not the case it would not be a contract of employment, and the worker would become a serf or a slave. It would be wrong to insist that the rights and freedoms of the worker are abolished entirely within the sphere of capitalist production; although, of course, the sphere of capitalist production is authoritarian and hierarchical: unlike the 'very Eden' of the capitalist market.

It is beyond the scope of this present work to discuss all the ways in which, in order to maximize profits, the capitalist tries to dominate and intensify the performance of labour, subject to the constraints, or limits, of the employment contract. For example, the capitalist will attempt to increase the intensity of work by reducing lapses of time between successive operations, or to increase the care with which raw materials or fixed capital are used, so as to avoid waste and unnecessary damage.

It is also beyond the scope of this work to discuss the various ways in which the workers resist the intensification of labour, even within the limits of the employment contract, or may relax their vigilance in controlling quality when possible, in order to relieve themselves from sustained, high-intensity work.

The neglect of these issues in this book does not mean that they are not regarded as important. It is more to do with the fact that an adequate treatment of the labour process requires extended discussion of *concrete* situations. (For an example of an excellent study of the labour process in modern capitalism see Braverman (1974) and for a good case study of the motor car industry see Friedman (1977).)

Further remarks on the variability of labour

In recent years there have been moves within mainstream economics to incorporate the essential variability of the labour performed in the capitalist labour process. One of the most notable of these attempts is by Leibenstein (1976) with his concept of 'X-inefficiency'. Leibenstein recognizes the variable element in labour but sees the variation as resulting from vaguely specified 'motivational' factors, drawing no distinction between the motives of manager and worker, and paying little attention to the real labour process. Leibenstein compares actual labour performed with a more-or-less arbitrary standard of what would be performed if all the elements of X-inefficiency were absent. The fact that the labour process is *dominated* by the capitalist, who attempts to impose the pace and efficiency of work upon the worker, is ignored. (For other criticisms of Leibenstein see Loasby, 1976.)

Leibenstein's work is an inadequate attempt to understand and draw out the implications of the variability of labour. The concrete issue should be of increasing concern to all economists. We are faced with such facts as the motor car worker in the United States being *five times* as productive as his or her colleague in Britain, and even with similar plant and equipment the difference in productivity in certain comparative industries is 50 per cent (Caves and Krause, 1980, pp. 137, 194). The black-box view of production cannot explain such phenomena. In the search for theoretical explanations, and with the distinction between labour and labour-power, Marxian analysis should be at an advantage.

However, the distinction between labour and labour-power does not encapsulate all aspects of the struggle between capital and labour. Strictly speaking, the struggle over the variable pattern of labour performed is post-contractual, i.e. it lies within the bounds of the agreed contract. Other, pre-contractual, struggles are also extremely important, i.e. struggles over the terms of the contract itself. Pre-contractual struggles would include, of course, the fixing of the level of the wage, the length of the working day, the timing and extension of meal-breaks, and so on. Once again, the fact that these have not been discussed does not mean that they are not important. It is more to do with the fact that they do not relate to the distinction between labour-power, and the variable element labour, which we have sought to emphasize. Pre-contractual struggles do not vary labour performed *directly*; they impinge instead on the terms of hiring of labour-power.

In practice, however, the distinction between pre- and post-contractual struggles is obscured because the labour contract is frequently renegotiated during the period of production itself. As new techniques and new demands are imposed on the workers they respond by clarifying, and often changing, the terms of the contract. It is often in the interests of the capitalist to keep the contract of employment vague, and workers often have the choice of either responding in the above manner or accepting a deterioration of conditions of work.

The realization of profit

In the textbook models of production, where inputs of factors of production lead to the production of a homogeneous, physical output, such as corn, and a quick shift is made to the distribution of that product, a crucial step is ignored. This step is the sale of the product on the market under uncertain conditions, with the outcome of an uncertain realized price or quantity sold. Marx recognized this point (but expressed it misleadingly in labour theory of value terms) when he wrote of the *salto mortale*: the 'death leap' taken by the commodity from the sphere of production to the market (1976, p. 200). In this leap, the capitalist stands to make an immediate gain, or an immediate loss, compared to his or her expected level of profit. The outcome is essentially uncertain. In contrast, the worker does not bear an immediate gain or loss, according to the outcome of the *salto mortale*. Wages are contracted *prior* to the sale of the commodity. Actual profits are realized at the point of sale, they are the final outcome of the process.

Capital goods, to a large degree, are fixed and non-variable (i.e. fixed capital); but profit is not. In contrast, labour is variable but post-contractual wages are awarded according to a fixed formula. To anyone accustomed to thinking in terms of the classical, long-run, stationary state, or neoclassical general equilibrium, these propositions may come as a bit of a shock. Steady-state and general equilibrium models impose a strict, determinate, magnitude on prices and profits. The analysis in chapters 14 and 15 should undermine this view. Prices and profits depend on elements, such as uncertainty and liquidity preference, which cannot be appreciated in long-run, stationary state, or Walrasian general equilibrium, terms. A grasp of the variable character of profits, contrasted with fixed wages and variable labour, would appear to be essential to an adequate explanation of the process of the accumulation of capital. There are further notes on this point in chapter 19.

Unproductive labour

It is with some reluctance that we open the hornet's nest and discuss the difficult distinction between productive and unproductive labour. However, the distinction that has been drawn between production as such and production under capitalist conditions forces us to include a brief discussion of this point. The classic summary of Marx's position on productive and unproductive labour is by Gough (1972). It is made clear in Gough's work that, for Marx, labour is productive under capitalism if it produces a marketed use-value, and therefore, in the terms of this present work, produces surplus-value. However, it is also clear that Marx excludes 'workers in the sphere of circulation', e.g. commercial workers, salesmen, advertising agents, etc., from the category of productive labour. It is probable that these workers are excluded because, in Marx's view, they are not part of production as such, i.e. they do not produce use-values. Marx is thus excluding the labour of those who work to preserve, or work simply as a result of the existence of, capitalist relations of production, without producing use-values.

A number of criticisms can be made of this formulation. Two in particular are relevant here. First, Marx does not give adequate recognition to the role of those who process and supply information to producers and consumers. For this reason certain forms of advertising, and the activities of certain people in the distributive process, should be regarded as productive. Information, we contend, is a use-value.

Second, in making a distinction between marketed and non-marketed output within capitalism, Marx is focusing on the role of profit and the reproduction of the capital—labour relation. However, this is not the same thing as making a distinction between production as such, and production under capitalist conditions. By bringing the production of use-values into the picture as a central criterion, it seems that a confusion is being made. The choice is either to focus on the distinction between marketed and non-marketed output, or to focus on the distinction between the production of use-values and other forms of work within capitalism.

The following are examples of work within capitalism which do not produce use-values: financial speculation, the activities of insurance agents, many activities of the police and army, and the work of lawyers and tax consultants. It is not suggested that such work is unnecessary: it *may* be required in other economic systems as well as capitalism. It is simply suggested that such work simply preserves, or results from the existence of, specific social or property relations.

Within the sphere of production we follow Marx in making a distinction between work which is directly productive of use-values, including such work of the managers which coordinates production, supplies technical information, and so on, on the one hand; and work which simply involves the exercise of authority over the worker on the other. The latter does not produce use-values.

A significant proportion of the work done by teachers, psychological counsellors, nurses and doctors is productive of use-values, in the form of the labour-power of pupils, clients or patients. Housework is productive of use-values. So too is the labour of transport workers, because the use-value of a good in one place is not the same as in any other.

The work 'unproductive' has derogatory overtones. From a radical perspective it would seem preferable, if the word is to be used at all, that it were assigned to those activities which do not produce use-values, rather than those which do not produce surplus value. The disadvantage in this definition is that it is sometimes extremely difficult to draw a precise line between a use-value and a non-use-value. However, in essence, this distinction is essential to Marxian and post-Marxian political economy, and it relates, directly, to the distinctions between use-value and exchange-value, and production as such and production under capitalist conditions.

The above distinction is not without practical, as well as theoretical, applications. If the activities of a sector of the economy resulted simply from the existence of certain social relations, then the growth of this sector would be expected to be non-autonomous and largely a reflection of growth in the use-value producing sector. In an interesting analysis of data from advanced capitalist countries, Driver has shown that this happens with the commercial sector, whereas the manufacturing sector *initiates* the growth in the economy (Driver, 1980, p. 13). With a slightly different argument from that above, Driver concludes that most of the activities of the commercial sector are unproductive.

Conclusion

The above analysis has been somewhat sketchy, due to the broadness and complexity of the subject-matter, and the limited purpose of this present work. We may conclude, however, by emphasizing some of the important conclusions.

It should be clear that the black-box view of production found in neoclassical and other textbooks is unacceptable. This is for several reasons. First, production, involving intentional labour is teleological as well as causal in the physical–mechanical sense. Second, even with a fixed input of labour-power, it is in the nature of the employment contract that the pattern of labour performed is *variable*. Third, even with a fixed output the *value* of that output is never entirely certain and can be varied by market conditions, in terms of the price or the quantity sold.

This rejection of the black-box view has a number of consequences including the common view that production is the passive economic sphere whilst consumption is the active area: where 'choice' is made. The rejection of this view undermines the notion that the consumer is 'sovereign' in the market economy.

Another important consequence is as follows. If given inputs, i.e. labour-power and capital goods, can give rise to a variable and unpredictable quantity and value of output then there is no basis for the view that the provision of a certain input, in a certain quantity, has a determinate effect on output. This, surely, must undermine the whole of the marginalist theory of distribution. Second, there is no basis for the *marginalist theory of individual property,* which asserts, in the manner of Clark, Friedman and many others, that the provision of an input gives rise to a certain *definite* claim on a *share* of the output, i.e. the 'pie-shares' view.

Our discussion of the labour process under capitalism, whilst being abstract, has emphasized the effect of uncertainty in determining both the boundaries of the firm and the extent of the contract of employment. In addition the role of the authority of the employer, and possible resistance to that authority by the worker, has been noted. An important distinction between pre-contractual and post-contractual struggles between workers and management has been drawn.

Finally, using Marx's distinction between the general process of production of use-values, and the social relations surrounding this in a particular, capitalist, society, it has been asserted that labour is the only human and social agency within production itself. Capital goods may be important, but in the process of work itself they play a passive role: they do not act, they are acted upon. In contrast, in the sphere of exchange, capital and money appear to have an active and animated role. This point is clearly of relevance to the notion of exploitation, and it will be discussed further in the next chapter. We do not, however, make it the exclusive basis for a theory of exploitation, and we draw upon many of the other points above.

CHAPTER 18

EXPLOITATION

[E]mployers and workmen may be, in the eyes of the law, equal parties in a civil contract; but they are never equal parties in fact. The worker, under contract, is bound to serve his employer; the employer is entitled to order the workman about. The relation between them is thus essentially unequal.

G. D. H. COLE, *British Trade Unionism Today*

In the economics of orthodox Marxism the existence of exploitation under capitalism is assumed. In neoclassical economics it is assumed away. The former doctrine declares or defines labour as the source of all value, and thus espies profit as the fruit of exploited labour. The latter regards competitive market equilibrium as the best of all possible worlds; thus a world where exploitation does not exist. In this book, both such approaches are rejected, and we try to give a different substance to the notion of exploitation.

The chapter begins with a critique of the liberal—bourgeois view that exploitation disappears in a competitive market economy. We then move on to show that the concept of exploitation has several facets, and it is not simple and uni-dimensional. Finally exploitation is defined, and the question of its measure is discussed.

The neoclassical symmetry

Being based on many ideas of classical liberalism, neoclassical economics regards production and distribution as symmetrical between factors. If, for simplicity of exposition, we exclude land, then the neoclassicals see two 'factors of production'—capital and labour. Each of these two factors is privately owned. The owner of capital sells or hires his or her capital to the firm. The owner of labour hires out his or her labour. The two factors of production are brought into the firm and production takes place. An output is produced and it is sold. According to the neoclassical argument, the net revenue is then distributed between the two owners according to the principle of

202

marginal productivity: in a perfectly competitive economy, in equilibrium, the rewards given to the owners of capital and labour will be equal to their respective marginal revenue products. Each one, therefore, in the words of Milton Friedman, 'gets what he produces'. There is a perfect symmetry between the factors of production in this respect at least.

For Marx, however, there is no such symmetry: it is denied throughout *Capital*. In particular, the asymmetry is made clear in the distinction between labour and labour-power. Additional and related differences between labour and capital goods have been discussed in chapter 16 above. Let us focus here on the crucial distinction discovered by Marx.

Could symmetry be restored by making a distinction between the *capacity* of capital goods to produce services in production, and the *activity* or service provided in production? For ease of exposition we could call these 'machine-power' and 'machine-services' respectively. This distinction would precisely parallel the distinction between labour-power, i.e. the capacity to work, and labour, i.e. the activity of work. Symmetry, then, would appear to be restored.

However, the process by which machine-services are exuded from machine-power is not the same as the process by which labour is exuded from labour-power. The former process will not be thwarted by obstructions from within the machine itself unless there is some mechanical breakdown in the functioning of the machine. As long as the machine is in working order there is no reason why it cannot exude machine-services. The link, therefore, between machine-power and machine-services is merely a mechanical–causal one.

On the other hand, a worker can hire out his or her labour-power, and turn up at the firm as a fit and able individual, but the precise pattern of labour cannot, as yet, be determined. The worker is subject to the control of the capitalist, within the terms and limits of the contract of employment. The precise pattern of work will depend on the dynamics of resistance and control within the firm, the methods employed by management, the capacity of the worker to moderate that control, and so on. The exudation of labour from labour-power is not a mechanical–causal but a *social* process. The manager does not conflict in this way with the machine: it is a passive instrument. In contrast, workers and capitalists have an active relationship, involving the clash of different purposes and intentions.

If we possess machine-power and the machine is sound, then, as long as labour is provided as well, there is no reason why the machine cannot exude machine-services. In contrast, the hiring of labour-power does not predetermine the pattern of labour. The distinction between labour and labour-power remains vital, unlike the distinction between machine-services and machine-power. The symmetry of the neoclassical view is denied by an examination of the real process of capitalist production.

Wages, profits and property

In the liberal and neoclassical view the justification of distributive rewards, such as wages and profits, is based on the ownership of property. The provision by a person of his or her property, including possibly labour-power, gives that person a claim on the value of the output, depending, of course, on the productive characteristics of that property.

The distinction between labour and labour-power poses a problem for this normative theory of distribution. A factor of production under a sales contract, such as a machine, can be hired or appropriated. The contract ensures that the factor will be provided with its required services. Upon that basis a reward for the provision of the factor will be claimed. It is different for the contract of employment. The worker agrees to work, but to an *imperfectly specified* pattern. The mere provision of the object of property, i.e. labour-power, is not sufficient. The worker has to submit to the authority of the employer in production as well, and the required pattern of work has to be performed.

Labour-power can be hired, i.e. appropriated for a period of time, but *labour* cannot. Labour is an activity, and it cannot be the object of a property relation. It is in the nature of the employment contract that the pattern of work depends on the ongoing relationship between worker and employer, *after* the contract of employment is agreed. Labour, therefore, is never specifically hired or owned by the capitalist.

A recognition of these facts of capitalist production leads to a contradiction in the liberal–neoclassical view. According to the latter, the distribution of the product is carried out on the basis of ownership of factors of production. Yet in production the worker provides something which cannot be owned or appropriated; but is necessary for production to take place. The worker does not merely provide an appropriable object. The worker accepts the authority of the capitalist and performs an amount of labour imperfectly specified in the contract. In contrast, the owner of capital receives a reward for providing an appropriable object *only.* The view found in neoclassical economics, and classical liberalism, is logically unsound, at least when it is applied to capitalist production.

There can be no 'fair' or 'equal' distribution of the social product based on capitalist private ownership of the means of production. The only way in which this could be constructed would be by transforming the employment contract into a sales contract. This would, in practice, mean the abolition of production upon capitalist lines. The working class would, in effect, be self-employed. Labour-power, strictly speaking, would cease to become a commodity and the workers would be offering specific services instead. This would no longer be capitalism. Capitalism, according to its own criteria, cannot be completely 'fair' without abolishing itself.

The black-box view again

Liberal and neoclassical theories of distribution are, in part, based on two premises. First, the provision of a factor of production by its owner gives that owner a right to claim a part of the output which results, in some way, from the provision of that factor in the sphere of production. Second, the provision of a factor in the sphere of production has a definite and predictable effect on output.

The second premise is necessary to develop a consistent rule, such as 'marginal productivity', so that the first premise can be applied in practice. It has already been shown, above, that the mere provision of all required factors is not sufficient for production to take place: labour must be *performed* under the authority of the capitalist. A second line of criticism involves an attack on the 'black-box' view of production which is implied in the second premise. This attack is made in the previous chapter and we need not repeat it here. It was concluded there that neither the quantity of output nor its value was an automatic result of the mere provision of factors of production, and that labour, in particular, was a variable element. The variability of labour depends a great deal on the relationship of forces between capital and labour within the workplace.

The upshot of a rejection of the black-box view of production is that liberal–neoclassical theories of distribution cannot be sustained. *There is no way of ascribing a change in the value of output, or a change in its quantity, to a definite variation in the input of a factor.* Although such variations are likely to have an effect, this effect is not definite, and does not result automatically from the quantity and type of factors provided. The black-box view neglects the relationships and activities within production itself, and it is these which are crucial, as well as the provided factors, in determining the level of output.

Pre-contractual exploitation

We now move on to a reconstruction of the notion of exploitation, as applied to different facets of the capitalist system. A primary distinction is made between pre-contractual and post-contractual exploitation. The former applies, of course, to influences and relationships which bear upon capitalist and worker before the employment contract is agreed, and can influence that contract to the disadvantage of one or the other.

The notion of pre-contractual exploitation is found, implicitly, in the work of many economists, including Adam Smith. In chapter 8 of *The Wealth of Nations,* Smith discusses the determinants of the wage level, and points out several factors which influence the contract between employee and employer, usually in favour of the latter and to the detriment of the former. For example, 'the masters, being fewer in number, can combine more easily', whilst, at that time the combination of workers, i.e. trade unions, was illegal. Also, Smith points out that if the workers withdraw their labour, in an attempt to renegotiate the labour contract more in their favour, then the employers have greater resources with which to survive the strike. In contrast, 'many workmen could not subsist a week ... without employment'. Smith concludes that in general employers have the advantage in the hiring of labour.

Although, with the rise of the modern trade union, Smith's particular views as to the power of the working class would have to be modified, his general idea is still applicable. The general idea is that if the two parties which negotiate a contract have different costs and benefits in making the contract then one party can be at a disadvantage. Smith's idea could apply to the power of the modern capitalist monopoly, or bureaucratically administered state involvement in the economy. An *individual* has little power in relation to such bodies when negotiating a contract.

In particular, trade unions have an important countervailing influence on the employment contract. An individual worker, in a non-unionized firm, is at a disadvantage compared with another worker in a unionized firm. The reason for this is expressed neatly by M. W. Reder (1959):

as an employer usually employs many wage earners, each of whom works only for him, the percentage loss of income from ending an employment relation is much less to him than the worker. Consequently, in the absence of collective bargaining, the employer has more 'power' over any of his employees than they have over him.

Another example of this type of pre-contractual exploitation is found in the traditional marriage contract. Until very recently (and only within a few professions in a few advanced industrialized countries has it ceased to be the case) women have been at an economic disadvantage compared with men, in terms of wealth, average earnings, and economic discrimination. So, although both parties consent to a marriage, the man can have the balance of advantage because the woman is dependent upon him, and she would bear greater costs if she were not married. Our analysis here can apply to other contracts as well as the contract of employment, therefore.

We need to be more precise in our definition of this type of exploitation. We adopt Chamberlain's (1951) measure of bargaining power. Consider two parties, A and B, negotiating a contract. The bargaining power of A is, by definition,

$$\frac{\text{Cost to B of disagreement with A's terms}}{\text{Cost to B of agreement on A's terms}}$$

and the bargaining power of B is, on the same basis,

$$\frac{\text{Cost to A of disagreement with B's terms}}{\text{Cost to A of agreement on B's terms}}$$

Although this measure may sometimes be difficult to apply in practice, partly due to the difficulty of reckoning 'costs', it does give a convenient indication of relative bargaining strength, in relation to the terms of a given contract. Such a contract is here defined as *exploitative* if its terms are such that the bargaining strengths are unequal. This type of exploitation we shall call *bargaining exploitation.*

A less simplistic approach would abandon the attempt to compute costs, and examine the relative strengths of A and B in terms of general power relations. Perhaps the most fruitful approach would be to adopt Lukes' (1974) definition of multi-dimensional power. This includes the power that a party has to set the 'agenda' of decision-making, and to dominate or control the process of bargaining. Of course, it is the radical view, which we cannot elaborate in detail here, that the working class is subordinate in these terms. The capitalists have much greater influence on the media, the political process, etc., and thus dominate the process of bargaining.

Post-contractual exploitation: first dimension

We now turn to exploitation which relates to the employment contract in particular, and has reference to the role of the worker in the sphere of production.

The first dimension to such exploitation derives from a special quality, possessed by labour, which was discussed in chapter 16 above. Unlike other factors of production, labour cannot be disassociated physically from its possessing agent. In contrast, the capitalist is free to go elsewhere whilst his capital is utilized in the sphere of production.

There are a number of effects which result from this asymmetry. First, the worker, as a person, is robbed of his or her *time*. A contractor may hire out a machine but does not lose his or her time whilst the machine is being used. The worker, on the other hand, loses his or her time, as a possessing agent, as labour is being performed. The capitalist, having the benefit of greater time, can search out market information, negotiate new contracts, etc., thus obtaining a greater advantage in the pre-contractual bargaining process. This form of exploitation thus feeds back and reinforces pre-contractual exploitation.

Second, in being physically present within the sphere of production, the worker risks injury, disease, or even loss of life, if the working environment is not completely safe. In contrast, the capitalist, as an owner of capital, does not have to enter the sphere of production and is not subjected to such risks. Ever since Engels wrote his *Conditions of the Working Class in England in 1844* there has been an alarming documentation of the hazards of work, alleviated only partially by modern legislation and safer work practices.

Third, this peculiar feature of labour helps make it *less mobile* than capital. The worker's labour is confined, for practical reasons, to an area close to the worker's place of residence. In contrast, the capital owned by the capitalist can move quite literally round the world whilst its owner sits in an armchair. The capitalist can thus find the best possible rate of profit on his capital, without much inconvenience. The worker, however, must often tear up domestic roots, breaking ties of friendship and kinship, in order to find the best possible employment.

The one possible advantage that the worker can gain from this feature of labour, is a *net* enjoyment or satisfaction resulting from being present and involved in work itself. The joy of work must then be greater than the boredom, discomfort and tedium involved. This is very unlikely in most lines of employment; the exceptions being the highly rewarding and creative jobs of artists, writers, etc. The majority of professions are not in this class, even in advanced capitalist society, and this is not likely to change under this system in the near future. It would be even more unlikely that a positive net satisfaction would overwhelm the three negative features that result from this peculiar quality of labour. The exploitation that results cannot easily be compensated or eradicated. We shall call post-contractual exploitation of the first dimension *corporeal exploitation.*

Post-contractual exploitation: second dimension

We have shown that the worker is pre-contractually disadvantaged in the bargaining process, and, in addition, the worker suffers a disadvantage from being inseparable from his or her labour. The third aspect to the worker's exploitation is that within the sphere of production the worker is *dominated* by the authority of his or her employer. The worker is subjected to an authoritarian regime, after leaving the relatively equal and voluntary sphere of the market. After having exercised 'free choice' the worker is deprived of all sovereignty and subjected to the will of another.

It may be argued, however, that this deprivation of sovereignty is part of the explicit contract of employment and, therefore, endorsed by the worker in agreeing to that contract. In reply to this argument it must first be noted that although the agreement of the worker to the contract is technically voluntary, the worker has little choice but to be employed by someone, somewhere. The alternative is poverty or even starvation. In the last century in Europe, and in many countries today, fear of hunger is the force which pushes the worker to accept the authority of the capitalist. Rodbertus pointed this out most clearly: 'Thus, although the contract of labourer and employer has taken the place of slavery, the contract is only formally and not actually free, and hunger makes a good substitute for the whip' (Quoted in Böhm-Bawerk, 1970, p. 332). Although hunger does not enforce its will so dramatically within the modern welfare state, the effect of poverty, and loss of earnings and status, is very great.

Second, it is usually the case that the contract of employment is *imperfectly specified,* so the worker is not told in advance what precise pattern of work will be performed, or even the entire set of possible patterns of work which the employer may ask the worker to perform. In other words, the *limits* to the authority of the employer, as governed by the contract, may be unstated or stated unclearly. If this happens the worker will be subjected to an authority without clearly agreed limits to its power, and defiance of that authority would run the risk of arbitrary dismissal.

Third, the preference of the worker to be free of such authority at work can, to some extent, be measured within the existing system, with distribution and other factors remaining constant, by simply asking workers if they would prefer to have greater control of their working lives, and a clearer specification of their contract of employment. It is apparent, in many countries, that the resistance to such measures comes from employers rather than employees, and the voluntary nature of the present system of authority has to be qualified somewhat. Although there are often practical difficulties in the way, workers will frequently attempt to limit the authority of their employer. Trade unions are very important in this respect. Apart from the collective negotiation of wages, trade unions have an important role in checking the authority of the employer at work, and campaigning for a clear and more favourable contract of employment for the worker.

The other main method of limiting the authority of an employer is to cease to become employed and set up an independent business, as a self-employed worker or as a new employer. Although, for economic reasons, it is very difficult for most workers to take such a route, there is evidence that the desire 'to be your own boss' is widespread, even if it is clear that a higher income would not result. Such evidence again supports the view that the subjection of the worker to the authority of the capitalist is voluntary in a very limited sense only.

The above type of exploitation we shall call *authority exploitation.*

Post-contractual exploitation: third dimension

What is involved in establishing this particular dimension of exploitation is the adoption of one or two views of production, one of which, as we have argued above, is untenable.

The first view of production, held by the neoclassicals, is that output is the automatic result of the provision, or more generously the utilization, of different factors, in combination, within the firm. Each factor is as 'active' as another in the process, although, of course, the marginal productivity of each factor may vary. This view has already been criticized in this work, in a number of respects.

The second view of production was, in more or less rudimentary form, held by Petty, Locke, Smith and Ricardo. It was, to a great extent, clarified by Marx. It is also found in Keynes, who writes in the General Theory:

> *It is much preferable to speak of capital as having a yield over the course of its life in excess of its original cost, than as being* productive. . . . *I sympathise, therefore, with the pre-classical doctrine that everything is* produced *by* labour. . . . *It is preferable to regard labour, including of course the personal services of the entrepreneur and his assistants, as the sole factor of production, operating in a given environment of technique, natural resources, capital equipment and effective demand* (Keynes, 1936, pp. 213–14).

What is being asserted in this present work is similar to the above, but is different in its origin and sustaining argument. What is being asserted here is that labour is the active agency in production. This involves a Marxian view of production as a *labour process,* abstracted from the particular social relations in which it takes place. It is *not* being suggested that labour alone is productive of value, nor even that labour alone is productive of wealth; for capital goods can add to the value of the output, and nature can provide use-values, i.e. wealth. What *is* being suggested is that production, by definition, is a *human* activity which, in its most abstract form, depends upon human labour within the environment of nature. It is not a *naturalistic* activity in which human labour and other resources have an equivalent status. Human labour is the subject, not an object, of production.

Although real processes of production have to be considered in the context of a real socioeconomic system, with specific social relations, these social relations do not actually produce. They may ensure a more or less optimum allocation of resources, according to the relevant criteria. They may ensure the performance of a large amount of intense and efficient labour. However, they do not engage in production themselves. Under capitalism, for example, private ownership of the means of production may lead to a tremendous expansion of industry and output, but it does not itself *actively produce* anything. Capitalist property relations have functioned in such a way as to lead to a large output, but it is human labour, not social relations, which have actually produced that output. Note that this is not the same thing as suggesting that private ownership of the means of production can be dispensed with, or that it is inferior to another arrangement (although socialists will make precisely these arguments). No judgement is made as to the viability of alternatives to capitalism, or to the superiority of capitalism itself, at this stage. What is involved is a non-naturalistic view of production.

Let us use an example. In nature, bees gather nectar and create a form of honey. We could say 'produce a form of honey' but that would mean using 'production' in a naturalistic and non-human sense. If a bee-keeper is involved in maintaining the hive, and gathering the honey, then it is the bee-keeper, not the bee, that is the active human agency of production. And if the hive is owned by a second person who pays the wages of the bee-keeper, then that arrangement may help to ensure that the bee-keeper works on a regular and disciplined basis, but that arrangement does not, itself, produce anything.

It is the Marxian standpoint which is the most consistent and forceful in the above respect because it gives full recognition to the fact that private property is a *man-made,* not a *natural,* institution. In putting man at the centre of social science, as distinguished from nature, a number of things are achieved. First, for reasons we have discussed at several points in this work, the science finds its essential foundation. Second, social relations are seen as man-made and social, rather than natural in character. And finally, production is seen to be a *human* process in which labour, broadly defined, is the active agency.

We must distinguish, however, between the labour of the foreman or manager which is simply involved in giving instructions to the workforce, and labour which is necessary, in the abstract, for production to take place. Included in the latter is not only the labour of the manual worker, but also those who played a part in the rearing and education of that worker, those who supply information to the worker which is necessary for production itself, and those who co-ordinate the process of production.

We can now see the basis for this dimension to exploitation. *Exploitation exists in this sense if a class obtains a part of the product of collective labour purely on the basis of their ownership or control of the means of production.* We shall call this *class exploitation,* because it involves the appropriation of products of the labour process, in which the workers are the active agents, by another class. No theory of value is involved here. The working class is *collectively* responsible for the entire product. It is not necessary to attribute *value* to individual products.

Other modes of production

Before we return to exploitation under capitalism, and deal with some outstanding questions. We shall examine the relevance or otherwise of the four types of exploitation discussed above to other modes of production. The following modes of production will be discussed in brief: slavery, feudalism, simple commodity production, sovietism (i.e. the USSR, Eastern Europe, etc.), and socialism.

Under slavery it is clear that corporeal, authority, and class exploitation exist. The slave is exploited in all these ways. However, the slave does not have the legal right to make a contract, and therefore, the distinction between pre- and post-contractual exploitation, which applies to capitalism, breaks down. Also there is no such thing as bargaining exploitation *for the slave*; that is limited to the non-labouring classes.

Bargaining exploitation is *generally* limited under feudalism because *all individuals* have limited contractual rights. Also the feudal serf is allowed more autonomy in the sphere of production than the slave or the worker under capitalism. Direct and continuous supervision of the serf is not necessary, because for a part of the time the serfs work for themselves, and for the other part they work for a form of rent. Only when the rent was in the form of labour-services was authority exploitation the rule. Otherwise, authority exploitation was minimized. However, clear corporeal and class exploitation exist under feudalism.

Under simple commodity production, i.e. a society of self-employed workers, bargaining exploitation can exist in relation to the marriage contract and other contracts. However, it is not possible to own means of production other than for the use of the owner. Thus the accumulation of vast quantities of wealth in the hands of a minority is not possible. Bargaining exploitation, therefore, has practical limits. Under this system neither class nor authority exploitation exist; but corporeal exploitation is present.

It is not possible here to give a full analysis of soviet society. What follows is possibly a controversial statement. Within sovietism there are few contracts outside the labour contract. As this contract is between the individual and the state, and the state is not run on very democratic lines, bargaining exploitation exists. Corporeal exploitation is also present, along with authority exploitation. However, class exploitation would exist only if the system was class-divided, and the bureaucracy constituted a class. Even some critics of the Soviet Union, such as Leon Trotsky, do not hold this view; but there is a theory, developed by Max Shachtman and others, that the bureaucracy is such a class.

Like all the above systems, corporeal exploitation will exist under socialism, at least until the stage that the bulk of production is auto-

	CATEGORIES OF EXPLOITATION			
	Bargaining	*Corporeal*	*Authority*	*Class*
Slavery	Limited to non-labour-ing classes	Present	Present	Present
Feudalism	Generally limited	Present	Limited or absent	Present
Simple commodity production	Practically limited	Present	Absent	Absent
Capitalism	Present	Present	Present	Present
Sovietism	Present	Present	Present	Present if bureaucracy is a class
Socialism	Limited	Present	Limited	Absent

Figure 18.1
Exploitation in different modes of production

mated. Bargaining exploitation will be limited by a more equal distribution of wealth and power. Authority exploitation will be limited
by the extension of workers' control in production. Class exploitation will not exist, because incomes will not be derived from ownership or control of the means of production.

These results, along with the data for capitalism, are presented in
figure 18.1. It can be seen from this figure that corporeal exploitation is present in all the above modes of production. It must be
pointed out, however, that in modern industrial society, with the
development of sophisticated machines, at least the possibility of a
drastic reduction of this type of exploitation exists. Under slavery,
such exploitation was intense, and even under simple commodity
production it would exist to a large degree, because large-scale
mechanization is inhibited.

We have not discussed cooperative ownership of the means of
production because this is likely to exist only within a social formation dominated by a different mode of production. Cooperatives
under capitalism or sovietism usually have a degree of authority
exploitation in production. Under socialism such exploitation would
more likely be limited. Unless a maximum size was fixed for the co-

operative, then it could also subject smaller firms or individuals to bargaining exploitation.

It must be pointed out, in addition, that we have not discussed exploitation *between nations*. The above theory cannot easily be generalized to relate to all aspects of imperialism and colonialism because the theory applies to production only. Additional categories of exploitation would have to cover the subjection of a nation by force, or the seizure of its assets, in the absence of a supra-national state authority. If we are concerned with capitalist imperialism, then the term *extra-contractual exploitation* would be applicable to such phenomena. However, the category of bargaining exploitation could readily be applied to post-colonial capitalist imperialism. I refer to the asymmetry of bargaining powers and interests between a rich and a poor capitalist nation. In the modern capitalist world this asymmetry shows no sign of disappearing, and the rich nations use their superior powers to the disadvantage of the poor.

The measurement of class exploitation

In orthodox Marxian economics, the rate of exploitation is defined as a ratio between the amount of labour embodied in the surplus product, and the amount of labour embodied in the real wage received by the working class. No serious problem results from abandoning the labour-embodied measure of exploitation. In fact serious problems exist if it is retained. First, no-one has ever successfully computed such a rate of exploitation in a real economy, as far as this author is aware. Second, the precise social meaning of such a rate, if it were computed, would not be clear in the light of our previous discussion of the ambiguity of the category of embodied labour.

In class societies other than capitalism, class exploitation can be recognized in the surplus product that accrues to the class that owns or controls the means of production. Under capitalism there is no reason why this surplus product cannot be measured in terms of its value, i.e. in terms of equilibrium price. The rate of class exploitation could then be defined as, for example, the share of profits, interest and rent in total income. I simply do not understand why so much objection to measuring class exploitation in money terms is made by orthodox Marxists. First, all such statements of exploitation-rates in the literature are either directly or indirectly in price terms. Second, money is, after all, the universal material representative of wealth under capitalism and it is, therefore, *more meaningful* to calculate rates of exploitation in price terms. In contrast, socially necessary labour time is simply an *ex post* calculation, and the widespread view that it focuses on the labour process is without foundation.

In any case, as we have shown, exploitation is a complex and multi-dimensional phenomenon, and although one particular type of exploitation, class exploitation, has a homogeneous measure under capitalism, this does not mean that such a measure can encapsulate either that form of exploitation, or exploitation in the richest and widest sense.

Final remarks

It is the fourth type of exploitation, class exploitation, which would, arguably, be regarded as the most important by socialists and radicals. This type of exploitation relates to social classes, not individuals. It depends upon the existence of a class-divided society, and a surplus product; but no theory of *value* is involved, and it does not matter, crucially, how the surplus product is *measured*.

This is in contrast to the discussion of exploitation in the work of Morishima and Catephores (1978). In this and other similar works the approach is to generate a set of positive 'values' for each commodity, applying this to an economic system with positive prices and profits, and then declaring, triumphantly, that positive profits are related to positive surplus 'value'. As long as the surplus product, profits, and the contrived 'values' are all positive this must, by assumption, be the case. It is little more than a tautology.

This so-called 'fundamental Marxian theorem' tells us very little about the real social relations involved. The contrived 'values' bear no relation to real, operational magnitudes in the economy. Like the neoclassical notion of utility they are *imposed* upon reality. They are not abstracted from an analysis of real processes and relations. In contrast, in this work, an attempt has been made to uncover such relations and processes, and thereby give substance to the notion of exploitation.

It is not suggested that a complete analysis of exploitation is provided here. In particular, the process of *production* and *reproduction* of exploitative *relations* has not been analysed. Such an analysis would involve, in part, the theory of distribution, and this is beyond the scope of this work. It is the social relations themselves that have been stressed here. In particular, it must be noted, class exploitation cannot be ameliorated by purely redistributive measures. Instead, social relations must be *transformed*.

CHAPTER 19

NOTES ON CAPITAL ACCUMULATION

Accumulate, accumulate! That is Moses and the prophets! ... Therefore save, save, i.e. reconvert the greatest possible portion of the surplus-value or surplus product into capital! Accumulation for the sake of accumulation, production for the sake of production ...

KARL MARX, Capital, vol. 1

It is impossible, in one chapter, to give a full account of the issues relating to the accumulation of capital. However, there are a few implications which can be drawn out of the foregoing parts of this work, and some outstanding issues which require clarification. We deal with these in little more than note form, as it is beyond the scope of this work to give a complete picture.

Profits as a mark-up

It should be clear from chapter 17 that profits cannot be regarded as a *residual* element. That is, profits are not the simple result of a process which consists of deducting wages and other costs from revenue. This view is based on the assumption that output and prices are fixed *before* profits, and it must be rejected if the process of capitalist production is seriously considered. The consequences of this are, quite simply, as follows: a reduction in wages will not necessarily lead to an increase in profits, and a rise in wages will not necessarily lead to a fall in profits. To determine the respective outcomes, changes in productivity and market conditions, amongst other things, will have to be considered.

A number of policy implications flow from the above. First, profitability cannot be restored simply by restricting or lowering wages in a capitalist economy. As Keynes pointed out, the reduction of wages is more likely to lead to a reduction in demand, a contraction in output, and a consequent fall in profits. Second, 'profits squeeze' theories of modern capitalist crisis, for example Glyn and Sutcliffe (1972), have to be severely qualified or even rejected. The

difficulty in such theories is that they underestimate possible increases in output, and thereby profits, through increases in productivity. Huge productivity differentials in different advanced capitalist
countries support the view that wages are less significant in determining the level, share, or rate of profits.

It is more plausible to follow Kalecki and regard profits as a *mark-
up* on costs. Rejecting the 'pie-shares' and 'black-box' viewpoints,
and recognizing that production is controlled and dominated by the
owners of capital who retain ownership of the product from the
sphere of production to the market, gives us a basis for seeing profits
in this light. Of course, there are restrictions on the ability of firms
to raise profits by increasing the mark-up on an individual product.
One of the most important is the degree of competition and the
firm's control over the market. If competition is fierce then a *unit*
mark-up will be restricted, and the firm will have to resort to an increase in productivity and a lowering of costs to survive.

For the firm, the rate of profit can be increased by raising the unit
mark-up, or by increasing productivity, or both. The former depends
upon the firm's control of the market or 'degree of monopoly' as
Kalecki put it. The latter variable depends upon access to new technology and the firm's control over the process of production. The
firm can also raise the rate of profit by lowering money wages. However, this requires a pre-contractual struggle, before production, and
it may defeat its own object by lowering productivity. It is more
plausible for the firm to adopt the other strategies: increased mark-
up or increased productivity. Although such attempts to confront
workers by lowering wages have occurred, such as in the 1920s in
Britain, the strategy does not often lead to success for the firm.
These factors help to explain the 'stickiness' of wages emphasized in
the literature of Keynes and his followers.

The conception of profit as a mark-up can be easily accommodated
in a Sraffian price theory. The approach developed in chapter 6
above was called a 'cost of production plus profit' theory for precisely this reason; and at first the mark-up profit-rates were not
assumed to be uniform, so as to show that a mark-up approach was
plausible even if the rate of profit was not equalized.

The 'degree of monopoly'

It is important to note that the profit mark-up is not rigidly determined by 'the degree of monopoly'. Such a misconception of Kalecki's

approach has led to the mistaken view that what is involved is simply a tautological definition. A careful reading of Kalecki's work (1968, 1971, for example), shows that the mark-up depends on, and is a symptom of, the degree of monopoly, rather than being a direct reflection of it. When placing the profit mark-up on the cost, the firm takes into account the prices of other sellers in the industry. The price can be higher than that quoted by competitors, but not too high as to drastically reduce sales and lose markets. Neither is the price set too low as to endanger safe profit margins.

It is clear that this is an imperfectly specified model. Orthodox theorists would regard it as pertaining to 'imperfect competition'. The fact is, however, that perfect competition has never existed nor is it ever likely to exist. In the heyday of *laissez faire,* i.e. Victorian capitalism in the nineteenth century, competition was limited by the fact that a large number of markets were local. There may have been thousands of shoe-makers, as opposed to a dozen or fewer large shoe-making firms today, but the Victorian cobbler sold largely to a local market and had a limited number of competitors. Secondly, financial institutions were less centralized and the smaller firms had less access to finance capital. Consequently, it has been pointed out, the forces leading to an equalization of the rate of profit were somewhat restricted. Imperfect competition is not the exception, it is the rule for capitalism.

This point is reinforced if we consider the firm itself. As we have seen, inside the firm the forces of the market are prevented from allocating resources: they are allocated according to the authority of the management. Furthermore, the employers use their authority relationship over the workforce to determine the pattern of work and, to a large degree, the quantity and quality of output. What happens within the firm, and what is produced by the firm, is not the subject of competitive forces only. They are partly the result of *power relationships.* It would be naive to assume that power relationships are absent from the sphere of exchange as well. The orthodox 'ideal type' of perfect competition is not merely unrealistic, it is inappropriate. Elements of oligopoly and monopoly are *built in* to capitalism from the start.

Our general standpoint, therefore, is to regard prices and profits as expressions of *relations of power* between firms and individuals in the system. This approach puts less emphasis on prices as allocators of resources, because if economic power is involved they cannot accomplish this task alone. Prices retain, however, their role as distributors of money incomes to firms, and these are likewise affected by power relationships. In turn, the firm's money income influences money wages and distributed profits. The way is open to regarding the distribution of income between labour and capital as the outcome of relations of power within a social structure where capital is the dominant relation.

The general rate of profit

Both Marx and Sraffa assume that within the capitalist system there is a strong tendency for the rate of profit to be equalized between industries and firms. Marx leaves the discussion of this process out of the first volume of *Capital*. It is in the third volume that he elaborates the concept of the 'general rate of profit' and discusses the forces that tend to equalize rates of return on capital outlay. This is no accident. A discussion of this question belongs, quite properly, to a level of abstraction at which a number of critical categories and relations have been established. For this reason, strictly speaking, it is beyond the scope of this present work. It would be useful, however, to include a brief discussion of this subject.

Usually it is argued that if rates of profit are unequal then investors will shift their capital from unprofitable to profitable industries. In a competitive equilibrium a general rate of profit will be formed, i.e. an equalized rate of profit across the entire economy, and no investor will have an incentive to shift capital from one sector to another.

This argument depends upon the assumption of capital mobility, including the transfer of capital from one sector to another. It is important here to distinguish between *finance* capital and capital *goods,* such as machines. Finance capital can move into a firm by the creation of credit with a bank by the firm itself, or by the purchase of stocks or shares by an outside body. This mobility of finance capital gives a strong incentive to compare rates of return on different investments in stocks and shares, and to compare these rates of return with the rates of interest. There is a forceful argument, by Clifton (1977) and others, that the role of finance capital has been extremely important in modern international capitalism, and has created a strong tendency to equalize rates of profit. Clifton argues that despite the growth of monopoly and multinational firms, capitalism has not decreased in competitiveness since the last century.

Capital goods are much less versatile, and much less mobile, than finance capital. Given plant and machinery can sometimes be switched from the production of one commodity to another, but the choice of output will be limited. The existence of barriers to entry is also possible. A particular firm will hold a monopoly of certain skills, patents, resources etc., and be able to exclude others from the production of a particular commodity. Barriers to entry do not apply to finance capital in the same way. Even if the firm concerned was a monopoly, if financiers can buy its stocks and shares then finance capital can move into the monopoly firm.

It would seem at first sight, as Marx suggested, that finance capital acts to create a general rate of profit within capitalism. This would imply a strong relationship between the rate of profit and the rate of interest, and not necessarily with the rate of interest as the determining variable as Sraffa (1960, p. 33) has remarked. It would be more plausible to assume an interaction between the two, but with the rate of interest more dependent on the rate of profit than *vice-versa*. This would be consistent with the Marxian position that *production,* and thereby profit, is the predominant element. In any case, however, there are a number of factors which would cause rates of profit and interest to diverge. Interest and profits are paid over different periods of time and subject to different degrees of uncertainty. In general, interest-bearing assets are more liquid than stocks and shares. A single rate of interest, therefore, cannot be regarded as the basis of a general rate of profit.

In a brief article, Levine (1980) has argued that if the real nature of *fixed* capital is taken into account, rates of profit will be calculated on the basis of historic rather than replacement cost. This would suggest that if prices were changing over time, rates of profit, in firms identical in all respects except the age of their capital equipment, would be unequal. This argument led to an exchange with Roncaglia (1980), without clear or satisfactory resolution.

To resolve the question it seems essential to make a distinction between short-run and long-run competitive behaviour. In the short run, by definition, the fixed capital in different firms remains unchanged except by wear and depreciation. Finance capital moves from firm to firm and from industry to industry in search of the highest rate of return. In moving around their units of finance capital, the financier will be primarily concerned with the expected return on his or her money-capital, not the rate of profit of the *total* capital in the firm concerned. In the short run it will be this adjustment 'at the margin' which will be paramount. Hence comparisons will be made between the ratio

$$\frac{\text{Expected } extra \text{ profit}}{\textit{Increment} \text{ of available money-capital}}$$

and *not*

$$\frac{\text{Total profit in the firm}}{\text{Value of firm's advanced capital}}$$

The former ratio, not the latter, will be 'compared' with the rate of interest. Any difference between the two ratios will thwart a rapid equalization of the rate of profit, because this is defined in terms of the latter, not the former.

In the long run, however, comparisons are relevant between expected rates of profit on total capital. Complete replacement of plant and equipment bring such long-run considerations into play. This usually occurs with a change of production technique, for rarely is machinery replaced with new but identical equipment. This, in turn, questions the theoretical use of a version of the Sraffa system where techniques are fixed.

To summarize, the notion of a general rate of profit has to be qualified, at least in the short run, but there are arguments to suggest that the concept has meaning, and corresponds to real forces which tend to equalize the rates of profit in real and modern capitalist systems. As yet, the balance of argument suggests that the concept of the general rate of profit should be qualified rather than abandoned. This would allow the discussion of value-theory models with an equalized rate of profit, but also suggests that much more work should be done on the dynamics of the capitalist economy to establish the reasons for divergences from the general rate of profit in different industries and firms.

Profits and growth

From an analysis of the behaviour of the firm, Wood (1975) has developed an explanation of the level of profits. In simple terms, according to Wood, the rate of profit for the firm is that which is required to finance and accommodate economic growth:

The central principle of the present theory, therefore, is that the amount of profits which the firm sets out to earn is determined by the amount of investment that it plans to undertake. Naturally enough there are restrictions on the individual firm's desire to invest. In particular, competition from other firms limits both the rate of expansion of its sales and its ability to make profits (Wood, 1975, p. 4).

According to this theory, the profits made by the firm are determined by its plans to invest, not *vice-versa*. As Wood points out, the approach behind this theory can be detected in chapter 25 ('The General Law of Capitalist Accumulation') of vol. 1 of *Capital*. In an aggregate form, pertaining to the economy as a whole, it was developed by Kalecki, but it is absent from the neoclassical tradition.

Wood's theory follows from an analysis of the financial behaviour of firms and the short-run and long-run profit margins. It is then used to explain the share of profits in the national income. Kalecki's theory starts from the economy as a whole, but comes to strikingly similar conclusions. We shall briefly discuss the basis and development of Kalecki's theory here.

Although Kalecki published some of the main ideas of the *General Theory* in advance of Keynes, having developed these independently in Poland, his approach differs from Keynes in a number of respects (see Feiwel, 1975). First, Kalecki rejects marginalism and is more influenced by Marx than Marshall. Second, Kalecki divides economic agents into two social classes: capitalists and workers, treating their consumption and saving behaviour as different. This enables him to derive an important result connecting profits and investment.

If workers do not save then their wages are spent on consumption goods and services. Capitalists can spend their profits on either consumption or investment, or a mix of both. The money spent by the workers, although it may pass through the hands of the capitalists, returns to the workers in the form of wage payments. Workers' income is virtually a closed circular flow, without leakages. In contrast, capitalists may save, and withdraw money from circulation. What they do not save they will spend, on either consumption or investment, and this will return to the capitalist class. The money spent on consumption and investment by the capitalist class *as a whole* will return to the capitalist class *as a whole*. If money is saved by the capitalists then this will not return as income until it is eventually turned into investment or consumption expenditure. Hence, in a well-known aphorism which summarizes Kalecki's theory: *workers spend what they get and capitalists get what they spend*.

Consequently, investment expenditure will, for the capitalist class as a whole, return as income for the capitalists in the form of profit. Hence profits, after a time-lag, are determined by investment, not the other way round.

Clearly, this picture is oversimplified and must be extended from a simple model to a model with exports, imports, government expenditure and taxes. Nevertheless it is an important model in determining the relationship between profits and the accumulation of capital, and it is confirmed by Wood's more complex analysis of the firm.

A general rule can be suggested: the faster-growing and heavily-investing economies will be the more profitable capitalist economies. This can, to use Mary Kaldor's phrase, be called the law of *the survival of the fastest* (Kaldor, 1978, pp. 52–5). Or, in the words of Marx, it can give substance to his description of capital as 'self expanding value'.

If profits are determined by investment, then what determines the latter? It is here, I believe, that Keynes has the greatest insight. Investment is determined by expectations, particularly *expectations of future profits*. These expectations do not follow automatically from observed conditions, they are dependent upon guesses regarding an essentially uncertain future.

Keynes proposed that aggregate effective demand should be stimulated by government expenditure so as to encourage expectations which lead to high investment. However, although this *may* work, there is no reason why it *necessarily* should do so. If, for example, inflation is created in the economy then capitalists may be deterred from long-term investment projects even in the presence of high effective demand. Inflation may annul any optimistic expectations created by that demand.

We shall briefly return to the issue of inflation at a later stage. Another factor which influences effective demand and thereby expectations is the level of employment. We now turn to the interaction between employment, wages and economic growth.

Accumulation and employment

Assume that the capitalist economy is growing at a certain rate. As a result, there is an increasing demand for labour-power. If the rate of increase of this demand for labour-power exceeds the rate of increase of the available labour force then workers will be in an improving bargaining position and wages will be pushed up. In the absence of inflation and rapid changes in productivity, this will mean that workers will have a larger share of the real product, and less will go to capitalist consumption and investment. Profits will fall, expectations will be revised, and accumulation will slow down. As a result, the increase in employment will be reduced, and eventually overall employment may fall. The supply of available labour-power will move well in excess of demand and wages will rise slowly or fall. In turn, investment may then be stimulated and the process will repeat itself. The trend of employment growth will be the same as the growth of available labour-power.

Clearly, this model is based on restrictive assumptions, in particular an extremely simple model of expectations-formation, and a neglect of some of the effects of increases in productivity. However, it is one of the most useful models to explain the interaction between accumulation and employment. In essence, it is found in chapter 25 of the first volume of *Capital,* and it has been expressed elegantly, in a mathematical model of the trade cycle, by Goodwin (1972).

The model is used by Marx to explain aspects of the relationship between wages, profits and accumulation. The rate of accumulation affects the difference between the supply and the demand for labour, i.e. the level of unemployment. In turn, unemployment affects the wage level. Thus: 'the rate of accumulation is the independent, not the dependent variable; the rate of wages is the dependent not the independent variable' (Marx, 1976, p. 770).

This is the reverse of the Ricardian view where, implausibly, profits are seen as a residual, after wages and costs, which are independently determined, are deducted from output. Statements in this present work, which describe wages as 'fixed' or 'sticky', are not to be confused with this Ricardian view. The notion that output, and its value, can be regarded as fixed is rejected in this present work. The sense in which wages are described as sticky is *relative to profits,* and in the short run. In contrast to wages, profits can oscillate wildly from month to month, depending with sensitivity upon variations in output and sales. Wages are contracted in advance of production, and involve regular payments, which legally must be met by the employers. Wages respond only slowly to changing conditions of unemployment and inflation.

Furthermore, as well as the price of labour-power being slow to respond, there are enormous barriers to the enlargement or contraction of the quantity of labour-power supplied. Assume, for example, that an excess demand for labour-power exists. This demand can be met by extending working hours or by bringing more people on to the labour market. There are clear social and physical limits to the extent of overtime working. The labour force can be enlarged by moving peasants off their land, by employing female or child labour, by immigration, or by an increase in the birth rate. These depend upon political, social, cultural, biological and other considerations. The supply of labour-power, therefore, will not readily increase when an excess demand for labour-power exists on the market.

When labour-power is in excess supply, wages will not quickly adjust in response. Even if they did, the reduction in wages may be perceived as a reduction in demand and employment and investment may be reduced as a consequence. The quantity adjustment is even more problematic; women and children may be able to withdraw themselves from the labour market because they can be supported by the family, but whole families of peasants cannot go back to the land, nor immigrants so easily cross the sea. The supply of labour-power can only be reduced within limits, short of famine or war, if it is in excess relative to demand.

Other commodities are quite different. Their price will adjust more readily to excess demand or excess supply. An excess demand for bread will pull up its price, and signal to the producers that more bread should be supplied. In pursuit of extra sales and profit, more bread will be manufactured. If bread is in excess supply, then less will be produced.

Not so with labour-power. It is not produced under capitalist conditions. Its supply does not readily adjust via the mechanism of the market. Other factors determine its supply. It would appear that this is one of the most significant properties of labour-power within a capitalist society: its supply is not smoothly, wholly, or mainly regulated by the market mechanism.

The above discussion has a great deal to do with Marx's conception of unemployment as a 'reserve army'. Quite early on in his writing, Marx seems to have drawn the kernel of truth from Malthus' theory of population: that the supply of people does not relate proportionally or directly to economic conditions. He uses this to show the deficiency of the market mechanism with respect to the commodity labour-power:

When political economy claims that demand and supply always balance each other, it immediately forgets that according to its own claim (theory of population) the supply of people always exceeds the demand, and that, therefore, in the essential result of the whole production process—the existence of man—the disparity between demand and supply gets its most striking expression (Marx, 1964, p. 155).

Keynes read very little of Marx, and significantly more of Malthus. It was in the latter that he found a precedent for his theory of effective demand: 'in the later phase of Malthus the notion of the insufficiency of effective demand takes a definite place as a scientific explanation of unemployment' (Keynes, 1936, p. 362). It was unfortunate that Keynes did not incorporate the Marxian notion of

mode of production, and the Marxian emphasis on the social relations of production. If he had done so, he would have been able to
explain, even more clearly than he did, that chronic unemployment
is a condition of the capitalist system; a system which reduces almost
everything to a commodity, but which cannot produce labour-power
under its own conditions, on pain of self-destruction. Capitalism
produces *by* the people, it is a system *of* the people, it dominates
over people, and it makes profit and value *via* the people. But it cannot, itself, produce people. Instead it produces mass unemployment.

Inflation and accumulation

Money in its modern form, i.e. token and credit money, etc., has one
important thing in common with labour-power. It too is not produced under capitalist conditions. It is produced directly by, or its
production is controlled by, the state. There are important consequences for the theory of accumulation and inflation.

As Keynes and Marx both showed, a capitalist economy can
remain with a large level of unemployment, without an automatic
tendency to move back towards full employment. If there is an
excess supply of labour-power then there must, by Walras' Law, be
an excess demand for other commodities: either goods and services,
or money, or a combination of these. We shall briefly consider two
cases: *first*, when goods and services are generally in excess supply, as
well as labour-power, and money is in excess demand; and *second*,
when goods and services are generally in excess demand, unlike
labour-power, money being in either excess demand or excess supply.
Both cases are being considered in conjunction with widespread unemployment.

The first case is a classic crisis of overproduction. The aggregate
supply of labour-power, goods and services exceeds their aggregate
demand. The Keynesian remedy to a crisis of this type, as in the
Depression of the 1930s, was to pump up aggregate effective demand.
This could have been achieved by the remedies of extended public
works, higher unemployment benefits, greater government expenditure, etc. It is generally held that such measures will push up the
supply of money. Logically, in any case, according to Walras' Law, an
excess supply of non-money commodities must be matched by an
excess demand for money, and as the excess supply is reduced, so
too must the excess demand for money. The actual mechanism involved is more complex. It should be clear, however, that as money
does not take the form of gold in a modern capitalist system, its

increased production does not stimulate demand by expanding employment in the sector of the economy concerned with increasing credit and token money. Effective demand increases *via* the route of capitalist expectations under these Keynesian policies. Government intervention is responsible for a small increase in demand, but the explicit objective is to stimulate the *private* sector. The hope is that the small increase in demand created by the government will 'pump prime' the system, raise capitalist expectations, and cause capitalists to take advantage of the increased availability of money. This money is then expressed as augmented demand for labour-power, goods and services. With their hopes raised, capitalists expand production and effective demand is increased, cumulatively, to full employment. The Keynesian solution to a crisis of overproduction depends, crucially, upon this uplift in capitalist expectations. If the uplift does not occur then the remedy will not work.

Given that the supply of labour-power is not adjusted primarily through the market mechanism, it is likely that Keynesian policies will, at first, bring an excess demand for goods and services rather than an excess demand for labour-power. This is the second case. If the government is bent on the objective of full employment then its demand-stimulating policies will continue. Inflation is likely to result, because goods and services are now in excess demand, and the government continues to pump money into the economy.

Let us summarize the argument: Keynesian policies work *via* an essential uplift of capitalist expectations. The Keynesian objective is full employment. There are two serious problems in the consistent application of this policy. First, capitalist expectations are unreliable, beyond direct control within a private enterprise system, and may require increased doses of demand-stimulation to be affected. Second, the supply of labour-power will not adjust readily to increased demand. This could create shortages of certain types of labour-power whilst other workers are unemployed. Wages could be pushed up even before full employment is reached.

When full employment *is* reached then the problems are exacerbated. Labour-power is no longer in excess supply, but the excess demand for goods and services has to be counterbalanced by the excess supply of money alone. Furthermore, workers will be in a stronger position to push up wages. The inflationary juggernaut will pick up speed.

In turn, inflation will act to depress capitalist expectations. For example, in an inflationary context, long-term investment projects will look increasingly risky, because it will be more difficult to pre-

dict future revenue and costs. The time-horizon of capitalist operations will move from the distant to the not-so-distant future. The
pace of technical progress and investment will be reduced.

As a result, a government operating Keynesian policies will have to
rely on larger and larger doses of government expenditure to stimulate the economy. In turn greater inflation will result, and if expectations are then sufficiently depressed, this inflation will be combined
with unemployment. The inflation that results from Keynesian
policies is intimately connected with corresponding problems in the
process of capital accumulation.

The partial effectiveness of Keynesian policies, for over two
decades after the Second World War, has to be recognized; but so too
do the long-term problems. The central weakness in the Keynesian
method of economic regulation is that it chases the will-o'-the-wisp
of capitalist expectations, with an initial or sustained burst of state-
induced demand. However, even real effective demand, from the
state or any other body, does not necessarily increase capitalist
expectations. Instead, it is more likely to give firms greater scope for
a profit mark-up, especially when aggregate supply lags behind
demand. And when unemployment is reduced to a certain level,
workers will have greater confidence and bargaining power to push
up wages. The consequence, as those who have lived through the
1960s and 1970s know too well, is inflation.

Recently, sophisticated theories of inflation have begun to appear
which recognize the modern conditions, and key mechanisms, in the
creation of inflation. One of the best examples is found in the work
of Rowthorn (1980). However, it must be added that inflation, in
part, is a result of the fact that money is no longer produced under
predominantly capitalist conditions, and the excess demand for
money is not quickly followed by a rise in the number of persons
employed in the production of this demanded commodity. Money,
when it is gold, produces a gold-rush; but when it is mere credit and
paper within a capitalist world, it produces inflation.

The limits to capitalism

These problems arise because money is not produced under capitalist
conditions yet is being produced for a capitalist market economy. It
was noted above that the Keynesians took the route of demand-
stimulation rather than interfering in the hallowed sphere of capitalist production. The alternative strategy to reduce unemployment
would be to intervene at the level of production and to produce an

increased output. This, however, would solve the problems of capitalism by undermining capitalist production itself. Today we have this disharmony: on the one hand most goods and services are produced under capitalist conditions and distributed *via* the capitalist market; on the other hand, money and labour-power are not produced under capitalist conditions, yet they are both central to the functioning of capitalism. The radical solution is to overcome this disharmony by moving *all* production away from the dominance of capitalist relations.

It is important to note that the state plays a central role in both the production and regulation of both labour-power and money. Public education had emerged in several advanced capitalist countries before the end of the last century. A few decades later followed the creation of the welfare state (see Gough, 1979). Both the health and the education of labour-power is a concern of the state in many of the more advanced capitalist countries. In addition, in the post Second World War period, there has been considerable state intervention in the monetary sphere. It is almost as if capital, in failing to subdue the unruly provinces of money and labour, invited the state to move in and take over. In doing this, capital visibly demonstrated its own limitations.

Furthermore, as each recession or crisis causes the smaller capitalist firms to fail whilst the larger survive, the concentration of capital proceeds apace. Fewer and fewer firms dominate the globe. We move from the large firm to the near-monopoly, from the near-monopoly to the national monopoly, and from the national monopoly to the multinational corporation. As the firm grows larger and larger it increases its own domain of production. As we have seen, however, within this domain of production resources are not allocated according to the pricing mechanism of the capitalist market. The firm itself is a domain of planning (albeit not socialist planning) within a capitalist world. The firm itself is testimony to the limits of capitalist relations.

The survival of domestic production within the family; the role of the state in education, health, economic regulation and the monetary sphere; and the rise of the huge corporation: these are all testimony to the non-universality of capitalist production. In the case of labour-power, there are logical limits to the encroachment of capital (if labour-power were produced under capitalist conditions then the whole system would cease to be capitalist). In the case of money and the firm there are clear practical and institutional limits. Capitalism cannot, logically, exist in a pure form; historically it has never done so, and with the rise of the modern state and the modern multi-national corporation it is highly unlikely now to develop in that direction.

It is here that we find a flaw in Marx's analysis. Although he gave a vivid and brilliant prediction of the process of centralization of capital, Marx omits the state and the domestic sphere from his analysis. He planned, in the 1850s, to write a book on the state, and along with the fact that the state had generally retreated from the economic sphere in Britain in the nineteenth century, little blame can be put on Marx for this particular omission. However, both the structure and content of *Capital* seem to indicate that Marx expected capitalist relations steadily to undermine all others, including, for example, those involved in the production of labour-power. With certain important qualifications, on the whole the family has survived the hundred years following the publication of *Capital.* (For an important discussion of this point see Humphries, 1977.) More generally, the whole drift of *Capital* is to show that capitalism, *in its pure form,* will lead to an impasse. This suggestion is confirmed, in part, by a passage in the Preface to the first edition:

The physicist either observes natural processes where they occur in their most significant form, and are least affected by disturbing influences, or, wherever possible, he makes experiments under conditions which ensure that the process will occur in its pure state. What I have to examine in this work is the capitalist mode of production, and the relations of production and forms of intercourse that correspond to it. . . . Intrinsically, it is not a question of the higher or lower degree of development of the social antagonisms that spring from the natural laws of capitalist production. It is a question of these laws themselves, of these tendencies winning their way through and working themselves out with iron necessity (1976, pp. 90–1).

The impression of the capitalist system working towards an impasse is found in several passages in *Capital* (e.g. 1976, p. 929) and in Marx's famous 'law of the tendency of the rate of profit to fall', which has been found to be theoretically misconceived and empirically unconfirmed.

Although it is necessary to begin an analysis of capitalist society from the capitalist mode of production, it has to be recognized that the analysis of the system cannot be completed from the mode of production in a pure form. A full recognition of this point would have led Marx to abandon his catastrophist vision of capitalist development. Furthermore, more attention would have been paid to questions of economic policy, in particular the precise method of transition from capitalism to socialism. But Marx was too imbued with Victorian determinism to move in this direction, and we cannot help but remark that one of the barriers to his movement was the classical analysis of value. The latter hangs like an albatross round his theory of money and employment, almost preventing the revolutionary message from getting out. As a result, the bulk of the Marxian tradition has wasted enormous amounts of time salvaging the labour theory of value, promulgating and inventing theories of capitalist collapse, and generally defending the faith. In the meantime, issues of immediate and concrete policy have been left on the side, and with very few exceptions real historical and theoretical analysis has remained undeveloped.

The limits to capitalist development are found within the capitalist social formation itself. Like all economic systems, including slavery and feudalism, capitalism contains within itself both remnants of the past and the seeds of the future. Elements of Roman law are central to the capitalist legal system. Vestiges of feudalism exist within most advanced capitalist countries. Seeds of possible alternative future societies can also be found; perhaps a form of state totalitarianism, perhaps a form of post-capitalist corporatism, and, hopefully, democratic socialism. There is a need to categorize these, and analyse their development.

Finally, to make our position clear, a smooth and gradualist transition from capitalism to a future society is not being proposed. Any transition will involve disruption, crisis, and social and political convulsions. The tired old debate between naive reformist gradualism and romantic insurrectionary politics is not being repeated here. It is simply being suggested that capitalism is not an express train on the track to its inevitable and fatal crisis; and if we want vehicles to an alternative future then they can be found within the system, moving, in conflict, in a number of directions.

CHAPTER 20

TOWARDS A RADICAL POLITICAL ECONOMY

Thus, for all the virtuosity of effort that has gone into the last fifty years, I cannot discover in the chapter of modern economics a depth or breadth that would raise it above the level of attainments of previous chapters. . . . Perhaps this is a consequence of living in a period of transition, when the hidden problems of the market system are giving way to those of a nascent planning system. What visions will emerge to help us comprehend this period of transition we do not yet know. Beginnings of a new orientation for economics lie here and there, but they have yet to be gathered into a new 'doctrine'. Dusk is falling, but the owl of Minerva has yet to spread its wings.

ROBERT L. HEILBRONER, *Modern Economics as a Chapter in The History of Economic Thought,* 1980

If a new radical political economy is to be constructed, its two main components will be the works of Keynes and Marx. From Marx it will derive the elements of a theory of production, and a historical perspective of capitalist development based on the crucial concept of a mode of production, consisting of a structure of social relations. From Keynes it will derive a theory of money, the elements of a theory of employment, and an emphasis on practical economic policy.

Unfortunately, these foundations are not enough. First of all, as we have tried to indicate in this present work, there is a need for a new theory of value. There is a striking congruence between Marx and Keynes in this respect. Each of their theoretical structures sits awkwardly on an outdated and inadequate theory of value. In the case of Marx, he rests his work on a modified version of the classical theory of value of Smith and Ricardo, but stretches out, almost off balance, towards a theory of production and money which would sit more securely on a quite different theoretical foundation. In the case of Keynes, despite his efforts to 'escape' from the theoretical tradition of the neoclassical economists, much of his argument is still cast in a marginalist problematic. Quite rightly, Keynes rejects the Ricard-

233

ian theory of value, but he failed to notice that, in many respects, he was reaching out in the same direction as that of Marx.

It would be wrong to give the impression that the theory of value is the magic key to economic science. The advances made by Keynes and Marx, despite an inadequate value theory, should help to counter that view; but one is still led to the conclusion that many of the shortcomings of those two great theorists stem from their fractured value-theoretic foundations. In the case of Marx, his deterministic leanings, and his failure to develop a theory of economic policy, stem, in part, from his naturalistic theory of value. In the case of Keynes, his defence of private property and the market system of resource allocation (1936, pp. 377–81) flows, in part, from his continuing adherence to marginalism.

A systematic and new radical political economy will have to start from a new theory of value. The formal elements of this, as we have tried to show, are provided by Sraffa. However, it is clear that Sraffa's theory is much closer to the classical and Marxian tradition than to that of the neoclassicals. Whilst it does mark a new and radical break, it emphasizes, in the classical and Marxian tradition, costs of production, rather than the interaction of supply and demand.

In addition to a theory of value the new radical political economy will require a theory of production, a theory of money and a theory of property. The first of these will rely a great deal on the central sections of *Capital* and recent work on the labour process. The second will rely on the work of the modern neo-Keynesians. (However, it must be noted that in the absence of a corresponding break from neoclassical theories of production and property, much neo-Keynesian work, such as that of Clower, retains a conservative bias.) The third will have to chart new ground, for, apart from recent neoclassical literature on property rights, there is little work on this topic. In finding this new ground, radical property theory would still continue a tradition of 'utopian' socialist thought, such as that of William Godwin, Thomas Hodgskin, and William Thompson. It may, in addition, draw on important work in the Marxian theory of law (Pashukanis, 1978).

In addition to Marx, Keynes and Sraffa, two other figures should be influential in the creation of a new radical political economy: Kalecki and Robinson. Their works cover a wide field, but perhaps, in both cases, their contribution to macroeconomics will be the most significant. Figure 20.1 gives a schematic picture of the history of economic thought since Adam Smith. Heilbroner's remark that economics is not at a zenith but in an age of transition is confirmed by

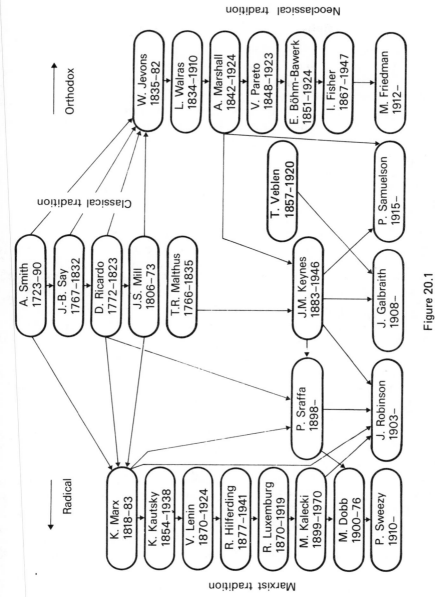

Figure 20.1
Diverging and converging traditions in the history of economics

this picture. The twin orthodoxies of Marxism and neoclassicism have been gradually eroded; and now, with the work of, in particular, Kalecki, Robinson and Sraffa, the basis for a new 'left of centre' tradition can be described.

An obvious question emerges. Will the new economics lie mainly or wholly within the Marxian tradition, and be seen as a continuation of it? It is difficult to give a straightforward answer. The positive side of Marx's analysis has been emphasized in this work. The negative elements—an outdated value theory and a deterministic or catastrophist vision—have also been mentioned. Unfortunately, in the Marxian *tradition,* such positive elements as an emphasis on the labour process and the social relations of production, have been highlighted only recently. As a consequence, Marxian theory carries a burden of mechanical and determinist thought which is, in practice, proving difficult to dislodge.

Furthermore, no economic analysis can be separated from its epoch. The catastrophist outlook to be found in *Capital* may apply, more appropriately, to an epoch where public intervention in the economic sphere was more limited than it is today. In the 1860s the *laissez-faire* policies of the Manchester School were still the prevailing doctrine, and it was all the more appropriate for Marx to suggest that market forces, in the absence of state intervention or guidance which was not widely foreseen at the time, would lead to inevitable disaster. Today, not only can we foresee the economic role of the state, but it is there, in the midst of economic life.

Yet traditional Marxism still advocates, either explicitly or by default, the free play of market forces in the pre-revolutionary period. The argument is this: market forces will develop the forces of production and hasten the transition to a new society. It is like giving capitalism enough rope to hang itself. As a consequence it is not uncommon for Marxists to support free trade rather than import controls, to suggest that all governments, from left to right, are powerless to alter the course of economic development, and to show a general indifference to state intervention or economic reform. These are the fatalistic policies of nineteenth-century political economy, having their say in the twentieth, in false radical guise.

For Marxism to survive it must break through into the post-Keynesian era. The acid test of its survival is this: it must produce radical and realistic policies which can be applied to the *existing* situation in advanced capitalist countries and which can begin the transformation of capitalism, both politically and economically, into a more progressive and humane society. If it fails on this, and this test alone, it has no future relevance, and should justly be superseded.

During the 1970s it has become to be widely accepted that the era of Keynesian 'demand management' is dead. The Achilles' heel of Keynesianism is inflation. High levels of government expenditure have pumped up effective demand, but failed to raise capitalist expectations and produced inflation instead. Inflation, in turn, has deterred long-term investment and exacerbated recession. After these Keynesian policies were seen to be failing, the first response of several capitalist governments was to abandon the objective of full employment and adopt, with Milton Friedman's blessing, tight controls of the money supply. At the same time, lost faith in the market mechanism was restored, and economic policy moved notably to the right. It did this, however, on the basis of conservative, pre-Keynesian policies.

By 1980, however, there were signs that this first pre-Keynesian reaction was beginning to be superseded, although still on a conservative basis. It was recognized that the key failure of Keynesian policies was to stimulate demand without at the same time stimulating supply. Being conservative, however, this second reaction did not take the obvious course. The suggestion was made that the objective of policy should be to stimulate supply (that is the obvious part) but to leave demand well alone (that does not logically follow). Hence we have observed the rise of the 'supply side' economics of Arthur Laffer, Robert Mundell and others. Strangely, however, this 'new' brand of economics does not concentrate on the supply side of the economy. Instead it concentrates on proposals to reduce marginal tax rates and to increase capitalists' *demand* for investment goods. Admittedly, the idea is that workers will work harder or longer as the marginal tax burden is reduced. However, the evidence for this is hard to find, and workers may just as well use their increased real disposable income to increase their leisure, and, as a consequence, to increase their *demand* for consumer goods. 'Supply side' economics turns out to be age-old conservative talk of 'individual incentives' in reaction to the growth of the economic role of the state.

If the substance is false, however, the slogan rings true. The new post-Keynesian economics will involve intervention and planning on the supply side of the modern capitalist economy. The real supply side is not the taxation system, but the sphere of production. It is here that radical political economy has developed some theoretical tools which can begin to make an impact, and to move the modern world out of the trough of unemployment and stagnation.

	Radical political economy	Orthodox economics
Status of subject within social science as a whole	Political economy as basis of unified social science	Economics as distinct discipline within social science
Main objects of analysis	Social relations, social classes	Abstract choice between things
Characteristic concept	Mode of production	Abstract individual
Aim of subject	To explain laws of development of economic systems	To make economic predictions
Applicability of principles of analysis	Applicable to one mode of production only	Applicable to all economic systems
Emphasis of analysis	Change, conflict, crisis	Social harmony, equilibrium
Basic sphere of analysis	Production	Exchange
Basis of theory of value	Costs of production	Interaction between supply and demand
Major topics	Labour process, role of money, economic crisis, role of the state	Market equilibrium, relative prices, perfect competition, welfare economics
General policy stance	State intervention, planning, and/or industrial democracy	Laissez faire: reliance on markets, restricted role for the state

Figure 20.2
Orthodox economics and radical political economy contrasted

With its basic sphere of analysis in production rather than exchange, and with a theory of value based on costs of production, radical political economy would have the new foundation to complete the structure of Marx and Keynes. With little faith in the ability of the market mechanism to adjust to need, radical political economy would instead put emphasis on the transformation of social relations. The central concern would be to revitalize production by a transformation of both the economic and political structures of power. It is reassuring to note that a number of works by economists have appeared with this objective in recent years (see, for example, Carnoy and Shearer, 1980; ETUI, 1979; Holland, 1975, 1979; LCC–CSE, 1980; and Rowthorn, 1980, ch. 3. See also Hodgson, 1979).

In figure 20.2 a comparison is made between the radical political economy which we have attempted to develop in this book and orthodox, or neoclassical, economics. It should be clear that the radical political economy here proposed is derived from the tradition of economics which has been neglected in the three decades following the Second World War. Concepts such as the mode of production, social classes, and social relations of production, and phenomena such as crises and chronic unemployment, do not enter into the neoclassical way of seeing things. Instead, an implicit faith in the virtues of the market is expressed in unrealistic models of market equilibrium, perfect competition and social harmony.

It is in one sense fortunate that, with the end of the Keynesian era, neoclassical economics has the chance to demonstrate the impotence of its remedies. It is with this impotence that the radical opportunity lies.

GLOSSARY

The following definitions are either unique to this work, or are not widespread in the literature, or are terms which require the most clarification. Other terms, of a more standard nature, have been omitted.

Abstract labour
Abstract labour is the set of qualities which are common to labour-power and all forms of concrete labour. Namely, labour is an intentional activity; labour-power has a degree of versatility generally exceeding machines; and labour and labour-power cannot be separated from their possessing agent. Furthermore, under capitalism, labour-power is not produced under capitalist conditions. The capitalist mode of production itself produces an enhanced form of abstract labour by, for example, creating a highly versatile labour force.

Agent of possession
An agent of possession is a person with legal rights of ownership, i.e. individual and absolute property rights. Under modern capitalism, most persons are agents of possession. Although being an agent of possession does not imply actual ownership, most persons, as a minimum, possess their labour-power under this system.

Capitalism
Capitalism is generalized commodity production. It is a mode of production in which most goods and services take the form of commodities. In particular, labour-power is a commodity. For this to occur, the workers must be separated from the means of production, ownership of the latter being concentrated in the hands of a minority class.

Capitalist production
Capitalist production involves the hiring of labour-power by an employer who, either personally or through his agents, supervises the production process, and who retains ownership of the finished product. Capitalist production is a form of commodity production in which the product is intended for sale on the market at a profit.

Commodity
A commodity is a good or service which is destined to be brought to the market for exchange. It is important to note that under capitalism, according to this definition of a commodity, both labour-power and money, even token money, are commodities, even if they are not objects of capitalist production.

Exploitation
Exploitation can take a number of forms. Class exploitation is the appropriation of a surplus product by the social class which owns or controls the means of production. Authority exploitation is the subjection of the worker to the authority of another person or group within production. Corporeal exploitation derives from the fact that labour-power, unlike capital, is inseparable from its possessing agent, and for labour to be performed the agent of possession is subjected to a number of risks and inconveniences. Bargaining exploitation results from unequal bargaining strengths during the negotiation of a contract; in particular, this type of exploitation can exist if the two parties to the contract are unequal in terms of wealth and power.

Labour-power
Labour-power is the capacity to perform labour. Unlike labour itself, labour-power can be traded on the market and be an object of possession. Unlike labour, labour-power is not an activity. The hiring of labour-power, at least under capitalism, is not the agreement to perform a specified pattern of labour. It is an agreement, on the part of the worker, to submit for a time to the authority of the employer who can then select a specific pattern of labour to be performed from a perfectly or imperfectly specified set. A distinction can be drawn between *potential* labour-power, which is the complete set of labouring activities which could be performed by the worker, and *hired* labour-power, which is the set of activities specified or implied in the contract.

Production as such
Production as such is the intentional creation, by human beings, of a good or service, with appropriate instruments of production. It is man's purposeful interaction with nature. It is the essential character of production in the abstract, without reference to a specific mode of production. Labour is the purposeful activity involved in production, i.e. the active, human element in the process of production as such. For this reason production can, in general, be described as the *labour* process.

Productive labour
Productive labour is here defined as labour which produces use-values and which would be required under any conceivable mode of production in which equivalent use-values were produced. Labour that is necessary simply because of the existence of specific relations of production, and which could be dispensed with under an alternative economic system, is unproductive. (This definition is very different from that of Marx.)

Rate of (class) exploitation
The rate of (class) exploitation is the ratio between the value of the surplus product under capitalism, and either the value of the real wage, or the total value-added in production.

Real wage
The real wage is the set of goods and services purchased by a worker with his or her wages. It is often assumed that the purchase of commodities in the real wage precisely exhausts the wage itself, i.e. there is no saving or dissaving.

Reproducible commodity
Under capitalism, a reproducible commodity is a commodity which is capable of being reproduced by the economy at a given stage of development. A commodity is reproducible if its likeness can thus be produced within a finite period of time under those conditions. Contrary to a popular view, wine is generally a reproducible commodity. Most types of labour-power are reproducible, and so too are the majority of commodities under modern capitalism.

Say's Law
Say's Law is used in a number of senses in the literature. Here it is used in the following sense. Say's Law involves the implicit assumption that the supply and demand for money are equal. If this were

the case it would follow, by Walras' Law, that the magnitude of the total excess demand for non-money commodities in the economy would be precisely equal to the magnitude of excess supply. In such circumstances it could be expected that both excess demand and excess supply would, through the market mechanism, diminish to zero. In the long run excess supply, including unemployment, would not exist. Say's Law thus implies no overproduction and no unemployment in the long run. Excess supply creates an equivalent excess demand.

The validity of Say's Law depends upon the validity of the assumption that the supply and demand for money are, or tend to be, equal. This is a falsifiable proposition, and in accord with both Marx and Keynes, in this work the assumption, and Say's Law itself, are taken to be generally false.

Shifting equilibrium

Capitalist expectations affect investment behaviour. In turn, investment leads to changes in the supply, demand, and prices of commodities, and these changing conditions will generally lead to an adjustment of expectations. Thus, if changing expectations are capable of influencing entrepreneurial behaviour, and in turn this behaviour affects future expectations, the economy will be chasing an ever-changing equilibrium. It will be in equilibrium in the short term only, before capitalist behaviour has worked through the system to prompt a revision in expectations. This ever-changing equilibrium was described by Keynes as a shifting equilibrium.

Simple commodity production

Simple commodity production is a form of commodity production, distinguished from capitalism, in which labour-power is not a commodity, because each individual worker owns his or her means of production.

Surplus product

Consider the gross product of an economic system over a given time-period. Deduct from this gross product the goods and services required to replace used-up raw materials and worn-out means of production. (What now remains is the net product.) Deduct the real wage. What remains is the surplus product. It consists of goods and services required for investment in additional means of production, and luxury goods to be consumed by non-members of the labouring class.

Surplus-value
The category of surplus value applies to the capitalist mode of production. It is the value of the surplus product, measured in monetary units. (Note that value is defined in a specific sense below.)

Training experience
A training experience consists of an activity which augments potential labour-power. This could include activities within the family, or education, or learning-by-doing at the point of production.

Use-value
The set of useful qualities found in a good or service consist of its use-value. Although use-values are intrinsic to goods they relate to a specific social culture and even specific persons. However, use-value is an objective, rather than a subjective concept. It is not to be confused with utility.

Utility
Utility, a concept used in neoclassical theory, is the individual satisfaction obtained from the consumption of a good. Unlike use-value, utility has a homogeneous measure in the ordinal or cardinal sense. However, it is a subjective rather than an objective concept.

Value
The value of a commodity is its price, expressed in money units, in some form of monetary equilibrium. The most general form of equilibrium to which it could be applied would be the shifting equilibrium of a monetary economy.

Value added
As in orthodox economic theory, value added is the value of the net product. It is the source of all incomes within a capitalist system, including wages, profits, interest and rent.

Wage
The wage is a money payment for employed labour-power. It can be on a time, piece-work or other basis. A salary is a type of wage. In equilibrium, total wages plus surplus value will equal total value added.

Walras' Law

Walras' Law is the following proposition: *if* the total supply and total demand for money in the economy are equal *then,* as a consequence, the total price of non-money commodities supplied will be equal to the total price of non-money commodities demanded. As such, Walras' Law is a logical result, rather than a statement about the real world. Note, however, that different uses of the term exist in the literature.

BIBLIOGRAPHY

Albert, M. and Hahnel, R. (1978) *Unorthodox Marxism*, South End Press, New York.

Althusser, L. and Balibar, E. (1970) *Reading Capital*, NLB, London.

Armstrong, P., Glyn, A. and Harrison, J. (1978) In defence of value: a reply to Ian Steedman, *Capital and Class*, no. 5, Summer.

Arneson, R. J. (1981) What's wrong with exploitation?, *Ethics*, 91 (2), January.

Becker, G. S. (1965) A theory of the allocation of time, *Economic Journal*, 75.

Benassy, J.-P. (1975) Neo-Keynesian disequilibrium theory in a monetary economy, *Review of Economic Studies*, October.

Beneria, L. (1979) Reproduction, production and the sexual division of labour, *Cambridge Journal of Economics*, 3 (3), September.

Blackburn, R. (1972) Introduction, in Blackburn, R. (ed.), *Ideology and Social Science*, Fontana, London.

Blatt, J. M. (1979) The utility of being hanged on the gallows, *Journal of Post Keynesian Economics*, 2 (2), Winter.

Blau, P. M. (1974) *On the Nature of Organisations*, Wiley, New York.

Blaug, M. (1968) *Economic Theory in Retrospect*, 2nd edition, Heinemann, London.

Bleaney, M. (1976) *Underconsumption Theories*, Lawrence and Wishart, London.

Böhm-Bawerk, E. v. (1970) *Capital and Interest*, Augustus Kelley, New York.

Böhm-Bawerk, E. v. (1975) Karl Marx and the close of his system, in Sweezy (1975).

Bose, A. (1975) *Marxian and Post-Marxian Political Economy*, Penguin, London.

Bowles, S. and Gintis, H. (1977) The Marxian theory of value and heterogeneous labour: a critique and reformulation, *Cambridge Journal of Economics*, 1 (2), June.

Braverman, H. (1974) *Labor and Monopoly Capital*, Monthly Review Press, New York.

Bródy, A. (1970) *Proportions, Prices and Planning*, North Holland, Amsterdam.

Bukharin, N. (1972) *Economic Theory of the Leisure Class*, Monthly Review Press, New York.

Burawoy, M. (1979) *Manufacturing Consent*, University of Chicago Press.

Burkitt, B. and Bowers, D. (1979) *Trade Unions and the Economy*, Macmillan, London.

Cairncross, A. K. (1958) Economic schizophrenia, *Scottish Journal of Political Economy*, February.

Carnoy, M. and Shearer, D. (1980) *Economic Democracy*, Sharpe, New York.

Caves, R. E. and Krause, L. B. (1980) eds. *Britain's Economic Performance*, Brookings Institution, Washington.

Chamberlain, N. W. (1951) *Collective Bargaining*, McGraw-Hill, New York.

Clark, J. B. (1899) *The Distribution of Wealth*, Macmillan, New York.

Clifton, J. (1977) Competition and the evolution of the capitalist mode of production, *Cambridge Journal of Economics*, **1** (2), June.

Clower, R. M. (1965) The Keynesian counter-revolution: a theoretical appraisal, in Hahn and Brechling (1975). Reprinted in Clower (1969).

Clower, R. W. (1967) A reconsideration of the microfoundations of monetary theory, *Western Economic Journal*, **6**. Reprinted in Clower (1969).

Clower, R. W. (1969) ed. *Monetary Theory*, Penguin, London.

Coase, R. H. (1937) The nature of the firm, *Economica*, November.

Cohen, G. A. (1979) The labour theory of value and the concept of exploitation, *Philosophy and Public Affairs*, **8** (4), Summer.

Colletti, L. (1972) *From Rousseau to Lenin*, NLB, London.

Colletti, L. (1973) *Marxism and Hegel*, NLB, London.

Crocker, L. (1972) Marx's concept of exploitation, *Social Theory and Practise*, **1**.

Cutler, A. (1978) The romance of 'labour', *Economy and Society*, **7** (1), February.

Cutler, A., Hindess, B., Hirst, P. and Hussain, A. (1977) *Marx's 'Capital' and Capitalism Today*, vol. 1, Routledge and Kegan Paul, London.

Cutler, A., Hindess, B., Hirst, P. and Hussain, A. (1978) *Marx's 'Capital' and Capitalism Today*, vol. 2, Routledge and Kegan Paul, London.

Davidson, P. (1974) 'A Keynesian view of Friedman's theoretical framework for monetary analysis', in Gordon (1974).

Davidson, P. (1977) *Money and the Real World*, 2nd edition, Macmillan, New York.

Davidson, P. (1980) Post Keynesian economics, *The Public Interest*, Special Issue.

Dobb, M. (1940) *Political Economy and Capitalism*, Routledge and Kegan Paul, London.

Dobb, M. (1973) *Theories of Value and Distribution Since Adam Smith*, Cambridge University Press, London.

Driver, C. (1980) *Productive and Unproductive Labour: Uses and Limitations of The Concept*, Thames Papers in Political Economy, Thames Polytechnic, London.

Eatwell, J. (1975) Mr. Sraffa's standard commodity and the rate of exploitation, *Quarterly Journal of Economics*, November.

Edwards, M. (1979) *Contested Terrain*, Basic Books, New York.

Eichner, A. (1976) *The Megacorp and Oligopoly*, Cambridge University Press.

Ellerman, D. P. (1978) *On Property Theory and Value Theory*, unpublished mimeo.

Ellerman, D. P. (1980) Some property theoretic aspects of orthodox economic theory, in Nell (1980b).

Elson, D. (1979) ed. *Value: The Representation of Labour in Capitalism*, CSE Books, London.

Elster, J. (1978) The labour theory of value: a reinterpretation of Marxist economics, *Marxist Perspectives,* **1** (3), Fall.

ETUI (1979) *Keynes Plus – A Participatory Economy,* European Trade Union Institute, Brussels.

Feiwel, G. R. (1975) *The Intellectual Capital of Michal Kalecki,* University of Tennessee Press.

Ferguson, C. E. (1972) *Microeconomic Theory,* 3rd edition, Irwin, Illinois.

Fine, B. and Harris, L. (1976) Controversial issues in Marxist economic theory, *Socialist Register 1976,* Merlin, London.

Fine, B. and Harris, L. (1977) Surveying the foundations, *Socialist Register 1977,* Merlin, London.

Fisher, I. (1906) *The Nature of Capital and Income,* Macmillan, London.

Friedman, A. L. (1977) *Industry and Labour,* Macmillan, London.

Friedman, M. (1962) *Price Theory: A Provisional Text,* Aldine, Chicago.

Galbraith, J. K. (1962) *The Affluent Society,* Pelican, London.

Garegnani, P. (1978) Notes on consumption, investment and effective demand, Part I, *Cambridge Journal of Economics,* **2** (4), December.

Garegnani, P. (1979) Notes on consumption, investment and effective demand, Part II, *Cambridge Journal of Economics,* **3** (1), March.

Georgescu-Roegen, N. (1978) Mechanistic dogma in economics, *British Review of Economic Issues,* no. 2, May.

Glyn, A. and Sutcliffe, R. (1972) *British Capitalism, Workers and the Profits Squeeze,* Penguin, London.

Goodwin, R. M. (1972) A growth cycle, in Hunt and Schwartz (1972).

Gordon, R. J. (1974) *Milton Friedman's Monetary Framework,* University of Chicago Press.

Gorz, A. (1976) ed. *The Division of Labour: The Labour Process and Class Struggle in Modern Capitalism,* Harvester, Sussex.

Gough, I. (1972) Marx's theory of productive and unproductive labour, *New Left Review,* no. 76, November–December.

Gough, I. (1974) *Wants and Needs,* unpublished.

Gough, I. (1979) *The Political Economy of the Welfare State,* Macmillan, London.

Hahn, F. (1980) General equilibrium theory, *The Public Interest,* Special Issue.

Hahn, F. and Brechling, F. (1965) *The Theory of Interest Rates,* Macmillan, London.

Harcourt, G. (1972) *Some Cambridge Controversies in the Theory of Capital,* Cambridge University Press, London.

Heller, A. (1976) *The Theory of Need in Marx,* Allison and Busby, London.

Henderson, J. M. and Quandt, R. E. (1971) *Microeconomic Theory: A Mathematical Approach,* McGraw-Hill, New York.

Hilferding, R. (1975) *Böhm-Bawerk's Criticism of Marx,* in Sweezy (1975).

Himmelweit, S. and Mohun, S. (1977) Domestic labour and capital, *Cambridge Journal of Economics,* **1** (1), March.

Himmelweit, S. and Mohun, S. (1978) The anomalies of capital, *Capital and Class,* no. 6.

Hindess, B. and Hirst, P. (1977) *Mode of Production and Social Formation,* Macmillan, London.

Hirshleifer, J. (1970) *Investment, Interest and Capital,* Prentice-Hall, New York.

Hodgson, G. (1974a) The theory of the falling rate of profit, *New Left Review,* no. 84, March–April.

Hodgson, G. (1974b) Marxian epistemology and the transformation problem, *Economy and Society,* 3 (4), November.

Hodgson, G. (1974c) The effects of joint production and fixed capital in linear economic analysis, unpublished MA thesis, University of Manchester.

Hodgson, G. (1976) Exploitation and embodied labour time, *Bulletin of the Conference of Socialist Economists,* March.

Hodgson, G. (1977a) Papering over the cracks, *Socialist Register 1977,* Merlin, London.

Hodgson, G. (1977b) Sraffa, value and distribution, *British Review of Economic Issues,* no. 1, November.

Hodgson, G. (1979) *Socialist Economic Strategy,* ILP Square One, Leeds.

Hodgson, G. (1980) A theory of exploitation without the labor theory of value, *Science and Society,* Fall.

Hodgson, G. (1981a) On exploitation and labor-value, *Science and Society,* Summer.

Hodgson, G. (1981b) Money and the Sraffa system, *Australian Economic Papers,* June.

Holland, S. (1975) *The Socialist Challenge,* Quartet, London.

Holland, S. (1979) ed. *Beyond Capitalist Planning,* Basil Blackwell, Oxford.

Hollis, M. and Nell, E. (1975) *Rational Economic Man,* Cambridge University Press.

Holmstrom, N. (1977) Exploitation, *Canadian Journal of Philosophy,* 7.

Homans, G. C. (1961) *Social Behaviour: Its Elementary Form,* Routledge and Kegan Paul, London.

Horowitz, D. (1968) ed. *Marx and Modern Economics,* Modern Reader, New York.

Howard, M. C. and King, J. E. (1975) *The Political Economy of Marx,* Longman, Harlow.

Humphries, J. (1977) Class struggle and the persistence of the working class family, *Cambridge Journal of Economics,* 1 (3), September.

Hunt, E. K. and Schwartz, J. G. (1972) eds. *A Critique of Economic Theory,* Penguin, London.

Hunt, E. K. and Sherman, H. (1975) *Economics: An Introduction to Traditional and Radical Views,* Harper and Row, New York.

Jonsson, E. (1978) Labour as a risk-bearer, *Cambridge Journal of Economics,* 2 (4), December.

Kaldor, M. (1978) *The Disintegrating West,* Pelican, London.

Kalecki, M. (1968) *Theory of Economic Dynamics,* Modern Reader, New York.

Kalecki, M. (1971) *Selected Essays in the Dynamics of the Capitalist Economy,* Cambridge University Press, London.

Kamenka, E. and Neale, R. S. (1975) eds. *Feudalism, Capitalism and Beyond,* Arnold, London.

Kenway, P. (1980) Marx, Keynes and the possibility of crisis, *Cambridge Journal of Economics*, **4** (1), March.

Keynes, J. M. (1936) *The General Theory of Employment, Interest and Money*, Macmillan, London.

Keynes, J. M. (1937) The general theory of employment, *Quarterly Journal of Economics*, **51**. Reprinted in Clower (1969).

Koestler, A. (1967) *The Ghost in the Machine*, Macmillan, New York.

Kregel, J. (1973) *The Reconstruction of Political Economy*, Macmillan, London.

Kregel, J. (1976) Economic methodology in the face of uncertainty, *Economic Journal*, **86**, June.

Kurz, H. D. (1979) Sraffa after Marx, *Australian Economic Papers*, **18**, June.

LCC–CSE (1980) *The Alternative Economic Strategy – A Labour Movement Response*, Labour Coordinating Committee and CSE Books, London.

Laidler, D. and Rowe, N. (1980) George Simmel's 'Philosophy of Money': a review article for economists, *Journal of Economic Literature*, **18**, March.

Lebowitz, M. (1977) Capital and the production of needs, *Science and Society*, **41**, Fall.

Leibenstein, H. (1976) *Beyond Economic Man: A New Foundation for Microeconomics*, Harvard University Press.

Leijonhufvud, A. (1968) *On Keynesian Economics and the Economics of Keynes*, Oxford University Press, New York.

Lenin, V. I. (1964) *The Development of Capitalism in Russia*, Lawrence and Wishart, London.

Levine, D. P. (1976) A critical note on the theory of production, *Australian Economic Papers*, **15**, December.

Levine, D. P. (1977) *Economic Studies: Contributions to the Critique of Economic Theory*, Routledge and Kegan Paul, London.

Levine, D. P. (1978) *Economic Theory;* Volume 1, *The Elementary Relations of Economic Life*, Routledge and Kegan Paul, London.

Levine, D. P. (1980) Production prices and the theory of the firm, *Journal of Post Keynesian Economics*, **3** (1), Fall.

Lippi, M. (1979) *Value and Naturalism in Marx*, NLB, London.

Lipsey, R. G. (1975) *Positive Economics*, Weidenfeld and Nicholson, London.

Loasby, B. J. (1976) Review of Leibenstein (1976) in *Economic Journal*, December.

Lukacs, G. (1972) *Political Writings 1919–1929*, NLB, London.

Lukes, S. (1974) *Power: A Radical View*, Macmillan, London.

Lupton, T. and Bowey, A. (1974) *Wages and Salaries*, Penguin, London.

Maarek, G. (1979) *An Introduction to Karl Marx's 'Das Kapital'*, Martin Robertson, Oxford.

Machlup, F. (1967) Theories of the firm: marginalist, behavioural, managerial, *American Economic Review*, March.

Macpherson, C. B. (1962) *The Political Theory of Possessive Individualism*, Oxford University Press.

Macpherson, C. B. (1973) *Democratic Theory: Essays in Retrieval*, Clarendon Press, Oxford.

Mandel, E. (1967) *An Introduction to Marxist Economic Theory,* Pathfinder, New York.

Mandel, E. (1968) *Marxist Economic Theory,* 2 vols, Merlin Press, London.

Mandel, E. (1971) *The Formation of the Economic Thought of Karl Marx,* NLB, London.

Marcuse, H. (1968) *One dimensional Man,* Sphere Books, London.

Marglin, S. A. (1974) What do bosses do? The origins and functions of hierarchy in capitalist production, *Review of Radical Political Economics,* **6** (2), Summer.

Marshall, A. (1920) *Principles of Economics,* 8th edition, Macmillan, London.

Marx, K. (1976) *Capital,* vol. 1, Pelican, London.

Marx, K. (1961) *Capital,* vol. 2, Lawrence and Wishart, London.

Marx, K. (1962) *Capital,* vol. 3, Lawrence and Wishart, London.

Marx, K. (1964) *The Economic and Philosophical Manuscripts of 1844,* (ed. D. J. Struik), International Publishers, New York.

Marx, K. (1969) *Theories of Surplus Value,* part 2, Lawrence and Wishart, London.

Marx, K. (1972) *Theories of Surplus Value,* part 3, Lawrence and Wishart, London.

Marx, K. (1971) *A Contribution to the Critique of Political Economy,* Lawrence and Wishart, London.

Marx, K. (1973) *Grundrisse,* Pelican, London.

Matson, F. W. (1964) *The Broken Image,* New York.

Meek, R. (1973) *Studies in the Labour Theory of Value,* 2nd edition, Lawrence and Wishart, London.

Menger, A. (1899) *The Right to the Whole Product of Labour,* Macmillan, London.

Merrett, S. (1977) Some conceptual relationships in 'Capital', *History of Political Economy,* **9** (4).

Mill, James (1821) *Elements of Political Economy,* London.

Mini, P. (1974) *Philosophy and Economics,* University of Florida, Gainesville.

Moggridge, D. E. (1976) *Keynes,* Fontana, London.

Morishima, M. (1973) *Marx's Economics,* Cambridge University Press.

Morishima, M. (1974) Marx in the light of modern economic theory, *Econometrica,* July.

Morishima, M. and Catephores, G. (1978) *Value, Exploitation and Growth,* McGraw-Hill, London.

Nell, E. J. (1978) The simple theory of effective demand, *Intermountain Economic Review,* Fall.

Nell, E. J. (1979) Changes in productivity and real wages, *Economic Forum,* **10,** Winter.

Nell, E. J. (1980a) Value and capital in Marxian economics, *The Public Interest,* Special Issue.

Nell, E. J. (1980b) ed. *Growth, Profits and Property,* Cambridge University Press, New York.

Neumann, J. v. (1945) A model of general economic equilibrium, *Review of Economic Studies,* **13.**

Nuti, M. (1972) Vulgar economy in the theory of income distribution, in Hunt and Schwartz (1972).

Pashukanis, E. B. (1978) *Law and Marxism,* Ink Links, London.

Preiser, E. (1952) Property and power in the theory of distribution, *International Economic Papers,* no. 2. Reprinted in Rothschild (1971).

Putnam, T. (1978) Mode of production—out?, *Capital and Class,* no. 4, Spring.

Reder, M. W. (1959) Job scarcity and the nature of union power, *Industrial Labour Relations Review,* **13**. Reprinted in B. J. McCormick and E. Owen Smith, eds., *The Labour Market,* Penguin, London, 1968.

Ricardo, D. (1971) *Principles of Political Economy and Taxation,* Pelican, London.

Robinson, J. (1964) *Economic Philosophy,* Pelican, London.

Robinson, J. (1951) *Collected Economic Papers,* vol. 1, Blackwell, Oxford.

Robinson, J. (1960) *Collected Economic Papers,* vol. 2, Blackwell, Oxford.

Robinson, J. (1965) *Collected Economic Papers,* vol. 3, Blackwell, Oxford.

Robinson, J. (1973) *Collected Economic Papers,* vol. 4, Blackwell, Oxford.

Robinson, J. (1977) The labour theory of value, *Monthly Review,* December.

Roemer, J. E. (1978) Differentially exploited labour: a Marxian theory of discrimination, *Review of Radical Political Economics,* **10** (2), Summer.

Roemer, J. E. (1979) *Origins of Exploitation and Class: Value Theory of Pre-Capitalist Economy,* Department of Economics, University of California at Davis, Working Paper no. 125.

Roll, E. (1973) *A History of Economic Thought,* 4th edition, Faber, London.

Roncaglia, A. (1974) The reduction of complex labour to simple labour, *Bulletin of the Conference of Socialist Economists,* Autumn.

Roncaglia, A. (1978) *Sraffa and the Theory of Prices,* Wiley, New York.

Roncaglia, A. (1980) Production prices and the theory of the firm: a comment, *Journal of Post Keynesian Economics,* **3** (1), Fall.

Rosdolsky, R. (1977) *The Making of Marx's 'Capital',* Pluto Press, London.

Rothschild, K. W. (1971) ed. *Power in Economics,* Penguin, London.

Rowthorn, R. (1974) Neo-Classicism, Neo-Ricardianism, and Marxism, *New Left Review,* no. 86, July—August. Reprinted in Rowthorn (1980).

Rowthorn, R. (1980) *Capitalism, Conflict and Inflation,* Lawrence and Wishart, London.

Rubin, I. I. (1972) *Essays on Marx's Theory of Value,* Black and Red, Detroit.

Rubin, I. I. (1979) *A History of Economic Thought,* Ink Links, London.

Sahlins, M. (1972) *Stone Age Economics,* Tavistock, London.

Samuelson, P. (1975) *Economics,* McGraw-Hill, New York.

Schwartz, J. (1977) ed. *The Subtle Anatomy of Capitalism,* Goodyear Publishing, Santa Monica.

Sen, A. (1978) On the labour theory of value: some methodological issues, *Cambridge Journal of Economics,* **2** (2), June.

Shachtman, M. (1962) *The Bureaucratic Revolution,* Donald Press, New York.

Shackle, G. L. S. (1967) *The Years of High Theory,* Cambridge University Press, London.

Shackle, G. L. S. (1972) *Epistemics and Economics,* Cambridge University Press, London.

Simmel, G. (1978) *The Philosophy of Money*, Routledge and Kegan Paul, London.

Simon, H. A. (1951) A formal theory of the employment relationship, *Econometrica*, July.

Smith, A. (1970) *The Nature and Causes of the Wealth of Nations*, Pelican, London.

Sraffa, P. (1960) *The Production of Commodities by Means of Commodities*, Cambridge University Press, London.

Steedman, I. (1975) Positive profits with negative surplus value, *Economic Journal*, 85, March.

Steedman, I. (1977) *Marx After Sraffa*, NLB, London.

Steedman, I. (1979) *Marx on Ricardo*, University of Manchester Department of Economics Discussion Paper, no. 10.

Sweezy, P. M. (1968) *The Theory of Capitalist Development*, Modern Reader, New York.

Sweezy, P. M. (1975) ed. *Karl Marx and the Close of His System*, Merlin, London.

Tortajada, R. (1977) A note on the reduction of complex labour to simple labour, *Capital and Class*, no. 1, Spring.

Trotsky, L. (1965) *The Revolution Betrayed*, Merit, New York.

Van Parijs, P. (1980) The falling-rate-of-profit theory of crisis: a rational reconstruction by way of obituary, *The Review of Radical Political Economics*, Spring.

Weiser, F. (1930) *Natural Value*, Stechert, New York.

Wood, A. (1975) *A Theory of Profits*, Cambridge University Press.

Wright, E. O. (1978) *Class, Crisis and the State*, NLB, London.

Wright, E. O. (1979) The value controversy and social research, *New Left Review*, no. 116, July–August.

Yaffe, D. S. (1975) Value and Price in Marx's 'Capital', *Revolutionary Communist*, January.

Younes, Y. (1975) On the role of money in the process of exchange and the existence of a non-Walrasian equilibrium, *Review of Economic Studies*, October.

INDEX

Use-value, 34–44, 134, 183, 185, 190, 198–200, 244; of money, 124–7
Utilitarianism, 28
Utility, 7, 15, 28–9, 34, 41–4, 46–51, 53, 77, 114, 146, 216, 244
Utopian socialism, 111

Valorization, 183, 187–98
Value, 10, 86–7, 149–53, 185, 212, 216, 244; and exploitation, 215–16; in Marx, 80, 149–51
Value-added, 244
Van Parijs, Philippe, 112
Variable capital, 195–7
Veblen, Thorstein B., 235
Voltaire, F., 116

Wage–profit frontier, 66, 160–2, 181
Wages, 55–6, 168–9, 175, 180–1, 193, 204–5, 217–18, 223–9, 244

Walras, Léon, 4, 140, 144, 148, 152, 198, 235
Walras' Law, 123–4, 129, 227, 243, 245
Wants, 31, 40; double coincidence of, 120–1
Water embodied, 78
Welfare state, 230
Whitehead, Alfred N., 75
Wicksteed, P. H., 68
Wilde, Oscar, 104
Wine, 68–70, 78
Wood, Adrian, 222–4
Workers' control, 214, 238–9
Working class, 51–4, 182, 187. *See also* Class, Labour, Labour-power, Wage
Work-study, 175
Wright, Erik Olin, 87, 89–94, 97, 182

X-inefficiency, 62, 196–7

Yaffe, David, 86
Younes, Y., 144, 152